THE EROTIC SCREEN

THE EROTIC SCREEN
Desire, Addiction, and Perversity in Cinema

Thomas Wolman

PHOENIX
PUBLISHING HOUSE
firing the mind

First published in 2020 by
Phoenix Publishing House Ltd
62 Bucknell Road
Bicester
Oxfordshire OX26 2DS

British Library Cataloguing in Publication Data

A C.I.P. for this book is available from the British Library

ISBN-13: 978-1-912691-27-2

Typeset by Medlar Publishing Solutions Pvt Ltd, India

www.firingthemind.com

Contents

Part II
Portraits of Addiction in Hollywood Melodramas

Part III
Perverse Desire in Mainstream Cinema

Acknowledgments

In addition to the help I received, this book is the result of a fortunate alignment of the planets, a conjunction of desire, opportunity, and resources. It could not have happened without access to a vast library of films instantly available for study on a laptop computer, without the time to pursue the project unhindered, and without the matching of a new author with a new publishing house.

First and foremost I would like to thank Salman Akhtar, my friend and colleague. Salman has been critiquing and later editing my writings since 1982, when I published a book review on the life of Harry Stack Sullivan. He has been encouraging me to write a book for a decade, and when I started to write about movies from a psychoanalytic perspective, we both saw something begin to take shape. Among his prodigious talents is the ability to pull a table of contents out of a hat and sketch it on a dinner napkin. The title, *The Erotic Screen*, I owe to him, a triple entendre on the psychoanalytic, cinematic, and sexual connotations of the word "screen".

I would like to thank friends and colleagues for discussions I have had over the past two years working on this project. I thank Gregg Gorton, Henry Bachrach, and Kenneth Weiss for their encouragement. I thank my friends for their suggestions on promoting and circulating the book.

I especially want to thank Kate Pearce for her belief in the book and for her helpful editorial advice at every step of the process.

I thank Taylor and Francis, publishers, for permission to reprint the chapter on greed.

With all my heart I thank my wife Julie for her patience during the year-long gestation of this book and for tolerating me for being even more "inside my head" than I usually am.

And finally I thank my children, Daniel and Jessica, for including me in their lives, which is for me essential for everything else I do.

About the Author

Thomas Wolman, M.D., was born and raised in New York City, where he now lives after residing in Philadelphia, PA, for forty-four years. He attended Johns Hopkins University and the Pennsylvania State University Medical College. Subsequently, he trained at the Philadelphia Psychoanalytic Center, where he taught in both the psychoanalytic and the psychotherapy training programs. Until his move, he held the title of assistant clinical professor of psychiatry at the University of Pennsylvania School of Medicine. He has written on Winnicott, Mahler, Kohut, and Lacan, as well as on contemporary films, and more recently on greed, bereavement, and privacy issues. Currently, he teaches a course on the history of psychoanalysis at the New York Psychoanalytic Institute.

Introduction

Movies have depicted sexuality in one form or another since their inception in 1896, when Thomas Alva Edison produced *The Kiss*. Despite its brief duration of 18 seconds, this film proceeds in three acts. In act one, a man and a woman nuzzle each other around the lips and cheek, while engaging in intimate conversation. In act two, the man abruptly steps way, ostentatiously grooming his moustache—a sign of his virility. In act three, he leans in for a deep kiss, while nibbling the edges of his partner's lips. Thus the sheer length of the kiss, its formal progress from foreplay to climax, and its in-your-face close-ups make its sexual implications unmistakable. And the sexual aspect was not lost on the film's audience. The disgust it aroused in many reflected moral outrage, but also the perception that something "excessive" was invading the viewer's imaginary space. Indeed, some even branded the film as pornographic (Wikipedia)—or at least as its precursor. And even after the screen kiss had become an acceptable symbol of movie romance, it never quite shed its prurient undertones.

It is therefore not surprising that *The Kiss* (1896) gave rise to the first calls for movie censorship. Censorship—official or unofficial—has always regulated the relationship between movies and sexuality. It must be understood that censorship originated in the collective mentality of filmgoers—in the moral restraints imposed by individual minds acting in concert and as a national consensus. Hollywood responded to this consensus with a set of self-imposed restrictions known as the Motion Picture Production Code. Of the code's eleven prohibitions and twenty-five constraints, at least thirteen pertained to sexuality (Wikipedia). The consensus upon which the code was based remained in effect from 1927 until 1945, with the year 1934 serving as a fulcrum. After this date, any film that did not receive a certificate of approval could not be released. Thus 1934 can be considered the high-watermark of Hollywood censorship. And almost four decades later, after the code was abolished, we could say that censorship reached its nadir.

But, in another sense, the year 1934 simply changed the battle over censorship into a guerilla war waged by filmmakers. In *It Happened One Night* (1934), for example, the Director—Frank Capra—*exploits his own compliance with the Censor* in order to put across his own subversive message. Early in the film, the screenwriters introduce a running gag involving the walls of Jericho whose hilarity is only enhanced by its biblical roots. The censorship expressly forbade the depiction of unmarried couples sharing a bed or even a bedroom where proximity offered too great a temptation. Hence it sought to exclude the mere suggestion of premarital sex. Capra solves this problem by having his male lead, played by Clark Gable, hang a somewhat threadbare blanket between the two beds that he and his future bride were compelled to share due to lack of funds. He then depicts his two stars—the newspaperman and the runaway socialite (Claudette Colbert)—behaving *like an ordinary married couple*. They bicker, they haggle over money, and Gable's character cooks his "wife" breakfast. Meanwhile, the blanket satisfies the censorship and probably fools the naïve and the willfully ignorant. But does any thinking person believe this flimsy piece of cloth poses a real barrier? Thus Capra gently mocks the censor *sotto voce*, so to speak. Specifically, he places a "screen of propriety" over a scene whose sexual possibilities are transparent. In this way, the threadbare blanket unconsciously suggests the titillating image (especially for male viewers) of Gable's character "deflowering" his future wife in an obscure hotel room. Eventually the two get married and we chuckle when "the walls of Jericho" do come tumbling down.

But in 1934 a mass movement was under way that would decisively alter the dynamic interplay between censor and moviemaker. I refer to the immigration of the German film industry, the majority of whom were Jews, to Hollywood. These filmmakers brought with them a European sensibility quite at odds with America's dominating strain of Puritanism.

During the pre-code era, the most avant-garde films were being made in Berlin. Hollywood responded to these films with admiration and envy in equal measure. The industry knew—even in the 1920s—it was barred from making such sexually candid movies. But the Berlin output had a powerful effect on the studios' collective psyche.

During this era, three groundbreaking films depicted sexuality in a manner that would have been considered brazen—if not salacious—in America: *Pandora's Box* (1929), *The Blue Angel* (1930), and *M* (1931). On this side of the Atlantic, directors marveled at the screen presence of two actresses, Louise Brooks and Marlene Dietrich. Dietrich was invited along with her director Joseph von Sternberg to Hollywood where the pair made a string of successful movies together in the 1930s. Brooks on the other hand (an American actress), never found her footing in Hollywood after her brief run in Europe. Their contrasting fates reveal Hollywood's contradictory attitudes toward women who choose not to hide their sexuality.

The most shocking of the three—*Pandora's Box*—is a kind of sexual three ring circus portraying every variety of illicit coupling. But what was most disturbing to viewers, then as now, is Brook's out-and-out naturalism. She approaches every sexual encounter with the innocence of a child. On an unconscious level she evokes the way children gleefully engage in sexual games without any awareness of transgression. Another factor affecting viewers was the state of psychosexual disorder in the film that led some writers to cite it as a symptom of the even greater decadence in Weimar society (Weir, 2018).

But it would be wrong to view the film as devoid of restraint. There is a famous scene, for example, that shows Brook's character dancing with a lesbian woman during her own wedding reception. Her husband stands with his back to us, signaling: "his back is up." The woman shoots him a proprietary look that challenges his virility. The two seem to be sparring over who has the phallic member—or who may claim rights to Brooks as the universally desired object. But the film never makes this encounter explicit. The viewer is free to infer that the woman is, or is not, a lesbian. There is thus an element of self-censorship at work: it is OK to insinuate sexual liaisons so long as their nature remains tacit. Early American talkies of 1930–1933 adopted this attitude up to the point of mild suggestiveness.

Starting in the late 1930s (with rare exceptions such as *Sunrise* (1927)) European filmmakers got their first crack at making films in Hollywood (or, to a lesser extent, in London, as was the case with Alfred Hitchcock, who served his apprenticeship in Berlin). The most successful practitioners, such as Billy Wilder, made films infused with a European sensibility while still adhering to the letter of the law. In the case of film noir—arguably their own invention—they injected low budget crime thrillers with a super-charged eroticism that no amount of censorship could erase (Naremore, 2019). In the process, they imported the idea of sex as an irresistible force that overrides considerations of conscience, propriety, and even self-preservation. It was the concession that illicit sex always brings about its comeuppance that satisfied the censors. And after a steady diet of bland optimism, a dose of European fatalism gave post-war audiences a twinge of *Schadenfreude*.

The year 1934 also ushered in other means of circumventing the censor by exploiting loopholes in the code. With the repeal of Prohibition in 1933, a national mood of indulgence set in regarding the representation of alcohol consumption. *The Thin Man* (1934), for example, presents a running gag wherein the married sleuths solve a crime while visibly intoxicated for much of the movie's running time. In this film, and others like it, we are invited to revel in the loss of inhibitions and the barely hidden assumption that such loosening might lead to sexual activity.

Another "loophole" was onscreen violence in films such as *Scarface* (1932) that stirred audiences with their gleeful mayhem. And ever since 1922's *Nosferatu*, the vampire genre was "cloaked" in a penumbra of dark sexuality. In the 1950s filmmakers amped up the element of horror in science fiction movies to induce "spine tingling" thrills and chills. The basic idea was that any visceral "kick" or thrill—whether emanating from violence, exuberant imbibing, bloodsucking, or the shock of horror—gave sexual satisfaction in displaced form. Two such films discussed in this book—*The Thing from Another World* (1951) and the *Invasion of the Body Snatchers* (1956)—deploy this trend in low budget vehicles that flew under the censor's radar. In a later film discussed herein—*Alien* (1979)—the director consciously exploited the psychosexual potential of the alien entity.

Meanwhile, however, World War II had changed America into a global society and weakened the national consensus that had supported censorship since 1934. Thus it is perhaps not just coincidence that the first to challenge the Production Code head-on was Otto Preminger, an Austro-Hungarian by birth. He had already raised eyebrows with his film *Laura* (1944) that subtly tweaked gender stereotypes, and in the waning years of the Production

Code, his *Anatomy of a Murder* (1959) found a way of presenting sexual content in a context that demanded truthfulness: the courtroom.

But his most direct challenge to the censorship involved a rather tame romantic comedy—now remembered more for its moment in history than its artistic merit. In 1953 that film, *The Moon Is Blue*, was rejected for its treatment of "illicit sex." The official reason for the ruling was a "light-hearted" attitude toward sexuality, but the Breen Office might never have taken this position if not for the use of the words "virgin," "pregnancy," and "mistress" in the script. And in just this way, they pushed their mission to the point of absurdity and self-mockery. They were asking producers to censor words that even in 1953 were part of everyday speech. And they were behaving as if adults were incapable of judging these matters for themselves (or as if children harbored no doubts regarding the stork myth). The censors were also accused of extreme literality since the context of these allegedly "forbidden" words was a completely innocuous plot in which the female lead fends off two male admirers until one of them proposes marriage to her.

The release of the film after a court battle paved the way for further weakening of the censorship in the following decade and its eventual abandonment in 1968. The new MPAA rating system instituted by Jack Valenti attempted to eliminate the code's major abuses (Wikipedia). And for the critical years 1968–1972 it succeeded. For the first time since the 1920s mainstream movies were free to address sexuality in a free and open manner. During these years, filmmakers experimented with sexual themes and in many cases their sheer exuberance caused them to include nude scenes that in retrospect seem gratuitous. This trend in world cinema led in turn to the first non-pornographic film incorporating explicit sexual acts: *Last Tango in Paris* (1972). Setting aside the question of artistic merit, this film was widely regarded as a historical turning point and a trendsetter. Instead, it hit a dead end. In an ironic sense it performed the necessary "last tango" of unfettered sex.

Many reasons have been proposed for this outcome, but I would claim that *Last Tango in Paris* butted against a contradiction inherent in cinema as a mass medium: that the voyeuristic delight in seeing requires that the so-called "primal scene" be barred from view (Žižek, 1991). In the context of mainstream cinema the "primal scene" means sexual intercourse or its equivalent. And from this requirement it follows that mainstream movies will henceforth impose some degree of censorship upon themselves even while retaining a greater frankness toward psychosexual themes.

The new censorship emerged from several sources. For audiences, it was not so much they disapproved of explicit sex per se. After all they had lined up in droves to see *Deep Throat* (1972) released the same year as *Last Tango in Paris* (1972) and the first pornographic film to reach a wide audience. No, it was more the feeling that explicit sex was occurring *in the wrong place*. In one sense it was as if such scenes breached the protective "screen" guaranteeing privacy to moviegoers. And the non-acceptance by audiences went hand-in-hand with a renewal of official censorship when the "X" rating was abandoned in favor of the NC-17 (Wikipedia). From that point on, filmmakers strove for the coveted "R" rating, mainly by eliminating or abbreviating nude scenes.

A new movie genre arose that portrayed men and women struggling to place a limit on the unfettered expression of their sexual drives. Since prototypes like *Carnal Knowledge* (1971), these films give a more nuanced and certainly more problematic take on the role of sexuality in human relationships. Even in the earlier sci-fi movies, that limit is implied in the decision to shield the alien sexual object from full exposure. In the more contemporary *Secretary* (2002) and *Little Children* (2006), that limit is reached when the participants realize that their miniature sexual utopia fails to provide the be-all and end-all of their respective lives.

The genre revealed a kinship to the pioneering *The Lost Weekend* (1945) both in its reaction to excess, and its explicit linkage of alcoholism and sexuality. Two parables of greed directed by John Huston—*The Maltese Falcon* (1941) and *The Treasure of the Sierra Madre* (1948)—depict men whose overwhelming drive to possess an impossible object (a mythical statuette or the mother lode of gold) leads to ruin. In the succeeding decades the cyclical ups and downs of excess and reaction—comparable to the earlier vicissitudes of censorship—re-emerged in exposés of alcohol and greed in films like the *Days of Wine and Roses* (1962), *Leaving Las Vegas* (1995), and *Wall Street* (1987). And in each succeeding reiteration the relationship between addiction, greed, and sexuality became more apparent. Thus the cycle of overreach and correction grew into an attempt at self-regulation.

My first close encounter with film censorship occurred during repeat viewings of *The Thing from Another World* (1951). I had always marveled at its ingenious special effects but now I sat in awe at its accomplishment in the face of burdensome constraints. These constraints were of three kinds: official censorship, budgetary limits, and pressures to conform to studio expectations. The movie's romantic sub-plot, for example, was designed to suggest—but not to exclaim—issues of male harassment, sexual bondage, and reversal of gender roles. The budget required the film to be finished in record time (a few weeks). Hence there was neither time nor money to build a detailed replica of a spaceship nor to design elaborate costumes for the alien creature. The cinematographer got around these restraints by giving us only brief glimpses of the alien entity. And finally, the Studio executives put pressure on the producers to include a happy ending—which in this case meant the destruction of "The Thing".

It then became evident to me that these internal and external restraints resembled the effects of censorship in so far as the central "thing" remains invisible—or at least ambiguous in shape and form—and only its effects on crew members' minds can be inferred. Moreover, if we assume that "The Thing" is in some sense a sexual "thing", then that "thing" is literally eclipsed from the movie. Moreover, the film's B movie status, its escapist appeal to teenagers, and its remoteness from the concerns of everyday life allowed it to fly under the radar. But on a deeper level it dawned on me that the film delves into the problems humans face when confronting an alien force in their midst. Readers of the chapter devoted to "The Thing" will decide for themselves whether I have made the case that the "thing" is the elusive sexual object. But I believe most will concur that the filmmakers' efforts to accommodate the restrictions imposed upon them can add layers to a film's subtext that, like impasto, enriches its artistic texture.

One idea threading its way through all the chapters of this book is the idea of human sexuality as both a *force majeure* and a conundrum challenging the human mind. In response to this challenge, the films raise questions about the nature of sexuality. *The Thing from Another World* (1951), for example, asks: what is the nature of the sexual object? In the case of *Invasion of the Body Snatchers* (1956), it could be: what if desire was eliminated from our collective mentality in favor of mass sexual surrender? And does *Alien* (1979), for its part, ask whether it is possible to expel the alien aspect of sexuality from the psyche? And picking up the alien theme, is Mark, the serial killer of women in *Peeping Tom* (1960), a monster—an alien in human form? Or is he a human being struggling against an alien force? And finally, the films *Secretary* (2002) and *Little Children* (2006) make explicit their question: If the infantile roots of human sexuality are inherently "poly-morphous and perverse," who then is the true pervert?

Of course the films decline to say whether these questions can be answered to our satisfaction. Indeed their ambiguity on this point adds to their enduring achievement. Hence, the assertions and conclusions to which I am led in my explorations of these movies are mainly intended to stir up discussion and debate—to help these movies live on in our minds.

Part I

The Nature of Desire in a Trio of Science Fiction Thrillers

CHAPTER ONE

The Object of Desire: *The Thing from Another World*

Near the beginning of Howard Hawks' *The Thing from Another World* (1951) we join the Air Force crew of a C-47 cargo plane, huddled around the controls. Present are: Captain Patrick Henry, his co-pilot, radioman, chief engineer, and Carrington, the chief scientist. They are en route to an area near the North Pole where a mysterious object has crashed. During the flight, the plane encounters unusual headwinds and a powerful electromagnetic force, causing the compass reading to deviate by twelve degrees.

The men realize they are dealing with no ordinary object. Carrington immediately deduces from its upward vector right before the crash that it is not a meteor. And its powerful effect on the compass suggests a capability for disruption. By causing the plane to veer off course, it interrupts the "flight plan" and seems to defy the laws of nature. It certainly upends the crew's expectations and their assumptions of a predictable world view. And yet, while its behavior is no doubt disturbing to the men, it is also intriguing. It challenges them and sets their minds to work. It stimulates the free exchange of ideas about the nature of The Thing. Captain Henry, however, limits himself to the practical task at hand: locating the object. And with this aim in mind, he plots a new course using "known landmarks."

Upon landing, and without delay, the group locates the alien entity as a bottle-shaped outline on a patch of ice. A tiny portion of what is assumed to be a spaceship protrudes above the surface. It appears to be some kind of stabilizer. The men fan out to the dark edge of the ship with their hands outstretched. From above we see them arranged in a circle. This discovery prompts Captain Patrick Henry, the team leader, to deploy "thermite" bombs in an effort to melt the ice. We hear two explosions, the first when the bombs detonate, and the second when the entire ship explodes. When the smoke clears, the men realize too late they have inadvertently destroyed the very thing they were charged to investigate.

But if their actions seem premature, let us note that the "thermite" bombs have provided the filmmakers a solution to a technical problem. Without the production budget to construct a spaceship, or even a scale model, they opted instead to indicate its broad outline and reveal only a tiny part or appendage. Then, by destroying the ship, they removed the possibility of ever having to reveal it.

But if these measures were driven by necessity, they have also advanced the film's aesthetic. On the one hand, they introduce a policy of postponement that will successively defer the actual appearance of The Thing. By the time the ship explodes, we are already twenty-four minutes into the movie. On the other hand, by offering up approximations of The Thing that never amount to a complete picture, they elicit curiosity, encourage speculation, and invite questions.

And not least of these questions asks why they committed such a precipitous and premature act in the first place. The rationalization that they were following "standard operating procedure" seems lame. It only highlights their failure of judgment. Yet the action advances the film's aesthetic by exposing human recklessness. It seeds the idea that the mad pursuit of mayhem for its own sake comes from us.

Of course the shape of the vehicle offers one loose approximation of The Thing. Its ovoid perimeter prompts one of the men to call it a "flying saucer." That phrase was not as hackneyed as it is today. Yet as speculation it is certainly premature: it offers an answer before the proper question has even been posed. This popular fantasy reduces the unknown Thing to an ordinary household object. A "flying saucer" may evoke fear but it doesn't evoke dread or horror.

Interestingly, the image that stays in the mind is the one shown right before the explosion: the circle of men and women, arms outstretched, forming a human chain around The Thing. Their hands almost touch but leave a small gap in between. This broken line depicts the ties that bind humans together and the gaps that prevent absolute solidarity. The roughly circular shape follows the outline of the spacecraft and also establishes the human perimeter. And at the center of the circle lies a dark shadow, an area of obscurity. Although it sits right underneath their feet, it remains inaccessible. Thus the human chain circumscribes an area of impenetrability, the boundary of the unknown.

And this cloak of invisibility persists when the crew unearths the occupant (or an occupant) of the ship encased in a block of ice, and transports him (or it) to the camp's storeroom. Like the ship, only the creature's bare outline is visible through the ice. He appears humanoid, and this fact alone is enough to stimulate interest. Wanting to investigate further, the men bring the creature inside the compound for more detailed observation by the combined group of scientists and military personnel. Curious but wary, the group places the visitor under twenty-four-hour guard while they grapple with the problem of thawing him out.

The alien gaze

But as the ice begins to melt, the creature's eyes become visible and its gaze exerts a disturbing effect on the guards.

The sergeant relays this news to Captain Henry. He suggests that the intervals of guard duty be reduced from four to two hours, and the captain readily agrees. But even this remedy proves insufficient. The corporal guarding The Thing becomes so anxious he drapes his electric blanket over the creature to block its gaze.

His actions precipitate a crisis. The camera pans to the electric switch and then the bottom edge of the blanket where melting water is dripping down. The film then cuts to the corporal standing up and blindly firing his weapon at The Thing. We viewers never see the toxic gaze first hand. We are meant to infer that The Thing has gotten up and escaped its restraints. In recounting the event to the captain, the wild-eyed corporal becomes visibly distraught. When his agitation threatens to spin out of control, the captain throws a glass of water in his face to "snap him out of it".

Now, to clarify the destabilizing effect of the gaze, let us rewind to the moment when the visitor escapes his shackles. In that instant, he goes from being literally frozen in time and space to rapid movement. The corporal shoots wildly—that is, he "sees" The Thing, but he cannot bring it in to single-point focus; he cannot "take aim" or keep the visitor in his sights.

In other words, he cannot "fixate" upon The Thing. To fixate means to make stable or stationary.

Thus his emotional disarray matches the breakdown in perception. He literally "loses focus." The film depicts this state in a montage of single shots showing the corporal firing in seemingly random directions. These directions simply do not line up. We can imagine the corporal feeling lost among these static figures. His dismay comes from the realization that he is missing in action; that the agency he thinks of as being in charge of his mental faculties has faded from the scene.

In a certain sense, therefore, the corporal—and by extension anyone exposed to the alien gaze—has *himself* been "fixated" by the gaze. Just as the creature was "fixated" inside the block of ice, so the corporal has become "fixated" by the creature's gaze. In other words, he has become at once fascinated, enthralled, and immersed, just as if he were watching a movie called The Thing. The word "petrified" conveys both the sense of horror and the resulting paralysis of the will. Perhaps the latter is most destabilizing of all, for it reduces the corporal to that of a pure *object* of the gaze, striking him mute, and robbing him of any sense of agency.

The crew's evolving strategy

Mobilized by the toxic and fatal effects of any close encounter with the visitor (two scientists have been killed), the crew begins a methodical search of the rooms inside the compound, using a Geiger counter to track its movements. The Geiger counter allows them to track the creature through its indirect effects, thus avoiding exposure to its gaze. Their initial goal is one of *containment*. They intend to trap the creature within a closed space—and block all conduits leading in or out. By keeping The Thing behind closed doors, they plan to limit exposure to its effects.

Their method bears fruit when they locate their adversary behind a closed door. With guns drawn, the captain asks his sergeant, "Are you ready?" The sergeant replies: "No, but go ahead". This gives the sergeant a moment to process what they are about to do. He recognizes his unreadiness and yet that very avowal announces his readiness and his preparation. "I am ready in my unreadiness", he seems to be saying. In fact, the brief verbal exchange between captain and sergeant, with the crew in attendance, acts as a thin buffer of time between the intention and the action—in effect a kind of verbal barricade against what they (and we) are about to see.

The door opens and the creature strikes out with his clawed hand. In the same instant, the men slam the door, trapping the appendage just outside the door. The creature then pulls in his hand and retreats. In this brief interval of time, he appears directly for the first time, at fifty-seven minutes running time, well past the halfway point of the film. Already his grand entrance has been postponed as long as possible. In point of fact, the strategy of limiting contact with the visitor dictates that the actual "close encounter" be deferred indefinitely. But the delay is effective in ramping up audience anticipation to a fever pitch. Indeed the sudden shock of seeing the creature, even for a millisecond, releases pent-up tension. At this point the mere approximation of a bogeyman would be enough to trigger a response.

Hence the director has performed a neat sleight of hand: he has given us the illusion of a hideous thing without any "special effects". For no sooner does The Thing appear, than it shrinks from sight. The door slams shut before our minds have time to take in the shot. The slamming door is like the closing of a camera shutter taking a still photo or a "freeze frame" of the action. And within this now stationary frame, we think we see The Thing. The frame appears to capture—much like a camera with a fast shutter speed captures a phenomenon invisible to the naked eye—The Thing itself. The stability of such an image would appear to fix it indelibly in the mind.

But actually the reverse happens: the slamming of the door disrupts and dissipates our impression of The Thing, effectively blotting it out. It is almost as though the filmmakers replicate the effect of the alien gaze: in the moment of rapid exposure, the "ego" of the viewer—namely, that part of the mind that interprets and judges sensory input—disappears.

However, the space of this blot serves as a "screen" upon which each viewer may project his own private version of The Thing. And by steering clear of actually showing lurid scenes of mauling and dismemberment, they allow primitive fantasy to supply the missing horrific elements. In the scene in question, the effect is facilitated by the eye's natural focus on the clawed hand, the one element that remains inside the visual field. A viewer may then extrapolate from the hand to a plausible body schema—a hybrid of man and beast like a centaur, satyr, or sphinx, for example; or perhaps a creature with multiple appendages such as a cephalopod.

But once again the director's decision to sharply curtail our visual access to The Thing goes beyond mere technique. For had the cinematographer shot The Thing in a long take or, heaven forbid, in close-up, the result would have been very different. Instead of a brief glimpse of something truly uncanny, we would have peered at a tall actor (the young James Arness) in a funny looking monster suit. Think of the effect on viewers whose patience is already strained. In place of the thrill of having their deepest fears realized on screen, they would feel only the deflation of an anticlimax and the dismay of being deprived of satisfaction. In other words, the movie's whole edifice would collapse if The Thing loses its aura of the extraordinary. Seen merely as a "thing" like any other—even a dangerous being eliciting fear—it would no longer fill the billing of its grand title, *The Thing*.

The Thing and the sexual object

The opening scene of *The Thing* establishes a connection between The Thing and the sexual object. The officers sitting around a card table first refer to The Thing as an object of "secret research." In almost the same breath, they mention an attractive woman assigned to the research group, who is a person of interest to Captain Henry. The men kid him about this, but he warns them not to step over the line. He is usually loose about pulling rank, but in this case he is obviously sensitive on the subject. His cautionary attitude warns the men not to reduce his interest to a purely prurient attraction. He is no doubt thinking of how sexual fantasy can proliferate among men isolated from women.

In a later conversation between Captain Henry and his co-pilot, this connection is made explicit. The co-pilot compares the effect of The Thing to that of an attractive woman on a captive male population. And he observes that, for the scientists, it is like a new toy in the hands of eager young boys. In both cases, he stresses the *disturbing* effect of the object. It is a source of attraction, yes, but it is also capable of rattling a tightly knit group or a tranquil mind.

The romantic subplot between Captain Henry and Nikki, the stenographer for the scientific group, shows the pair struggling with the sexual "thing." They are attracted to each other from the start. But that attraction has already caused a potential rift: Henry has recently made a pass at Nikki while intoxicated.

To its credit, the film allows Nikki to speak frankly to Henry about this unwanted sexual encounter. She explains that, for her, it was like being set upon by "eight hands" at the same time. She compares the eight hands to some sort of octopus. And although she doesn't spell it out, she leaves it to us to imagine what that must feel like. What's creepy is the sense of being assailed by disembodied (or severed) hands, each possessing a mind of its own, and acting independently. The subject of the "eight hands"—Captain Henry—is missing in action, a temporary casualty of his intoxication.

From Nikki's point of view, the experience is like being reduced to the "thing" the hands are pursuing. In that moment, she does not recognize her pursuer, nor does she recognize herself as a co-participant. She responds, not with desire, but with disgust and horror. Part of her response perhaps stems from being too close to the raw, undiluted *physicality* of sex, as if she were viewing the sexual act in extreme close-up. Her ability to sustain pleasure and anticipation depends on some degree of distance from the sexual "thing".

And this is exactly what she advocates in her continuing dialogue with Henry. In a second scene, she presents to him an alternative approach to the same given: their mutual attraction and liking for each other. She proposes they acknowledge the danger posed by "the sexual thing" and treat it with caution and circumspection. She demonstrates her approach by playfully tying-up Henry's mischievous hands. In so doing, she also shows that she *desires* Henry. That desire is coded in the implicit sadomasochistic fantasy. In the fantasy, she reverses the "eight hands" scenario and gives herself the dominant position. But she does so in a spirit of teasing exploration that allows both partners to participate. Certainly, the tying up enhances the erotic charge between them, while still holding Henry's impetuosity in check.

Yet she also tells him that her action will make a civilized man of him. In this fitting sentence she raises the "tying of hands" to the level of a symbolic act. It first of all represents the joining of hands—the human ties—required of civilized life. We will soon see, for example, that these connections acting in concert empower the human group to successfully stave off the alien visitor. The tying of hands also conveys the loss of freedom involved in any formal arrangement or contract. Thus it plays with the idea of marriage, evoking for example, the image of "ball and chain." And on a deeper level still, the tying up reinforces the cornerstone of civilized society: the prohibition against incest. That fundamental prohibition gives rise to the sexual taboos of a particular time and place, viz. sexual relations outside marriage. In the 1950s exceptions were made if a couple were "engaged."

Yet it is equally important to emphasize that Nikki does not speak on behalf of conventional morality—although what she says is certainly consistent with it. On the contrary, hers is an independent voice. She implies that restraint will actually enhance their future sexual encounters because it amplifies desire and spices it up with just a dollop of sadomasochism. But, most importantly, restraint protects the couple from the unforeseen consequences of untethered sexuality, such as pregnancy (a real possibility in the era before the pill). Indeed, its disregard for consequence temporarily suspends the subjectivity of both parties—their very ability to take consequences into account or to make ethical decisions.

Interestingly, Nikki places the sexual "thing" outside the couple per se. Each partner may temporarily become a "thing" in the eyes of the other—an object of lust, say, or object of disgust and horror. But a person is not to be equated with the "thing" itself. And while the man and the woman may hold different attitudes toward the "thing," "it" must remain forever a "thing" apart. Nikki advocates that she and Henry approach "it" as a *couple*, their partnership in effect serving as a bulwark against the "thing."

The implicit critique of science

The Thing delivers a thinly veiled critique of science at a time when the angst of the atomic age was beginning to set in. The movie alludes to the consequences of atomic energy by making The Thing radioactive. It seems to be saying that science has inadvertently produced a "thing" that has terrible repercussions and which may or may not be containable by humanity. Note that in this context, The Thing is a product of the human mind rather than a visitor from another planet. It came from outer space only in the sense that its advent was completely unexpected and inimical to life on Earth.

The screenplay brings this critique to life as a growing rift among the scientists regarding the nature of The Thing and the best way to approach it. One camp—perhaps the majority—advises caution and circumspection. They want to balance their desire to investigate The Thing against their equal desire to do no harm. They recognize that the investigation must include certain constraints that protect the participants, and by extension, the wider human population.

The film depicts their approach in a brilliant tableau of the scientific enterprise. The creature's severed arm has been recovered, and the scientists are examining it intently. The military stand on screen left, the scientists on screen right. A double-jointed lamp dominates center frame, flooding the field with light. One scientist holds up a large magnifying glass. Then the scene cuts to a co-worker peering through a compound microscope.

The light conveys the intensity of the men's gaze and their rapt attention on the task at hand. What is it that attracts their interest? Or put another way, what is the object that evokes their fascination? That object—the severed arm—is first and foremost a *dead* object. The inertness of the severed arm keeps the scientists at arm's length from the potentially toxic effects of The Thing. But while an inert object may not be toxic, it is also not particularly exciting or disturbing to the men. The proof comes when the hand starts to move. The slightest movement of the hand is enough to "spook" the scientists and halt their investigation.

What then *does* excite the researchers? For we know that, according to Henry's co-pilot, their level of excitement rivals that of a gang of boys presented with a new toy. But if the severed arm—while not without interest—proves lukewarm, what then generates the excitement? I would suggest it is the various instruments on display in the tableau: the articulated lamp, the magnifying glass, the microscope, and ultimately the human eye itself.

Thus, what animates the scientists is the variety of instruments they can bring to bear on The Thing. Their pleasure arises from the exercise of their advanced technology. Psychically, these "toys" represent extensions and enhancements of the human body. Their imaginary potency evoked in the tableau by tenfold magnification, makes of them phallic objects. But in that case, should they not promise mastery over The Thing?

But these scientists do not indulge in bravado. Let us note that the phallic object is defined as much by its limitations and boundaries as it is by its imaginary powers. It is not the thing itself—the penis, for example—because it "stands in" rather than "stands up." And for this very reason, it serves as a buffer—a kind of phalanx, if you will, around The Thing. Consequently, there is always an instrument between the severed arm and the naked eye. Yet such a safeguard—much like a condom—carries a built-in restraint on the intensity of fulfillment, scientific or otherwise. The researcher must accept that curiosity will be only partially satisfied.

In contrast to this judicious and prudent approach, the alternative is pursued with greater passion and ardor. Its leading exponent is Carrington. In contrast to the more static approach of the others, he conducts an experiment on the *living substance* of the visitor. We see only its product: a litter of throbbing, pulsating, alien babies. When osculated by one of the scientists, we hear a dissonant mewling sound.

Thus, instead of a dead object, we are presented with the visitor's vital essence—its germ protoplasm—so to speak. When Nikki witnesses these creatures, she begs to be excused. Her feelings of horror and disgust register the powerful effects of the sexual object on the human subject. The vehemence of her reaction no doubt arises from her proximity to the object's immense *vitality*, as well as the infernal taint of incestuous couplings. And it further expresses her resolution to re-establish distance and thus reclaim her rightful human mindset.

Carrington, however, feels no such inhibitions. For him the object of science and the sexual "thing" are one and the same. The critique of science implies that his pursuit of The Thing at all costs constitutes a Frankenstein-like miscarriage of the scientific endeavor. His passion for the thing-in-itself may then represent an inherent striving within science. It suggests something relentless and "drive-like" in its makeup. We sense this rapacious tendency in the premonition that whatever is scientifically feasible will eventually be realized regardless of ethical reservations held by the scientists themselves. From the psychoanalytic perspective, this critique compares such strivings to the sexual partial drives (Freud, 1905d), which seek their object at all costs outside of any risk/benefit calculation and against the instinct for self-preservation.

Subjectivity: The ultimate defense against The Thing

The men and women of the compound are imbued with a strong sense of camaraderie and *esprit de corps*. There is a surprising loosening of strict hierarchy and an almost total absence of authoritarianism. A spirit of collaboration prevails both within and between the military and science groups. Among all the participants, discussion and airing of differing views is encouraged.

An early scene between Captain Henry and his sergeant illustrates this nicely. The sergeant offers the helpful suggestion that the length of time a man stands guard over the visitor in the storeroom be reduced to two hours. The captain accepts this suggestion. He does not counter it with one of his own. He is unfazed by a man of lesser rank taking the lead; indeed he commends him for it. The sergeant, in his turn, graciously hints that he would not take offence if the captain were to co-opt this suggestion as his own, in order to preserve the chain of command. Yet the captain, in his turn, returns the credit to the sender.

Thus the "credit" circulates between the two men. "Credit" is a purely verbal, hence symbolic, entity. Credit implies the absence of a "thing."

To purchase something on credit is to pay nothing. The only thing given and received is one's promise to pay. And as a non-thing, it is in the nature of credit—not to lie dormant in a vault, accumulating and solidifying as substance—but rather to circulate among men and women. Thus the giving and receiving of credit represents an act of faith for both parties. It establishes a bond between Henry and his sergeant that epitomizes the links between all team members.

The romance between Henry and Nikki—already discussed—is depicted as a tongue-in-cheek "bondage." Nikki offers this little game as a verbal "proposal." It underscores her aim to be treated as a full partner in the relationship. In pursuit of this goal, she "engages" Henry directly through her speech. She, for example, invites him to have a drink with her instead of waiting around for him to make the first move. She has the audacity to assess his handling of the group. And she does all this against the expectation that a woman working in a military setting in 1951 should be seen and not heard.

In a clever spin on the job of "stenographer," the screenplay gives Nikki the freedom to expand this traditionally female role into that of *liaison*. For as private secretary to Carrington and emerging partner to Henry, she finds herself in the unique position of mediating between scientists and military. She sees that Carrington and Henry hold diametrically opposed opinions regarding The Thing and she wants to keep the dialogue going between them.

But she soon discovers a glitch in the works. Carrington, in the course of pursuing his own personal agenda, conceals vital information about his actions in the lab, the reproduction experiment in particular. Upon discovering this break in communication, Nikki gives Henry the experimental notes. She does this not merely because she loves Henry. She respects and admires Carrington and declines to condemn him. But she sees the latter's action as a refusal to talk about The Thing—just as Henry was initially reluctant to talk about the sexual "thing" with her. The breach is less about withholding than the removal of an idea from circulation. As liaison, Nikki defines her mission as preserving the possibility that all questions can be openly debated. Ultimately, Carrington's decision to "go rogue" breaches the pact between speakers: the engagement of the listener in every act of speech. In healing this breach, Nikki ratifies her commitment to Henry, brings the scientists and military back into association, and acknowledges Henry and Carrington as worthy adversaries.

Consequently, the free circulation of words and ideas among the group is restored. The filmmakers emphasize that the group's successful stand against the invader is dependent on the free exchange of ideas, and the consequent ability to reach independent judgments. Captain Patrick Henry represents this freedom through his namesake, whose motto was, "give me liberty or give me death." His ultimate decision to destroy the visitor—against the belated orders of his own General—is entirely his own.

Censorship and The Thing

However, Henry and Nikki's promotion of free speech butts up against a countervailing force: the censorship. We have already noted two of its sources: the suppression of sexual content dictated by the Hays Office and the technical constraints imposed by the film's low budget. The Freudian usage refers to the blocking out or redacting of what cannot be explicitly stated or shown in the film. Hence we postulate that the omission of direct references to sexuality is analogous to placing an electric blanket over The Thing to block its gaze. Obviously, if we were to substitute "genitalia" for The Thing, the blanket would screen the viewer's gaze.

Censorship enters the picture when Henry prevents Scotty, the newspaperman, from sending out information about the spacecraft until official authorization is obtained. Scotty—who combines the function of photographer and reporter—has a natural interest in getting the story out as quickly as possible. In limiting such communication, the captain wants to prevent mass panic and hysteria. Indeed, the camp has just received a bulletin that sightings of "flying saucers" are the result of "mass hysteria." So the captain might think that if he informs the public he will be inciting such "mass hysteria." On the other hand, he might worry that outsiders will think he and his team are the victims of mass hysteria. His claims might therefore be met with disbelief, and his credibility impugned. In either case, he has every reason to postpone such communication until such time as definitive proof can be produced.

The censorship reaches a crescendo just as the combined military and science teams are preparing to annihilate the creature. Henry has just been made aware of Carrington's duplicity and betrayal. He responds to the threat by quarantining the scientist in a confined area. This action effectively keeps him incommunicado. Henry treats him as if he were "radioactive" like The Thing. Indeed, his primary aim may be to protect others—including the public at large—from toxic effects on a mass scale. Interestingly, the move also protects Carrington from further exposure to The Thing in an effort to halt his mania.

In the making of a movie such as *The Thing*, censorship is imposed at successive points in time. It is there from the beginning in the director's sophisticated knowledge of what is acceptable to the Hays Office and the sensibilities of a mass audience. It is exercised again by the studio's critique of the raw footage. They may demand omission of dubious content as well as additions such as happy endings that package the film as a generally acceptable fantasy: a product of the "dream factory." And still further cuts are made in the final editing of post-production. Indeed, these cuts sometimes render a film unrecognizable to the filmmakers and, at times, incoherent due to the loss of narrative continuity.

In parallel to these external acts of censorship are those within the film narrative. Here the equivalent of the director's mindset is the suppression of information already in place at the site of "secret researches" being conducted near the North Pole. The analogue to studio oversight is Captain Henry's total news blackout. The silencing of Carrington after his betrayal and Scotty's final press release correspond to "post-production" or after-the-fact revisions.

And it is this internal censorship conducted by the film's protagonists that raises barriers to open discussion of sexuality. The original mindset of "secret research" suggests the phase of infantile sexual researches discovered by Freud—a part of life history often forgotten in adulthood (Freud, 1905d). During this phase the child pursues sexual knowledge with the zeal of a Carrington and with the latter's naive arrogance that all questions can be answered. The suppression and redaction of news represents a conservative desire to evade subversive thoughts; but in addition, seeks protection from the toxic effects of excessive stimulation (which Freud discussed under the rubric of automatic anxiety). Interestingly, "news" or "thoughts" with a sexual content are treated as if they were as "radioactive" as The Thing itself. Thus word of The Thing might set off "mass hysteria" and Carrington's ideas could infect or "corrupt" others.

We see evidence of this concern in Scotty's final and somewhat tendentious news bulletin. In this narrative summary delivered after the final conflagration, Scotty offers a sanitized version of events to the world. In a display of patent revisionism, he repackages the narrative as a "war-of-the-worlds" scenario with a familiar ring. This is Hollywood shaping the material to resemble a fairytale or collective fantasy, a typical product of the "dream factory." In the fantasy a tightly knit band of intrepid men and woman triumph over a race of "super-warriors." Carrington's defection is omitted. Indeed, it downplays the role of dissent and freedom of thought in favor of mass consensus. And most strikingly of all, the precis fails to mention the subject of the movie; which is not a horde of alien marauders but The Thing of its memorable title.

This mode of censorship occurs at the transition between the climax of the action and the team's preparation to re-enter the world at large. In this sense, it resembles the censorship upon awakening from a dream, for it happens just when the ego is reassembling itself and reasserting its mastery. Part of that effort goes into denigrating the importance of the dream ("it is only a dream") or reimagining it as a daydream (Freud, 1900a).

The final conflagration

In two bravura set pieces, the men and woman of the compound carry out their plan to destroy the creature. But in engineering this final conflagration, the filmmakers also reassemble and consolidate the movie's principal thematic elements.

In the first scene, the men are poised to throw kerosene on the creature and ignite it with a flare gun. They kill the lights in order not to be seen. The creature next appears in the doorway, backlit, so that its entire frontage lies in deep shadow. At just the right moment, the kerosene is hurled, and the creature bursts into flame. The smoke and flames further obscure its features. Indeed, the shock and awe of the spectacle draws attention away from The Thing itself.

The flames do, however, suggest the idea of incendiary passion and excitement that is barely (if at all) containable. As if in support of such a premise, one of the men throws Nikki a flame-retardant mattress for her protection. The mattress beautifully materializes the buffer between human and Thing. But let us stop here for a moment. Remember that at the outset, Nikki herself was considered an exciting and disturbing object. Thus the mattress shields the others from Nikki's smoldering sexuality as well. Yet it also answers her own need for a defensive barrier against her passionate nature.

After the creature retreats outside, Nikki says, in a half-joking tone, "If I start burning up, who's going to put out the fire?" Of course she is all but admitting the connection to her own sexual desire. Her little joke makes a double entendre. It links the destructive element of fire with sexuality. And the words "put out the fire" equally suggest throwing cold water on desire or obtaining sexual satisfaction. Hence Nikki's jest nicely raises the question whether the crew is extinguishing or accelerating the fire. And the same contradiction pertains to the split between the crew at pains to extinguish the source of agitation and the audience's mounting excitement at this display of pyrotechnics.

In the second scene, electricity takes the place of fire. The room is rigged to complete a circuit when the alien walks along a designated central path— a kind of "track" with a third rail. We initially see the creature in long shot, at the far end of the track, and along a narrow corridor. The long shot gives the viewer a stable vantage point with which to follow the action. The vantage point is located where the two rails of the track meet at the horizon or converge at a point on the viewer's retina (fovea). The creature's face, however, is still obscured by shadow.

The visitor picks up a wooden plank or "tie" and approaches. This action will prove auspicious. At the least, it lends the visitor a sense of agency that up to now he has lacked. He does what any human would do if backed into a corner. This evidence of the visitor's subjectivity unsettles us because it implies kinship (perhaps hinted at by the railroad "tie") at just the moment when he is being kept at arm's length.

Suddenly the lights go out and Carrington appears, armed with a pistol. He is immediately and easily disarmed. He must have wanted to hold everybody at bay while he attempted to communicate with the visitor. His pistol and the creature's wooden plank cast the pair of them as strange bedfellows. Then in a *coup de foudre*, he rushes toward the visitor in a vain effort to make contact.

The alien pauses. He seems as nonplussed by the situation as we are. For the briefest of seconds, the two of them stand face to face. The tantalizing possibility of such contact is dangled before us only to be quashed when the creature swats Carrington away with his free hand. But note that the visitor does not hit him with the wooden plank that he holds in his other hand. And therefore he never uses the "tie" as a weapon.

In his pause and in his decision not to use lethal force, the visitor proves capable of restraint. In these actions the film implies there may be a split between the visitor as agent or potential subject and the alien "thing" he embodies. This separation of visitor from "thing" once again demonstrates the impossibility of identifying The Thing with any specific entity or being.

The visitor resumes walking but steps off the wooden pathway in the center of the corridor. One of the men throws another wooden plank in his direction causing him to "get back on track." At this point, the group has the alien just where they want him—at the ideal point where all their lines of sight meet. At the right moment, a switch is thrown, and artificial bolts of lightning leap from the creature's head and two hands. For its brief duration, all eyes are held captive, until The Thing shrinks down to a heap of ash. Then Scotty, who has been taking flash photos of the conflagration, collapses in a faint. His reaction affords everybody a much-needed bit of comic relief.

That comic relief arises in part from the note of anti-climax. Just at the moment when the human group has apparently achieved complete mastery over The Thing, the official witness to the electrocution is reduced to a senseless "heap," almost as helpless and inert as the incinerated creature. Indeed, his faint subtly underscores the crew's inability to master The Thing. For at the moment when they "fix" the creature in their sight—when all lines of sight converge on it—the sudden flash of electricity "trans-fixes" them. That flash momentarily blinds them with its intensity and with its display of razzle-dazzle, reducing them and us viewers to mere voyeurs. In this regard, the "flashes" of Scotty's camera—so neatly exploited by Alfred Hitchcock in *Rear Window* (1954)—mimic the effect of the electric arcs. And once again, the "flash" deflects attention from The Thing itself, which is never seen. Those photos are never shown in the film, implying that it is never possible to capture a stable image of The Thing on film.

And on a deeper level—further elaborated in *Invasion of the Body Snatchers* (1956)—the comic anticlimax of the faint suggests the possibility of a sexual climax followed by post-coital sleep. We have already introduced the idea that The Thing is related to the sexual object and that fire and electricity are common metaphors for human passion. In this light, the faint is a swoon of passion and the "heap of ash" the state of inertia left behind when satisfaction has been achieved. In this view, the destruction of The Thing is equivalent to being consumed in the heat of passion. And the apparent victory over it amounts to rendering it (temporarily) incapable of attracting, repelling, or exciting the human protagonists.

Conclusions

In the end, the team solidifies its position against the invader by "closing ranks." In promoting this policy, Scotty's official communiqué addresses the global threat with a worldwide network of sentinels intently watching the sky and maintaining constant vigilance. On a more intimate scale, the sergeant entreats his captain to "settle down" in marriage. In both cases, closing ranks means joining together the disparate parts. And given the importance of this impending marriage for the group, their wedding enacts the formal tie between all team members. The two scales intersect in Scotty's allusion to Noah's ark. In this image, he in effect advocates universal marriage: the organization of humanity into a collection of monogamous pairs.

We may compare "closing ranks" to the action of pulling tight the two leads of a net so that its lacunae shrink down to almost nothing. This tightening and shrinking will in turn envelope The Thing in restraining bonds that immobilize it (like encasing it in a block of ice) and keep it buried like a foreign body within its host. On the more intimate scale of the small group, or the individual psyche, the policy seeks to nip the sexual object in the bud, thus neutralizing its "radioactivity"—that is, its erotic charge. Thus the policy entails a loss of freedom for both human and "thing", and therefore hints that all of us are "tied up" irrevocably with the sexual "thing."

Accordingly, the giddy sense of triumph at the moment of apparent victory contrasts with the dire warning that The Thing will return. Captain Henry conveys this concern in his humble attitude toward The Thing. It surfaces in his decision not to retaliate against Carrington for his betrayal. On a deeper level he perhaps recognizes that Carrington "going rogue" in the grip of overwhelming passion is not unlike himself devolving into an eight-handed cephalopod. Consequently, he knows that some day a "rogue element" will break free of terra firma, take on a life of its own, and ultimately hijack the entire security apparatus. And he at least senses that the group's supposed unity is provisional and its mastery over The Thing ephemeral.

Yet none of the participants know from which direction it will come next. The warning points to the sky. And certainly they want it to next appear in the sky where they can see it coming from far away; where they can detect it with instruments even *before* they see it.

But suppose it were to come from the opposite direction, from within? This possibility is brilliantly visualized in the film as the circle of outstretched hands surrounding a dark shape in a patch of ice. This shot taken from above (the sky) shows The Thing at the very core and heart of the human condition from a point unattainable by the participants. Thus no one anticipates the possibility of such a return. And this disregard adds a dimension of dread to the warning that no amount of vigilance can dispel. The "return from within" will become a constant theme in the future sequels, prequels, and re-imaginings of The Thing. It is almost as if the question is not when will The Thing return but when will we realize it is already here.

CHAPTER TWO

The Sleep of Desire in *Invasion of the Body Snatchers*

One feature of a movie's classic status is that it never appears dated. It looks and sounds as fresh today as it did when first released. Such is certainly the case with the *Invasion of the Body Snatchers* (1956)—one of many low budget science fiction movies churned out in the 1950s. This film is effective, in part, because it manages to induce profound unease in the viewer with virtually no special effects. It succeeds by sowing discord by other means. It's rudimentary soundtrack, for example, plays three jolting bass notes on a piano. Its visual style employs jump cutting, atypical framing, close-ups, and chiaroscuro to create uncanny effects.

In one of his signature techniques, Don Siegel, the director, interrupts a scene with some seemingly accidental distraction. The disruptive element is often an object such as a ringing telephone or a chiming cuckoo clock. Or it could be a series of cuts that impart a jagged or fragmented quality to a chase scene. Siegel also plays upon the burgeoning anonymity and unpredictability of California's highways. Automobile traffic stands in for any mass-movement where every vehicle is moving in the same direction. He shatters that notion by arranging three near collisions during the course of the movie.

In a key early scene, for example, we see the lead character, Dr. Miles Bennell, driving to his office in the town of Santa Mira, California. Accompanied by his nurse, he is half-listening to her concern that something has happened to the townspeople while he was attending a medical convention. It seems that a mysterious malady has "taken possession" of them. But before she can say more, a young boy (Jimmy) suddenly dashes in front of the car, causing the doctor to veer away, barely averting a collision.

In the scene, the near-collision snaps the doctor out of his reverie and refocuses his attention. It forces a change in direction, and for Miles Bennell, a reappraisal of his immediate plans. His "path" had pointed toward a homecoming from his trip and a return to established routine. But the mishap with the boy shakes his composure, and prevents him falling into a false sense of complacency.

Shortly after his return to the office, the boy and his grandmother come to see him for a consultation. While questioning the grandmother, Miles hears the boy cry out "she is not my mother." The boy then implores the adults in attendance to "not let her get me." Miles is shocked by the boy's outrageous claim but he senses his distress is genuine. On first hearing, he thinks the boy must be mistaken and he offers friendly reassurance that would have been typical for a GP at this time and place. But the boy stubbornly rebuffs his efforts. He will not minimize the urgency he feels, and his vehemence testifies to the strength of his conviction.

Yet the boy's tenacity has an invigorating effect on the doctor. It goads him into asking questions. Fortuitously, his soon-to-be girlfriend, Becky Driscoll, tells him about her cousin Wilma, whose complaints mimic those of the young boy. In this case, it is her uncle Ira, who is "not her uncle."

When Miles meets her, he immediately asks: "How is he different?" Wilma's response, "that's just it," reveals that she has asked herself the same question. She concedes that the change is not one "you can actually see," but senses that "something is missing" nevertheless. She recounts that, since childhood, Ira had been a father figure to her. She came to associate their bond with a "special look in his eye when he talked to me." In a similar vein, she opines that there was "no emotion, only the pretense of it."

It is also relevant to consider Wilma's emotional state while answering Miles' questions. She seems both pensive and mildly baffled, as if Miles' question continues to haunt her. Yet the one thing that rings true in her mind is her *question* concerning uncle Ira. Ultimately, it is a question of identity: she no longer knows who or what he is. And this causes her to question who or what *she* is in his mind, adding to her sense of insecurity. Thus her responses to Miles' questions appear tentative and preliminary. They fall short of yielding a solution that would fully satisfy her.

Wilma's questions can be stated in another way: how can Ira be so outwardly identical with his former self and yet be so fundamentally changed? Her statement about his lack of emotion addresses this question. Yet while she perceives Ira through the lens of their shared personal history, the new Ira might view her from a different mindset. His inability to "see" Wilma could simply reflect his participation in a collective mood, a mass-mentality. That mood might convey smug superiority, for example, an unwelcome emotion but not an absent one.

In this regard, Wilma's unconscious word choice of "pretense" might imply "pretentious" as if Ira was looking down his nose at her (instead of looking her straight in the eye) from an elevated status. The use of the term "affected" for this attitude plays upon the two meanings of "put on" and "moved with emotion." But the assumption that Ira is feigning or pretending is unnecessary. From their point of view, they are entirely sincere. Indeed it is their monolithic solidarity behind a single shared viewpoint that may add to Wilma's unease.

But these barriers to the truth do not deter Miles from pursuing Jimmy and Wilma's line of questions and others that now occur to him. He will come to define himself as a one-man board of inquiry into the town's unknown malady. And in accordance with this aim, he will try to separate the questions from the answers and distractions that readily present themselves. Thus he will call upon both his innate skepticism and his growing malaise. His tenacious resistance against all efforts to quell his fears—borrowed in part from Jimmy Grimaldi—will inure him against any *idée reçue* promising to reinstate his own and the townspeople's original complacency. In the end he will employ questions not as a demand for answers but rather as the critical "disruptive element" that might shake loose the truth.

Miles and Becky

His first challenge arrives in the person of Becky Driscoll, an attractive woman and old acquaintance. When he encounters her in his examining room after a five-year absence, the attraction between them is clear. For this scene and this scene only, the director has her wear an especially fetching outfit that in a flash rekindles Miles' desire for her, and hastens the flirtatious mood between them.

And that erotic charge is heightened by the fact that both are now divorced. Each hints at their new status in joking allusions to Reno—at that time the Mecca for quickie divorces. Divorce—although widely recognized as an accepted life decision—still carried an air of social stigma in 1950s California. Yet paradoxically, the realization that they are both mature adults who happen to be unattached opens the door to a sexual relationship, provided they remain discreet.

Yet the very life choice that brings them together as "lodge brothers" also separates them from the freshness of an "innocent" relationship. For they now inhabit an ambiguous area: from a legal standpoint, their relationship is completely legitimate. Adultery does not apply. Yet they cannot escape a whiff of the illicit. Their relationship is still an affront to married people of Santa Mira who may envy the couple's sexual freedom and believe it to be undeserved. In a small town such as theirs, their relationship will undoubtedly become the subject of gossip.

We must also recall that Miles and Becky's meeting is a reunion of sorts. Their attraction toward each other pre-dates their meeting by years. For all we know, they could have had an affair while both were still married. And even if they didn't, they probably wanted to. Indeed, what might be fueling the current erotic charge is the sudden freedom to consummate a long anticipated liaison. Besides the fulfillment of a romantic fantasy, their meeting enacts the return to an earlier state of bliss that alleviates the pain of separation.

Now that they have reunited, their love affair takes on its own momentum. We see the couple sharing a drink at a nightclub. Later the scene shifts to Becky's house at night where the erstwhile lovers are about to consummate their affair. But just before they take the plunge, Becky makes the strange assertion that going further would be "madness." Her use of this word is striking and although we do not know exactly what she means, it expresses Becky's emotional qualms. It means that what they are about to do is reckless, foolhardy, and disregarding of consequences. Yet it also suggests bliss and ecstasy. It even suggests the pair has fallen prey to the "mass hysteria" pervading the town. At base, it warns of the imminent loss of the *couple's full awareness of what they are doing.*

And as if he knew of Becky's misgivings, her father appears and offers Miles a nightcap. His presence leaves Miles nonplussed. He politely declines the father's offer and leaves. One might assume that he feels barred by the oedipal father guarding his daughter or goading his own conscience. But Becky's father seems lackadaisical about Miles' presence at the threshold of her bedroom. He looks sinister without being either menacing or prohibitive. But his presence does underscore Becky's longstanding attachment to him. If anything, it is this paternal attachment that holds them back. But it also supports her infatuation with Miles. As a dedicated physician and somewhat older man, he certainly ranks as a father figure.

And the presence of Becky's father hints at yet another aspect of the "madness." We may guess that Becky has a "fixation" on her father and that she has always seen herself as his docile little girl. Perhaps she feels on a deep level an overpowering temptation to remain in this state even if it jeopardizes her independent existence. It is as if she allows her father to keep her locked up inside a "box" or trapped within an archaic self-image.

Perhaps Miles senses Becky's entrapment because once outside her home he has a premonition that she is in danger. That foreboding enters his mind when he thinks of her father working late in the basement. Upon entering the basement through a window, he opens a cabinet and finds a female body with eyes closed. In horror and dismay he realizes it is Becky—or her double. Thus his premonition is confirmed. Becky is indeed locked inside one of her father's "boxes." Also (and like Jack's double, still to be discussed) she appears trapped in a deathlike trance akin to sleep or suspended animation.

Miles rushes upstairs and sees Becky's father asleep in his bedroom. He then enters Becky's bedroom and finds her asleep as well. He is unable to arouse her. So he picks her up and carries her downstairs and out of the house. Then the scene dissolves. Thus in quick succession we see Becky's dormant double, the father oblivious to a home invasion, and Becky in a deep sleep from which she cannot be awakened. Hence the danger Miles senses must have to do with Becky's apparent helplessness.

Then it is the morning after, and Miles and Becky are having breakfast in his kitchen. They acknowledge their intimacy of the preceding night. That is, they have finally "slept together." Becky remarks that it was "too good to be true." This phrase calls to mind her earlier words "this is madness." It suggests a state of rapture that is impossible to sustain, one that holds the mind captive in a delusory state. Miles, for example, seems to have forgotten his premonition of the night before that Becky was in danger.

In order to dispel some of the illogicality of the preceding scenes, let us attempt a thought experiment. Suppose for a moment that Miles is not carrying Becky *out* of her bedroom asleep but instead carrying her *into* his bedroom very much awake. That is, instead of Becky being asleep first and then inexplicably awake, she is first awake and *later* asleep. But since we now know that she and Miles have "slept together," we may conclude that the deep sleep she falls into is post-coital sleep. This would account for her earlier inability to become "aroused."

Moreover, the idea of post-coital sleep itself implies a temporal sequence. It starts with the moment of sexual surrender, reaches a climactic lapse in consciousness during, and finally ebbs toward a feeling of languor. The languor in turn can devolve into lethargy and even a kind of cataplexy—a paralysis triggered by a sudden upsurge of emotion or while dreaming. I mention these sub-phases in order to suggest the various forms of psychical inertia they call to mind, including any mental state that lulls the mind to sleep and blocks it from processing disturbing thoughts and signals of distress.

Awakening

While having drinks at a nightclub, Miles receives an emergency phone call from his friend Jack. He and Becky rush over to his home. Next we see Jack, his wife Teddy, Miles, and Becky gathered around a billiard table. They now constitute an informal "cell" poised to investigate the strange events. On the table lies a figure draped with a cover. Miles pulls it down, revealing a man's body. Then in quick succession, the music ramps up, the light throws Miles' shadow on the wall, and a raucous cuckoo clock chimes.

The group examines the body. They notice its generic appearance, like the "first impression stamped on a coin." It lacks character. There are no details, no "lines." Miles takes fingerprints and discovers they are missing. In fact, there are no distinguishing marks of any kind.

Debate arises as to whether the body is alive or dead. Its immobility suggests the latter. But its appearance as a newly minted creation suggests some form of dormancy. It reminds Miles of a "new model" which has only to be activated in order to come fully alive.

Then Teddy asks the group how tall they think it is, and how much it weighs. She notes that Jack's measurements are roughly the same. And immediately, Jack and Becky disparage this idea as "nonsense." But Teddy's question still hangs over the group. Moreover, the moment Teddy asks her question, Jack drops a liquor bottle and cuts his hand. The mishap momentarily interrupts his wife's train of thought, while she applies a bandage to Jack's cut.

Irresolute as to their next move, the group disperses. Teddy agrees to watch over the body during the night to see if anything changes. She falls asleep slumped over a barstool. The body's outsize face and fixed stare dominates the frame. And once again the cuckoo clock sounds. Teddy awakes with a start. She nears the body. The camera zooms in to a cut on its hand identical to the one on Jack's hand. She grasps the import of what she sees. And in that moment her face reveals the wrenching agony she is undergoing. Almost in an effort to expel the thought from her mind, she cries: "It's you! Its you!"

In both these heavily fraught scenes, Don Siegel emphasizes the moment of awakening from sleep. Recall that Miles was alerted to the situation by a ringing phone. The viewers are alerted by the swelling music. The cuckoo clock chimes not once but twice. And along with sounds, Siegel's use of close-ups, odd camera angles, and shadows lends the scene a "hypnopompic" aura.

Let us first review Teddy's moment of awakening. In the pure state, sleep means the suspension of all mental activity. For Teddy, wakefulness entails the resumption and full engagement in mental processing. Thus upon awakening, Teddy is reminded of the *time* by the cuckoo clock. In her exclamation, she makes a *judgment*. Indeed it is the act of judgment itself, which separates the waking mind from the sleeping or dreaming state. And in the same act, Teddy re-establishes her identity, for the "you" of her statement implies an "I."

Moreover, Teddy's actions upon awakening are imbued with affect. Strong affect, like thought, is arousing and therefore incompatible with sleep. In her shining moment on screen, the actress, Carolyn Jones, imparts multiple tonalities to the scene. There is first the surprise and even shock of discovery. There is the accusatory tone of an indictment. She realizes on some level that Jack has betrayed her. And then there is the vehemence in her voice and in the repetition of "its you!" In her effort to expel the words and in her emphasis on the word "you" she avoids the realization that she too is the auditor of her own words—"you too," as it were.

And throughout, Jones makes us feel the pain and agony this discovery costs her. Psychic pain is the great disturber of sleep and the reason that we dream. Let us note that her pain rests on a kernel of reality. The craving for sleep operates in all of us to a greater or lesser extent. Thus in the moment of awakening, Teddy—like all of us—must wrench herself free of sleep's undertow—of its powerful pull toward a few more minutes of oblivion. This fact should remind us that Teddy's declaration works as an act of separation and a severing of ties. She is saying, in effect, and mostly on an unconscious level, that her image of Jack can never be the same again; that in a certain sense, their intimacy is tainted.

Teddy's shift from sleep to wakefulness also calls to mind the transition from sleep to dreaming. The popular view of dreaming still clings to the notion that dreaming is just another form of escape from reality. But Freud (1900a) reminds us that the exact opposite is true: *dreams are the true disturbers of sleep*. If anything, they differ from our waking tendency to lull our faculties of thought and judgment. Thus when Teddy awakes, Don Siegel places her inside the frame of a dream. The weird imagery of the body's looming head, the fixed and vacant stare, and its placement along the horizontal line of the frame as if levitating off the ground is clearly intended to disturb and alarm. In a sense we could say that Teddy goes to sleep with a rather bland and innocuous sleeping body, and awakes to a body transformed by the dream-work into a monstrous body that is wide awake and ready to strike.

And in yet a third comparison, the scenes show the interplay between a blank or vacant screen (or dream screen) and its occupants. The blank screen or "dream screen" (Lewin, 1946) refers first to the infant asleep at the breast after a satisfying feed and the surface upon which the dream is projected. It is depicted in the movie by the body-double under examination. Its blankness is first indicated by its "cover" and then by its lack of character or distinguishing traits. It further suggests the body's empty stare and lack of animation or facial expressions. The occupied screen on the other hand, refers to the dream state, the unsatisfied mind, and waking thought. In this sense, Teddy goes from a zero-point to near maximum intensity.

Consider also the counterpoint between the body before and after Teddy's discovery. In the first examination, we can assign the body a value of "zero." After Teddy's discovery, it warrants a value of "one." The "one" corresponds to the "cut on the hand" which is also a single mark or line. The "one" retroactively gives a meaning to the body previously devoid of meaning. For Teddy it constitutes a verbal connection or bridge. We can thus view her declaration as a quasi-psychoanalytic interpretation. She interprets Jack's bungled action of the night before—dropping the bottle—as an admission. We're not sure of its exact content but an approximation might be: "you have lied about your hidden agenda."

The kiss of death

A few scenes later, the last piece of the puzzle falls into place. In Jack's greenhouse, a large pod splits open revealing a creature emerging from foamy fluid. From this "birth" the foursome can now reconstruct the sequence of events. They see that the overriding purpose of the "invasion" is reproduction, or what Miles calls: "duplication"; in other words, proliferation of exact copies. "Duplication" also implies that the "units" share an identical mindset. Their ultimate goal is the creation of a monolithic "mass-mentality" or "hive-mind." The film gives concrete form to this idea via the "pods" which are lightweight, compact, and easily duplicated. At this point in the movie, the multiple pods anticipate the "hive-mind" while the original bodies—the last traces of human diversity—disappear.

The group quickly deduces that all ties to family, friends, and neighbors must be severed (or at least suspended) even if it means destroying them. But they do not take the mental leap of seeing themselves as possible victims. In fact, breaking these bonds will prove a wrenching task, as Teddy foresaw in the case of Jack. Miles, for example, takes a pitchfork and prepares to impale the likeness of Becky. But he is unable to follow through because of the resemblance. The agony shows in his face and eyes. He looks away. He wields the pitchfork on a male figure instead. Yet his hesitation regarding Becky reveals a potential weakness. Miles does not yet realize the alien "contagion" has already affected him (let alone her) and that he will have to fight tooth and nail to free himself from its grip. He is just as susceptible to it as any other citizen of Santa Mira.

At this point, Miles decides to get help. He pays a visit to his trusted nurse, Sally. However, he becomes wary when he sees several cars parked in front of her house. He stands in the doorway. Sally sits in the center of a little group, her baby on her lap. Miles asks, "Is the baby asleep yet?" Sally answers, "No, but she will be soon." Then a slight pause … "and there will be no more tears." Sally says they have been waiting for him, and invites him inside. Miles bolts from the house and flees in his car with Becky.

This brief scene is chilling in its serene domesticity. The baby is about to fall asleep. We already know that the erasure of mind happens at the moment of falling asleep, and this tableau links the idea to the pervasive role of sleep during infancy. Thus Sally—the "nurse"—slips into the role of the nursing mother whose baby has just been fed. Also let us note that Sally's remark is delivered to Miles himself, implying that he too is on the verge of sleep (with its resulting loss of mind). Her words after the pause, make sense in the feeding context as well: the baby's tears have been soothed away prior to her going off to sleep.

Miles reacts to Sally's appeal by bolting from the scene. He and Becky now enter a phase of headlong flight from the townspeople. In one of their hiding places, a window gives them a panoramic view of the town square. The townspeople are slowly converging from all directions upon a central hub. It looks as if they were responding to an irresistible call (or force). The "pod-people"—for each of them now carries one—sort themselves into awaiting trucks.

At this moment Miles and Becky still believe they have found a temporary place of refuge, but they are dismayed when they discover that Jack (and probably Teddy) has been turned. Jack offers Miles and Becky another version of Sally's utopic vision: the promise of being "reborn in an untroubled world." The apparent loss of individuality is really no loss at all, for the simple reason that in the proposed state of bliss, the burden of caring one way or another has been obliterated. And even if you reject the idea, "you can't fight it, because sooner or later, you'll have to go to sleep."

However, after sedating their captors in what seems an ironic twist on the power of sleep, Miles and Becky again take to the road. While holed up inside an abandoned mine, they briefly see each other's reflections in a pool of water. They hear a haunting melody coming from afar. Miles decides to investigate on his own. He discovers the source of the song in a radio broadcast near a huge incubation facility. Upon returning to the mine, he discovers that Becky has fallen asleep.

They kiss.

And in that moment the scales fall from his eyes. Her eyes widen and lose focus; his quickly fill with horror and dread. He realizes that the woman he thought he loved is gone. Her beauty hid the reservoir of emptiness she has become. Only now can he summon the courage to wrench himself away from her likeness. Only now does he steel himself to destroy that likeness— that wavering image in the pool of water—and transcend the impasse he encountered in Jack's greenhouse.

At this critical juncture, let us again reorder events just slightly. Suppose that instead of being lured *away* from Becky, Miles is being lured *toward* her by the song's siren call. The kiss then makes sense as the response to this powerful force of attraction. It thus brings the entire sequence to a powerful "climax." But as was typical in Hollywood films, the screen kiss also stands in for the "climax" of sexual passion. And if such is the case, then sleep should *follow* the kiss, not *precede* it. The change in Becky's eyes could then reflect the moment of orgasm and subsequent post-coital sleep. Hence that moment of being "lost to him" symbolizes the dissolution of his infatuation. Indeed it hints that his liaison with Becky has been leading them astray all along.

And if this kiss casts doubt on the foundation of their affair, then perhaps his regard for Becky dulled his judgment of his and Becky's partnership. The sticking points have been present all along, starting with their status as fellow divorcees. Miles resents, for example, the perceived inequity of his "paying dues" while his ex "collects them." He ruefully puts Becky in the same category. He and Becky are also divided over the issue of having children. Both are childless. Becky wants children; Miles does not say, but we can infer that he has reservations. He notes that he was married to his job, for example, and had little energy left to devote to his marriage.

In the light of his ambivalence, his near-collision with Jimmy Grimaldi is significant. Jimmy dashes in front of his car in a moment of inattention or distraction. In retrospect it might seem as if the child, Jimmy, is the accidental result of a moment of inattention to birth control. Moreover, by almost hitting him, Miles unconsciously reveals his desire to not have a child. Perhaps he and his ex considered terminating a pregnancy?

And these possibilities are later intimated when Miles and Becky discover two pods hidden in the trunk of his car. Miles sets them on fire. Considering that the "pods" are embryos-in-the-making, and that they have been placed in the trunk unbeknownst to the couple, this act could be viewed as a termination of pregnancy.

But lest these contingencies seem far-fetched, it is well to keep in mind that Miles has been conducting his affair with Becky without thinking too much about the consequences. Despite movie censorship, the couple never even alludes to the possibility that Becky could get pregnant. Yet that is what Becky wants. Still, she is probably more aware than Miles of the complications this would cause. Indeed, her warnings to Miles that "this is madness" and "it is too good to be true" may refer to this very result.

Just for the sake of argument, let us assume that Becky has discovered she is pregnant right before she falls asleep in the mine. Such a turn of events would impart a new meaning to her surrender. At the moment of their final kiss, Becky's empty eyes might signify her overpowering satisfaction at having her most cherished desire fulfilled. But her being pregnant does not have to be literally true in order for this interpretation to resonate. Keep in mind that reproduction on a massive scale constitutes the sole drive of the invaders. By falling asleep and succumbing to the invaders, she allows her body to be used for the sole purpose of reproduction. According to a twisted logic she would thus surrender her future life and individuality in favor of her unborn "child."

Thus the conflicts between Miles and Becky join those of society at large. Becky becomes the embodiment of the new mentality and the lure intended to bring Miles into the fold. Miles' refusal makes him the last holdout—the gadfly—the goad—and ultimately a Cassandra crying in the wilderness.

Miles Bennell—the last subject standing

Miles is the last of a small band of resisters who define themselves through their acts of speech. First there was Jimmy Grimaldi and Becky's cousin, Wilma, who can only say what they are not: "she is not my mother/uncle; therefore, I am not her son/niece." Then there is Miles whose identity as a doctor and humanist is tied up with his determination to raise questions. And finally there is Teddy who fearlessly exposed (accused? indicted?) her husband Jack, and in so doing showed her true colors.

Note, however, that in each case the speaker addresses her message to a listener. In the case of Jimmy and Wilma, the interlocutor is Miles; for Teddy it is Miles, Becky, and Jack himself. But Miles' ability to function as a subject falls into jeopardy the moment his potential listeners desert him.

When the aliens openly revealed their purpose through Sally, Miles "former" nurse, he does not bother arguing with her because he already realizes there is nobody there to receive his message. Nor does he attempt to coax or cajole Becky once she drops her disguise. It would be futile.

And when Miles runs out into traffic, desperately trying to warn the others, he puts his life on the line. The filmmakers depict his predicament by showing cars almost hitting him and drivers shouting at him to get out of the way. Nobody takes him seriously. In this powerful shot the director plays upon the previous near collision with Jimmy Grimaldi. Those breaks in continuity also acted as bids for the viewer's attention. In general, placing Miles amidst traffic disrupts its alignment along parallel lines all moving in the same direction.

Miles implores drivers to "listen to me", a plea he repeats three times. When he fails to get anyone's attention, he utters his famous line "you're next!" His vulnerability is patent. Unless he can reach the ears of at least one person he becomes nothing more than a prophet crying in the wilderness. His final line ups the ante: its imperative voice signals urgency but its use of the word "you" makes it difficult to ignore. It is not addressed to "everybody" but rather to each individual listener. And before "you" can push it aside you have already taken it in! Moreover, the line carries an air of inevitability that instantly induces dread in the audience—the last remaining pool of potential listeners.

The frame

Not surprisingly, Don Siegel wanted to end his film just there with the echoing words "you're next!" ringing in our ears. However, the studio heads felt that such an ending would be too despairing for audiences to accept. Siegel acquiesced. He re-shot a "frame" around the story centered on Miles having been taken to a hospital ER for psychiatric examination. At the start of the film, we see and hear him telling his story to a psychiatrist, and from that standpoint, providing the voiceover for the rest of the film. The film concludes with the other half of the frame, when he is first brought in and assumed to be "mad as a March hare."

Despite having to compromise on this issue, some critics such as Roger Ebert (1994) came to believe that in this instance, Hollywood's instincts were correct. Ultimately, that is, the film's effectiveness did not suffer from the addition of an artificial device, and may have benefited. This is true in part because Siegel adapted the frame to elaborate and extend the film's thematic range. From our point of view, it allowed him to flesh out two areas: the question of "mass hysteria" and the related quest for recognition.

In the first shot of Dr. Miles Bennell in the hospital ER, we see a close-up of his distraught face. His rumpled clothes, hair falling over his face, disordered gaze, and exaggerated gestures suggest emotional disarray. Clearly, he has been deeply affected by the events of the past few days. But consider the following questions: Is there any way of distinguishing his response to an "alien invasion" from his exposure to the "mass hysteria" sweeping through the town? Could he, in fact, be suffering from a panic episode or a bout of hysteria (conversion neurosis)?

If we define "hysteria" not as a medical diagnosis but rather as a way of responding to an existential threat, then Miles fits that definition. For Miles the threat is directed at his ability to ask questions about what he perceives. And a corollary to this threat is the refusal of all authorities (the police and the FBI) to validate his questions or take seriously what he has to say. Note here that what he is looking for is not somebody to *believe* him. Rather he seeks some person in authority to *recognize his question as a true question*. He wants his question to invoke a response from the other, to cause him to have second thoughts, and to disrupt that person's previously unchallenged assumptions.

On the psychical level, all questions address the questioner. To the questions Miles asks himself, the movie provides but a single hint: Do I want to have children? His near-collision with Jimmy Grimaldi suggests he does not—or at least he regards the matter with great ambivalence. And this question raises others that remain mostly fodder for the viewer's speculation: Are his patients—including Jimmy—serving as child surrogates? Does he envy the status of women, as seen in his snarky comment about Becky collecting alimony? Does his relative lack of personal ambition combined with an almost total dedication to the needs of his patients suggest a maternal identification? Does Sally, his nurse, a mother herself, acting as his auxiliary, buttress the latter? Does he need his romance with Becky to prop up his wavering virility, the latter barely hinted in the phrase "the draining away of humanity"?

These questions mainly add to the movie's psychic density without resolving the unease they induce. Yet in order to ameliorate the pathos of Miles wandering amidst cars on a busy highway, Siegel resorts to a *deus ex machina*. He and his colleagues concoct an artificial solution to his dilemma. While he is being interrogated by one of the psychiatrists in the ER, word arrives that a recent truck collision unearthed what looked like giant seedpods. This offers concrete evidence of Miles' story and leads immediately to a mobilization against the invaders. Miles' immense relief is visible on his face.

In a certain sense this "solution" runs against the entire thrust toward keeping the audience in a continuing state of dread. On the other hand, it demonstrates that the "pods" are the one element in the story that cannot be relegated to the purely imaginary. It is the little piece of the "real" that protrudes through the "hysteria" it induces. And the return of the pods gives the audience just enough relief to allow that "dread" to persist in their minds. Remember, too, that Miles' moment of recognition does not mean that the fight is won; only that its outcome remains in doubt.

What the movie does intend, however, is that its unconscious message reach a wide viewership. That message is conveyed in compact form by the imperative: "You're next!" Siegel clearly wants to wake us up from the cloud of complacency that descends upon us in the wake of powerful and divisive societal forces (of which the ongoing "red scare" was just one example). Hence, by granting this "hysteric" the recognition he/she deserves, he allows his message to get through, announcing a true emergency in the body politic.

Conclusions: the nature of the malady

To conclude, let us revisit the overriding question posed by the film: what is the nature of the malady afflicting the citizens of Santa Mira? The official explanation holds that aliens have transformed humans into "pods" for the purpose of mass reproduction. But as theory, this crude myth appears flimsy. Much of it must be taken on faith: there are no spaceships, no scary looking aliens, and—aside from the "pods"—no material evidence of an advanced civilization, all stock-in-trade of the science fiction genre.

In this chapter we have searched the movie's subtext for psychical equivalents of the invasion scenario. In the case of Wilma, for example, there is an obvious psychical aspect to her no longer being seen as special in her uncle's eyes. Previously, she could elicit his desire—or we would say that she embodied the object of his desire. It is thus the eclipse of that desire and the consequent collapse of her identity as this unique object, that provokes her dismay and sadness.

We can further deduce that Ira looks at his niece without the emotions associated with desire such as interest, anticipation, and excitement. Instead, he exhibits the feeling states in keeping with the complete fulfillment of desire. He may, for example, view her with the smug satisfaction of successfully bringing her into the fold, as if her surrender were already a fait accompli. Or perhaps his "look" reflects the glee of the cat who has already eaten the canary. In either case, Ira's attitude conveys his participation in a collective mood while expressing complete indifference to Wilma as a person in her own right.

In retrospect, we can draw similar conclusions from Jimmy Grimaldi's total repudiation of his mother. Perhaps his mother dissolved into a void or lethal vortex, threatening to engulf him. This void does not simply reside in the vacancy of her unblinking stare. It signifies the loss of the bounded space within the mother, which Jimmy inhabited. It therefore amounts to a radical *eviction*. It leaves Jimmy with no place to go and no place to *be*. Indeed, if he should in any way accede or surrender to his mother's looming presence; if he were to identify himself with her total self-containment/contentment, it would be tantamount to participating in his own self-immolation, and so losing any shred of separate identity he still possessed.

The *Invasion of the Body Snatchers* portrays the predicament facing Santa Mira as a battle between forces supporting desire and those promising absolute satisfaction. The film uses the metaphor of sleep to represent the force of desire as whatever gets you out of bed in the morning. Arrayed against it are those tendencies that in health allow us to fall asleep after an active and stimulating day. In the extreme, however, they press toward oblivion and the abdication of one's engagement in the struggle.

If the movie has an overarching message it is this: that the human condition is held together by the most delicate and precarious of threads. In order to ensure its intactness and integrity we must combat that most seductive of ideas: *that the human condition can be resolved*. Like all the characters in the film, Miles Bennell can only speak of this danger in general terms as the "draining away of humanity" and the associated degradation of humanistic values.

In essence the film suggests that the human condition is inherently problematic and incapable of being fully "resolved." Any attempt at radical simplification of human life must be rejected. The illusion that the gap or "lack" within each one of us and within society at large can ultimately be filled must be debunked. For without obstacles to satisfaction, what *would* get us out of bed in the morning? And yet without some small measure of fulfillment how would we ever go to sleep at night? And if *Invasion of the Body Snatchers* tends to foster insomnia, perhaps this is just the "correction" we need.

CHAPTER THREE

Female Sexuality in *Alien*

In this chapter I propose three ideas: that the main subject of *Alien* (1979) is female sexuality, that the male crew members of the *Nostromo* are selectively traumatized by it, and that Ellen Ripley, the ship's warrant officer, enjoys partial immunity to its effects by virtue of being a woman— and of being the particular woman she is. These three ideas, in my view, help explain why Ripley ultimately emerges as the crew's de facto leader by acclamation, why the other crew members are picked off by the creature one by one, and why she finally triumphs over her adversary. They further explain how the celebrated "chest-buster" scene derives its impact and its pivotal importance to the movie's outcome.

In my discussion of these hypotheses, I draw evidence from four sources: direct statements by the filmmakers; plot elements used in the four films that, in part, make up the *Alien* franchise; deleted scenes from the original; and thematic motifs within the film itself. The many deleted scenes, in particular, offer a rich subtext for the edited film. These scenes provide background to the movie's themes, and we will reference them throughout our analysis.

Quotations from the film's creative team show how deliberate their intentions were to load the movie with sexual imagery and symbolism. Indeed the film abounds in lurid sexual images and primitive fantasies, examples of which include—but are not limited to—phallic symbols, scenes of traumatic birth, rape, *vagina dentata*, and castration. The filmmakers freely admit to throwing every conceivable Freudian motif into the mix (wikipedia.org).

While this melange of imagery evokes the broadest range of primal fears, the screenwriter Dan O'Bannon is more specific. He states that: "I'm going to attack the audience. I'm going to attack them sexually" (*The Alien Saga*, 2002).

Thus it is not only that men are more susceptible to castration anxiety, but that Ripley's womanhood somehow protects her or at least gives her an edge. It is therefore plausible that female sexuality in its various guises and incarnations poses the biggest menace for the crew.

Regarding plot elements in the four other movies in the *Alien* franchise, consider the following, while keeping in mind that these subsequent films are as much re-workings and interpretations of the original as they are sequels. In *Aliens* (1986), the creature (or creatures) is explicitly female, depositing eggs in host bodies, and fighting tooth (*sic*) and nail for her brood. In *Alien 3* (1992), Ripley herself becomes a female menace to the penal colony on the planet Fiorina, whose male inmates have double-Y chromosomes and are sworn to sexual abstinence. Then in *Alien Resurrection* (1997) Ripley herself carries the "alien queen" within her. With Ripley embodying the alien, we seem to have come full circle. Hence in its basic set-up, this latter film seems to imply that Ripley's femininity is itself "alien"—or at least that her femininity has a strong affinity with whatever we consider "alien."

Sexual tensions

In the opening scene of *Alien*, Ridley Scott depicts the interior of the spaceship *Nostromo* as an oppressive emptiness and a malign *presence*. Although arising in part from M-o-t-h-e-r, the ship's female operating system, the charged atmosphere on board evokes the collective mentality of the crew at the outset of their mission. What can we infer about this mentality and the interrelationships that sustain it? The emptiness of the opening scene points to a condition of profound emotional and sexual deprivation. That deprivation is multi-factorial. There is, first and foremost, frank sexual deprivation. Of necessity, the crew must endure long periods of sexual abstinence. Second there is what I would call "cultural deprivation." There are no pictures adorning the walls and no pop music emanating from speakers. Clothing is drab, utilitarian, and androgynous. There is not a single book anywhere in the movie, despite the fact that Scott was inspired by the novels of Joseph

Conrad. And despite the sophisticated technology on board, there are no video games, or for that matter, no games of any kind. Hence the crew lack creative outlets other than work, which by this time, we have to assume is fairly routine.

The lack of photographs points to a third loss: familial. The only "mother" mentioned in the film refers to the aforementioned computer system that runs the ship. But their utter dependence on that "mother," while in the state of hyper-sleep, hints at infantile dependency needs. Yet even as fully formed adults they must feel the loss of their own families and of the chance to have children of their own. And the years and probably decades away from earth effectively make them orphans.

And hand-in-hand with familial loss is a dearth of affection and intimacy. That absence is embodied by their mutual love and solicitude of Jones the cat. Jones is semi-seriously included as an extra crew member, a hint that he is more than just a mascot. The crew members are free to express affection and intimacy to Jones in a way they are inhibited from showing to one another.

Now given what we know about the climate of sexual abstinence, what little can we say about the interrelationships among the crew members? Let us first review the various pairings and fault lines within the group. The crew subdivides into several factions. There is the natural division between the five officers—Dallas, Kane, Ash, Ripley, and Lambert (in descending order) and the NCOs, Parker and Brett. This division corresponds to that between the ruling class (officers) and the proletariat (NCOs). Then there are the men—Dallas, Kane, Ash, Parker, and Brett—versus the women: Ripley and Lambert. And finally, there is the split between science and commerce, in which Ash, the science officer, occupies a class of one.

Pairings and sexual scarcity

The tensions within the group flair into rifts between factions, and these rifts reflect competition over scarce sexual opportunities. These opportunities or lack thereof arise from the pairings or "couplings" among the crew members. Because Ash is the "odd man out" among the seven, the other six subdivide into four pairs: Parker–Brett, Dallas–Ripley, Kane–Lambert, and Ripley–Lambert. The second and third pairings are overtly sexual while the first and fourth are perhaps *covertly* sexual.

Of these couples, the most obvious is that between Parker and Brett. These two men function as a tag-team and are always seen working side-by-side.

To the rest of the crew, they are a recognizable "couple." Ripley, for example, teases Brett for reflexively agreeing with everything Parker says, as if the two were an old married couple. Interestingly, Brett doesn't disagree with this assessment, jokingly repeating the word "right" to Ripley's jibe. In actuality, Parker respects Brett's technical competence. When Brett says, "Right," he is in effect saying that he is Parker's "right-hand man" and implicitly that he is Parker's "man."

But in an atmosphere of scarcity and deprivation, Parker and Brett feel that they are getting the raw end of the deal. They feel used by their superiors in rank and inadequately compensated for their labor. Thus they rail against the inequities of the system and demand a "share" equal to the others.

Interestingly, when speaking of "shares" the word "money" is never used, for such a designation would unduly narrow its meaning. In the immediate context of the voyage "share" refers to the *values and commodities at hand and how they are divvied up*. For Parker and Brett that "value" refers to their hands-on technical labor, but also to their "share" in decision-making, and participation in high-status operations (such as the expedition to the alien ship). Thus for Parker and Brett, I would argue, their "share" refers to their overall value to their peers, to their status among the group, to their relative potency, and ultimately, to their male identities.

A deleted scene suggests that the "shares" refer to sexual availability and satisfaction. In the scene in question, Lambert confides to Ripley that she has slept with both Dallas and Kane, but not with Ash, who seems uninterested in sex. Ripley implies that she has slept with Dallas but not Kane (dailyscript.com). Despite its absence from the film, this scene adds to the subtext of the actors' interplay with each other. It would be plausible to assume that knowledge of these clandestine relationships would leak out within a group living in such close quarters. Thus Parker and Brett may know, or at least suspect, that they are barred from sexual opportunities available to the officers.

To put the matter more simply, Parker and Brett are denied access to the one means of confirming and asserting their heterosexuality, and thus, in their eyes, their sense of masculinity. Moreover, this unavailability of women emphasizes the dangers of their constant "togetherness." Hence their protest—their "masculine protest," as it were—aims to reassert their importance and their capability. Indeed it goes further, for their guardianship of the ship's engine and power plant puts them at the center of its beating heart.

But for the two men, it is enough that their objections are aired. They have no wish to sow mutiny (and as we shall see, neither does Ripley). When push comes to shove Parker and Brett accept the law. Indeed, in their heart of hearts they knew all along what they had signed up for and they honor their commitments. It is therefore likely that their protest serves as a kind of *symptom* of the group's unrest, its general unease in the face of sexual and emotional scarcity combined with the typical homoerotic currents of a confined group—that while it is not all male—perhaps merits the term "androgynous."

A link between the two same-sex couples

Unlike the bond between Parker and Brett, the intimacy between Ripley and Lambert is left unstated in the movie. However, their connection is established in two deleted scenes. The first scene—already mentioned—depicts the women sharing facts about their private life, contrary to the accepted norms aboard ship. The second scene makes explicit the tensions between the women, only implied in the edited film (dailyscript.com).

The second scene occurs in the wake of Kane being brought on board after his encounter with the alien, and against Ripley's wishes. In the scene, Lambert slaps Ripley hard across the face. The two exchange heated looks. After a pause, Ripley says, "That's settled then." She doesn't retaliate.

All three elements of the scene—the slap, the reply, and the non-retaliation—imply intimacy. A slap may happen between lovers. Ripley's reply suggests empathy and recognition that a dispute between the women has been laid to rest—perhaps by the slap itself, the gesture perhaps allowing Lambert to vent her spleen and to obtain a measure of satisfaction. (Note that a ritual slap will initiate a duel and a demand for "satisfaction.") The non-retaliation—besides indicating Ripley's general attitude of restraint—speaks of rapport and mutual respect.

The slap also introduces two other elements, emotionality and dominance versus submission. For Lambert, it is a way of discharging excess emotion—emotion that has boiled over because of Ripley's refusal to grant Kane admission to the ship. But a slap may also be used to snap someone out of an emotional state such as panic. It aims to break the spell of such states, and if successful, acts like a damper or short-circuit. And given Ripley's more temperate sensibility, we can readily imagine her delivering such a slap to Lambert—at the height of the latter's panic during the chest-buster scene for example.

Thus the slap suggests that emotionality is shared between the two women or toggles back and forth between them. Ripley might see in Lambert the consequences of her own emotional wattage, while Lambert uses Ripley as a barrier (the skin of Ripley's face) or buffer against her own excess. Thus neither woman can be strictly labeled as overemotional or inhibited, since their very connection is fraught with emotion.

Consider in this regard, Ripley's response to Lambert's plea at the airlock: "Open the goddamned hatch, we have to get him (Kane) inside!" Ripley responds with: "I can't. If you were in my position, you'd do the same." The "you" being "in my position" alludes to the fluidity of their respective "positions" within the relationship. Ripley no doubt already suspects that Lambert is in love with Kane and that she wants to "get him inside" regardless of the cost to others. Ripley speaks for the opposite "polarity": as a woman you also need to consider the consequences of "letting a man inside"—whether that inside refers to your body or your psyche. For it is you who will bear the brunt of whatever consequences arise from the "insemination." Moreover, some of those consequences may prove fatal, a reality which women are only too well aware of.

The same circulating bipolarity applies to the theme of dominance versus submission. We can view the slap as an assertion of dominance by Lambert but we could just as easily see Ripley delivering the blow. And we can conceive Ripley submitting to Lambert in this one instance just as Lambert later accedes to her friend's succession to group leader and alpha female. The S and M theme operates as a current or dimension pervading the relationship.

And it is just here where we find a direct link in the form of a switch-word between Ripley/Lambert and Parker/Brett. Of course we already know that both couples are same-sex, that the men and women are bonded to their counterparts, and that dominance/submission plays a role—overt in the one, covert in the other—in their interplay. But the incident that truly ties them together is when Parker attempts to assert himself with Ripley over the matter of "shares." In this case, Parker hardly expects Ripley to reverse official policy. His protest is meant as a taunt and a ploy to get Ripley to lose her cool. If that had happened, Parker and Brett might have enjoyed a moment of male triumph over their superior officer acting "just like a woman."

But Ripley doesn't back down. She simply fulfills her role in the chain of command by reminding the men of their signed commitment. Just as she is

FEMALE SEXUALITY IN *ALIEN*   **43**

leaving, but within earshot, Parker emits the epithet, "bitch!" Ripley neither retaliates nor succumbs to the need for self-defense. In this one word Parker establishes a bridge between the two same-sex couples.

In order to see this connection, let us review the relevant meanings of the word, some of which are recent additions. They include: 1. a woman; 2. a malevolent, mean or spiteful woman; 3. a sexually wanton woman; 4. a vagina; 5. a pushy or overly aggressive woman; 6. a fierce or ferocious woman as in the expression "a bitch on wheels"; 7. a person of either sex who assumes a submissive position with regard to a partner. And we can add the meaning of "to bitch": to complain loudly as when, for example, Lambert gripes about the rigors of the trek toward the alien ship.

The most obvious connection involves the question: Who is the bitch (submissive) in the relationship and who is the dom? For the two males, it is obviously Brett who plays the "bitch." But when Ripley exercises authority over Parker, he becomes her bitch. Therefore he must turn the tables and make *her* the bitch. His "verbal ejaculation" of the word seeks to restore his "potency" in the relationship. Yet despite these negative connotations, Parker ultimately embraces Ripley as the leader they need, and therefore as his "bitch"—that is, his fierce female warrior. Hence the movie anticipates recent usages of the word that express approbation.

Now given the affinities between the two couples, what is it that sets them apart? For Parker and Brett sexual roles are sharply and rigidly demarcated, while for Ripley and Lambert the relationship is more fluid. We see, for example, that Brett is always Parker's "bitch"—despite their relative equality while working together—and never the other way around. Whereas either woman can take a turn at being the "bitch," and likewise either can play the "dom." The same condition applies to emotionality. When Parker attempts to taunt and goad Ripley into "losing her cool" he naturally assumes that letting emotion get the better of you makes you a woman. The women, by contrast, embrace emotion and the need for restraint in equal measure and the couple alternate between the poles.

And utilizing the same either/or logic, the men assume that any homo-erotic impulse makes you a woman by default. The women, by contrast, can assimilate such an impulse without having to give up their femininity. For the same reason, their androgynous uniforms are for them mere window dressing. In short, their identity as women is broader and more inclusive than their male counterparts, whose sense of masculinity is narrow and exclusive.

Ripley questions Dallas' authority

Dallas and Ripley make up another fraught relationship. The one thing we know for sure about this relationship is that it undergoes a dramatic reversal after the alien extrusion, resulting in Kane's death. And based upon how it ends up, we may make some assumptions about what lies beneath its strictly professional façade from the beginning. We can assume first off that Dallas was nonplussed when Ripley—a woman—became a last-minute replacement for a male warrant officer whom Dallas had worked with previously. It is likely that Dallas was uncomfortable with a woman under his direct command (Lambert, as navigator, sat in a kind of lateral position in the command structure, as did Ash). In addition to this sort of uneasiness, there was mutual attraction between the two. We can therefore assume that Dallas was having trouble keeping this unstated bond separate from their professional relationship.

At the same time, there were sources of unease that affected his confidence as commander. The abrupt diversion of the ship from its course, and its reclassification as a search and rescue mission must have been disturbing to a man whose core competencies lay in running a space-tugboat. He now suddenly finds himself leading a search party into the unknown, a task for which he feels completely unprepared. Perhaps he inwardly questioned his deferral to Kane as the de facto leader of the expedition. Kane took the lead from the start and almost singlehandedly explored the alien egg chamber. Perhaps Dallas second-guessed not urging his first officer to take greater caution. And then when Kane sustained grievous injury, Dallas could not have avoided feeling some remorse. The code among the officers dictates that the commander take the greatest risk. And the potential loss of an esteemed comrade no doubt weighed upon his mind.

It is likely that some combination of these factors could have augmented the antagonism between Dallas and Ripley when he, Lambert, and the injured Kane sought re-entry to the vehicle. Ripley refused the demand, judging that Kane might unwittingly "infect" the other crew members, a decision backed up by the rules of quarantine. As senior officer on board Ripley felt fully justified in temporarily assuming command.

To Dallas, Ripley's refusal seems an act of defiance rather than a prudent judgment. He views her action as an attack on his authority. For one thing, the full deployment of the quarantine rule would have relieved Dallas from command for the duration of the quarantine—however long that interval were to last. And Ripley had already challenged his authority by failing to obey his direct order. Moreover, his rage is only fanned by Ripley's appeal to the law. Her accusation that his order is "illegal" undercuts the legal foundation of his authority. Dallas had always prided himself on fidelity to the law. He quotes the law in his discussion of the contract that binds the crew members together and that establishes the hierarchy among them. Now he is being confronted with a gross inconsistency in his application of it. And in the grip of intense anger and blind loyalty to his fallen comrade, he might fear that disclosing his inconsistency exposes his behavior as "unmanly."

Later, after questioning Ash, Ripley and Dallas have a more frank discussion. It turns out that Ash opened the hatch and that Dallas had pre-approved his authority in the matter. Thus when Ripley was challenging Dallas' authority, he had already divested that authority! In disbelief, she asks: "How could you leave this kind of decision to him?" And her aggrieved tone testifies to an established relationship with the commander. Her question—rhetorical by this point—expresses her shock and dismay that he has undermined her in this way. Clearly, she had held him in high esteem and counted on his support.

And Dallas' response and self-justification reveals just how different their two approaches are. Dallas explains his decision, as follows: "I just run the ship. Anything that has to do with science division, Ash has the final word." The key idea in this explanation hinges on the word "division." The word offers a clue to Dallas' modus vivendi. He prefers clear and sharp divisions between different sectors of his life. Thus we have the mechanical or engineering sector versus science, and in the context of his engagement with Ripley, between his personal and professional life, and we may add a division between "sex" and "love."

But this division of authority countermands the primary mandate of any ship's captain: whatever happens on his watch is ultimately his responsibility. In Dallas' case this amounts to an abdication—and toward Ripley, abandonment, if not an outright betrayal. Thus in matters vital to the crew, and to Ripley in her role as caretaker, Dallas will be "missing in action" as if nobody is "manning the helm." Thus for Ripley, the man to whom she looked to for "backup" and for the embodiment of law is nowhere to be found.

This flaw does more than undermine Dallas' authority; it renders him impotent. We cannot fully understand Dallas' self-imposed "unmanning," for he seems to follow the company's orders without ever questioning them. It almost seems as if he is in the thrall of the "Mother" who runs the ship and executes the company agenda. Thus one way of viewing his "impotence" is as a blind faith in the "company/other" that forms a kind of bedrock of his sense of security. Put another way, he serves as a mere tool of the "other's desire."

In exposing this critical flaw, Ripley gains no satisfaction. Instead she loses a pillar holding up her status within the patriarchal order. It would be a mistake to picture her as a "castrating bitch," for that honor will go to our alien visitor. However, the flaw in the order of compartmentalization does hint that certain phenomena—first among which is female sexuality—seem to defy the imposition of any such order. We have seen already that there is no clear line of demarcation—no "clear definition" between human and alien—between who is inside the ship and who is outside (and by extension inside and outside the body), and between the aims of science and those of self-preservation.

We shall assume—and hope to demonstrate in the movie's second half—that Ripley entertains a greater tolerance for such blurring of the lines than the men.

Ripley and Ash: the ongoing dispute with science

Ripley and Ash have their first encounter early on when Ripley receives information that the distress signal on moon LV-426 may be a warning. She volunteers to leave the ship in the hands of the science officer while she hurries to warn the boarding party. Ash dissuades her, but the seeds of suspicion are planted in her mind.

What predisposes Ripley to suspect Ash so early in the story? Several factors come to mind. For one thing, there is the plaintive tone in Ash's voice when he says: "What's the point?" He seems to be pleading with her and in so doing, revealing an existential threat: the possibility that if Ripley warns the others, Ash's quest will be thwarted and the very "point" of his existence rendered moot. Therefore she would likely wonder why this issue is so important to him.

For this reason, Ripley suspects that Ash is hiding something. At this early stage she cannot say what it is. But she picks up on it because she herself hides her femininity under an androgynous cloak. Hence she may wonder if Ash is hiding something sexual, something forbidden, say, or at odds with his scientific detachment. What doesn't add up is Ash's apparent lack of desire for any of the crew members. This in turn might lead her to question whether Ash is "quite human" or if his desires are of the human variety.

The one thing that is known about Ash is his association with the aims of science. And even at this early juncture, it is clear that those aims are not necessarily coincidental with the *Nostromo*'s commercial mission. However, the two agendas have overlapped up to this point. But the moment when Ash dissuades Ripley from warning the others, discordance appears. The possibility is raised that Ash could be hiding a potential conflict between the aims of science and the crew's human desire to survive the mission.

When the cephalopod is removed from Kane's face, Ripley and Ash assume different attitudes toward its investigation. Ash relishes the opportunity for making new discoveries, such as the alien's ability to incorporate non-carbon based compounds into its carapace. He offers Ripley a jargon-filled scientific explanation ("polysaccharides, amino acids"). She however avoids being taken in by the details, and simply asks for the upshot: What does it *mean*—what is its import for the humans on board, what kind of menace does it pose? Ash's honest answer, "It's a tough little son-of-a-bitch," immediately re-phrases the information in human terms. It even hints that the alien is a product of a "female" entity. Yet more generally their two approaches suggest that for Ash, science is a *thing-in-itself* whereas for Ripley it is simply a means to a more limited end.

Shortly thereafter, Ripley questions Ash about his decision to allow Kane re-entry in words that superficially resemble her previous interrogation of Dallas. She challenges him with the same two arguments: the quarantine laws and Ripley's executive authority in the absence of Dallas and Kane. Ash responds to these questions in a reasonable and forthright manner. But the tone of the argument is quite different. As noted, there is no underlying sexual tension between them and therefore there is not the slightest hint that Ash feels his masculinity under attack. Indeed he is the epitome of the ship's androgynous but non-gendered culture. Thus, while Ash fully recognizes Ripley as a speaker (and demands that she afford him the same consideration), he does not acknowledge her as a woman. In effect, her being a woman has no meaning to him (or as we shall propose, perhaps a debased meaning). Or perhaps it is more accurate to say that the tension between Ripley and Ash resides mainly in their existential antagonism. And it is this discordance—this emotional divergence—that cues Ripley that something is "off" about Ash. Thus outwardly she accepts his explanations without protest; inwardly her suspicions continue unabated.

Then something happens that illustrates Ripley's dispute with Ash, and by extension with science: the alien appendage drops on Ripley and she

screams. Certainly it catches her unawares but her response is still surprising. She is not the squeamish type. Her primal response to touching the
alien life form is disgust and repugnance as if it were an unwanted sexual
contact with an "organ." The thing is henceforth referred to as a "specimen"
and under Ash's direction it is closely studied. It appears to be dead but even
this determination is uncertain. And while the others examine it, Ripley's
sole wish is to *expel* it, expel it from the ship and expel it from her body.

Her attitude is just the reverse of Kane's enchantment with the egg-like
entity inside the alien ship. He is attracted to the thing; Ripley is repelled.
He is driven to explore and to have intimate knowledge of the thing; she
wants to keep her distance from it. He is rendered spellbound by the thing,
while Ripley will not allow herself to fall into a state of fascination with it.
He wants to understand this new phenomenon: when the crew indulges in
speculation about the alien's true nature—its sexuality, for example—Ripley
demurs. She senses that such thinking will draw them into a labyrinth from
which there is no escape.

She sees or intuits that what attracts the crew to the alien is its sexual
nature and that this very attraction engages human sexual drives. And she
believes that the core of sexuality is "alien" to the traditional methods of
science. Treating the alien sexual organ as a "specimen" whose components
can be classified within a system and whose structure can be compared and
contrasted with known templates will still fail to capture its inimitable reality. Her strategy therefore has but a single aim: to protect her womanhood
from becoming the object of science. Indeed, Ripley's logic proceeds from
this premise: we must renounce the impossible quest to "capture" the thing,
to domesticate it, to "take it in." The only viable strategy is to banish it to
the exterior—outside the ship and outside any conceivable human system.

The chest-buster scene as a sexual eruption

Let us first note that the celebrated "chest-buster" scene—according to many
observers—resembles a strange or pathological birth. A birth always disrupts the ordinary course of human life. And more concretely, the contortions and seizures that Kane undergoes before the eruption mime—albeit in
extreme form—the pains and contractions of labor, already foreshadowed
by the changes in the mother's body image during pregnancy. And as in any
mammalian birth, delivery is a bloody process. We should not be put off
because the infantile life form emerges from a man's chest. Children often

entertain the idea that men can have babies as well as women, and boys especially, unaware of the existence of the vagina, may theorize that a baby must be removed by cutting open the body (Freud, 1909b). Moreover, Cesarean births are now commonplace. But in Shakespeare's time they were an aberration, a child "ripped, untimely from its mother's womb." Moreover, mothers must endure various "alien" visitations: the umbilical cord suggested by the creature's snakelike tail, wrapped around a baby's neck, for example. Nor must we forget the "afterbirth"—the extrusion of a truly "alien" organ.

Now, within the conventions of the sci-fi film, the father or "inseminator" of this baby is the alien life form. But Lambert's reaction to the event implies human parentage. She, unlike her colleagues, is completely splattered with Kane's blood. The blood may stand for bodily fluids such as the creature's drooling saliva that are shared during lovemaking. Note also that Lambert screams throughout the scene. Her arms and hands move in all directions, her fingers splay, and finally fly upwards in a gesture of surrender. Her body language seems to mimic in empathy Kane's movements and agony. Thus of all the crew, Lambert is the most affected by Kane's ordeal and death. The subtext might therefore suggest that Lambert was in love with Kane and that the creature is the pathological product of a sexual encounter between the two.

We can also say in Lambert's defense that she bears the brunt of the trauma and guilt associated with Kane's sacrifice. In her guilt she might have imagined punishment in the form of stillbirth or an abortion. "Abortion" is sometimes used loosely to mean any misshapen or malformed infant. A monstrous birth is every mother's nightmare. The alien life form hints at every conceivable bad outcome, from extreme prematurity to every kind of birth defect.

More broadly, however, the alien life form is depicted as an *anomaly*. An anomaly may refer to an abnormal variant, an example lying outside expectable norms. But in a more universal sense, "anomaly" means original, inimitable, or beyond comparison. In that sense every infant represents a new beginning and a clean slate. But it also connotes an entity that is wholly itself, that is without precedent, and that lacks any relationship to a model or template. For these reasons, an anomaly can also suggest "original" as in "first in a series". As examples, we can cite birth, of course, menarche, first love, sexual initiation, and the "shock of the new." For the men witnessing the chest-buster scene, the novelty of the experience calls to mind the sudden exposure to female sexuality in its raw and undiluted form.

In this light, consider the diverse reactions of the crew members' witness to the scene. We have noted that, as the closest both in distance and intimacy, Lambert bears the brunt. By contrast, Ripley stays at the far end of the table, her eyes averted. This gesture is not one of avoidance, in our view. Rather, it approximates Perseus not looking directly at the Gorgon's head: a safeguard against being "petrified" (turned to stone) or transfixed by the sight. Of the three men, Ash is the least affected since he is not human, and also because, for him, the birth of the alien is a blessed event. Parker is strongly affected but is still able to respond with appropriate emotion. He slowly moves his hands over his torso as if ensuring the intactness of his own body. Brett appears to fade from the scene. In the starkest contrast, Dallas puts up his hands in a gesture of defense, and after the creature's escape appears stunned and immobilized by what he has seen. His barely audible order, "secure the area," seems almost laughable in its futility and sense of impotence.

The crew in the aftermath of the alien invasion

The impact of the alien invasion brings about a reconfiguration among the crew, of which the most important change involves Dallas and Ripley. In a dramatic reversal of their relationship, Dallas transfers the authority vested in him as commander to Ripley. For Dallas, the transfer represents an act of both homage and self-sacrifice; for by ceding the symbols of his authority, he makes himself expendable. Indeed his act of self-sacrifice—pursuing the creature and ordering Ripley to stay behind—creates the necessary condition for the transfer of power.

The fateful transfer of authority takes place in the ritual handing over of the master key to M-o-t-h-e-r (the ship's computer system). Dallas removes the key from its hiding place and entrusts Ash with the task of giving it over to Ripley in case of his death. This key clearly refers to the transfer of name and title to Ripley, promoting her to heir apparent. It also functions as a kind of phallic scepter. From the male perspective, the transfer "unmans" Dallas and transforms Ripley into a "phallic woman." And it is true that the transfer vacates Dallas' potency within the group and empowers Ripley. But the "key" also highlights the imaginary aspect of the transaction. Is there really such a "key" granting the complete comprehension of womanhood?

At the moment of Dallas' death, Ripley assumes command. The group immediately accepts her leadership. This new consensus coalesces around their acceptance of being led by a woman. Indeed the transfer of authority *reconciles* the crew to Ripley being a woman. We might say that the mantle of authority stabilizes their relationship to her womanhood by nullifying, or at least pacifying, the locus of turbulence her female sexuality posed for them. Thirdly, her new status as a "phallic woman" further mollifies and reassures them. For boys (and some girls) the fantasy of the phallic woman can act as a buffer against having to grapple with the threat to their world view presented by a woman's sexuality (Freud, 1909b). And in the context of this film, possession of the phallus removes the alien dimension of her sex and makes her "one of us." She may be a "bitch on wheels" but she is now *our* "bitch on wheels."

Let us apply these ideas to the reshuffling of the other crew members. Of these, the one benefiting the most from Ripley's ascent is Parker. Parker had shown his mettle as early as the chest-buster scene when he continued to respond in words, gestures, and actions (taking up the knife, for example). In the aftermath, he participates in planning and in technical support (the jerry-rigged flame-throwers). But he comes to full possession of himself the moment Ripley assumes command. In an instant, he accepts her as leader and pledges his support. He disavows his former antagonism based on her gender (deleted line: "drop the bullshit"). In effect Parker assumes the role of first officer originally occupied by Kane. His "field promotion" erases his lower status and even fuels his hope for a "full share." In consequence, he feels that his manhood has been recognized and is no longer threatened by taking orders from a woman.

There are, however, two casualties of the new regime. Parker's new partnership with Ripley comes at the expense of his bond with Brett. Brett is now uncoupled from his former protector and now seems hapless and overmatched, a fish out of water. His technical skills were never in question, but his capacity to function independently is limited. Hence, when sent on a mission to find Jones the cat, he wanders aimlessly and is easily ambushed by the alien. In a similar vein, Lambert is still mourning the loss of Kane. She too is a fish out of water looking to others for direction even though she is the titular navigator. She makes the mistake of trusting Ash in preference to Ripley, in part due to antagonism toward a rival, and because Ash is the only remaining male officer (even though she knows he cannot desire her). She too ends up being ambushed by the creature and, in an ironic twist, Parker risks his life trying to rescue her and dies in the attempt.

The unmasking of Ash

Ripley's assumption of command empowers her to procure the key to M-o-t-h-e-r that is now hers by right. The key allows her to bypass Ash for the first time and to obtain direct access to the ship's computer system. Once logged in, the screen displays special order 937, declaring that in order to ensure the safe return of the alien organism, the crew is expendable. Ripley and the others reach the inescapable conclusion that Ash has faithfully carried out this directive from the start. In an instant, the mask drops.

Once exposed as a traitor, Ash attacks Ripley and the pair fall to blows. At first Ash's superior strength gives him an edge, and he pins Ripley to the ground. We can see a pin-up photo of a scantily clad woman juxtaposed to Ripley's face, and behind, a series of other pin-ups. Perhaps Ridley Scott intended a visual pun on the word "pin." These pictures flash by in a trice and are never mentioned in the dialogue. But groping around for a weapon, Ash rolls up a magazine that, according to the visual cues, may have been a girly magazine (scifi.stackexchange.com). He then jams its round end into Ripley's mouth in an attempt to suffocate her and possibly to deprive her of speech. Then Parker jumps into the breach and struggles with Ash. Parker retreats and picks up a makeshift club and strikes Ash in the head several times. The head is suddenly ripped off revealing the inner workings of a robot: a second unmasking.

We gain some insight into the motives behind Ash's action, when the crew reactivates his "talking head" and he explains what drives him. It is nothing less than the perfection of the alien organism, a state to which he clearly aspires. Part of his attitude no doubt derives from a childlike idealization of the complexity and sophistication of the alien's resourcefulness. In this regard, he must admire its ability to evolve, just as *his* existence represents one stage in the evolution of artificial intelligence. In his view therefore, "perfection" applies to the anomaly that defies every known system of classification and that keeps reinventing itself.

But his attitude suggests a state of rapture and thrall toward the alien life form, not unlike Kane's with respect to the egg sac. Such emotions are similar to those evoked by a child's first encounter with a naked woman and they are indisputably charged with eroticism. Ash may be non-human but he is not asexual as Lambert believed. He is ambiguously attracted to the alien as woman and the woman as alien. And for this very reason, he views himself as a sexual being inferior to the alien but superior to Ripley. This may be why he is so determined to debase Ripley as a woman. By reducing her to a sexual object—a kind of male fetish—he deprives her of the same ability to evolve and transform that he so admires in the alien.

We may also view Ash's third unmasking as the sudden revelation of the drive—the thing that drives him—underlying his mission. That is, we witness a single-minded impetus to obtain satisfaction regardless of the consequences. In its pure state, the drive bypasses the subject—that is, it achieves its aim without our having any say in the matter. The "talking head" that Ash becomes *in extremis* suggests the partial nature of the drive, its ability to act as a rogue agent in defiance of any principle of organization or unity (Freud, 1905d).

Thus Ash's final confession is yet another sudden exposure of sexual reality. In other words, there is a raw and unadulterated quality to the drive that is lacking in desire. Desire engages a subject within the dimension of fantasy. The drive severs the subject (cuts off its head) and tears the veil of fantasy asunder. We can associate this real element with the underlying aim of science: to pursue its path regardless of consequences. The chilling factor lies in science pursuing its path despite the ethical reservations of scientists. At times it seems that whatever science is capable of achieving, it eventually will bring about.

The drives, however, are found in both genders (although there may be different fixations and modes of expression between them). The drive is thus an inexact representation of female sexuality. Indeed, we could say that its rawness, its extreme proximity to the witness, and its blatant exploitation of the object for the sole purpose of sexual satisfaction are precisely the elements that disrupt the fantasy envelope and that, for the woman especially, transforms erotic desire into frank disgust. Seen in this light, Ash's attempt to turn Ripley into a pure sexual object dovetails with his drive's aim. And it is through her primal response of disgust, horror, and revulsion—and the correlative desire to oppose the drive elements—that Ripley asserts herself as a woman.

Jones the cat: Ripley's familiar

We now take up a hitherto neglected character, Jones the cat. Jones enters the story as a seemingly minor figure and perhaps, a bit of comic relief. But his importance is signaled from the start: upon awakening from artificial sleep, the crew's first order of business is retrieving Jones. We have already noted his role as a universal object of affection. This role already elevates him to symbolic status: he is the crew's mascot, totem, touchstone, transitional object, and as we shall propose, Ripley's familiar. But the very act of retrieval indicates that Jones has the run of the ship and will often be found missing. His small size, unpredictable movement, and ability to hide within tiny alcoves make finding him a perennial challenge.

In her first attempt to locate and trap the alien, for example, Ripley runs into Jones instead. Jones screeches, hisses, and jumps away. This mishap reveals that Jones tends to appear when and where he is least expected. In this respect he is similar to the alien, which will also demonstrate the same elusiveness. And this encounter should have acted as a warning to the crew: the attempt to pin down Jones' (and the alien's) location within a grid of intersecting passageways may prove too approximate a method to trap him (it).

Shortly thereafter, Ripley deputizes Brett to find the cat yet again. We have already noted Brett's credulousness and his vulnerability in the absence of Parker. He wanders into the maze of corridors calling, "Here, kitty," and, "Jones-y." And here the viewer can already anticipate that Brett is being led into a trap. Jones is unwittingly acting as a "lure" that draws him well out of his comfort zone. We can imagine Brett's pursuit of Jones as a quest to replace his lost partner with the only other being offering some measure of succor. Hence when the creature menaces Brett from behind, all Brett can see is Jones. As viewers, we see the creature reflected in Jones' eyes and hear it in his hiss. The warning comes too late to save Brett.

But Jones faces the creature unflinchingly and eye-to-eye. His look conveys full attention and antagonism. And catching the light, his ellipsoid pupils reveal a foreignness that coincides with that of the alien, and which resonates with the time-honored symbolism of feline mystery and inscrutability. He is not intimidated. When Jones looks the creature dead in the eye, he seems to be saying: "I see you for what you are." Jones' gaze also offers a clue to his immunity to the alien. Part of the alien's advantage resides in the mixture of horror and fascination he evokes in humans. If one can set aside this enervating and insidious paralysis, half the battle is already won.

Once alone on the ship, Ripley pursues Jones and manages to put him "in his box." Thus of all the crew members, only Ripley succeeds in capturing Jones. She literally subdues and constrains a wild, unpredictable force. In so doing, she is also reining in her own wild impulses. The "cat-in-the-box"—a kind of "jack-in-the-box," or in the words of Dr. Seuss, a "cat-in-the-hat"—is a symbol of her femininity. She too totters on the edge between domesticity and ferocity. Heretofore, we have implied she needs to hide her womanliness behind a façade of utilitarian androgyny. But she also needs to hide that aspect of her womanhood that smacks of excess, a cloying intimacy, say, or the impetus to overlap, to spill over, to flow like water into the spaces between walls (like the alien's bodily fluid). Self-restraint has become her guiding principle and the way she shapes her own version of femininity. That version employs her body as a coiled spring whose erotic energy is barely held in check.

And it is just this affinity with Jones that makes him an ally, partner, and "familiar." For in the midst of Ripley's final battle with the alien, the creature strikes down the box containing Jones. Inside the box, we can hear Jones crying and banging around inside. Thus he expresses his resistance to being boxed in. But the ruckus he makes distracts the alien. For a moment the box captures its attention and seems to befuddle and confound it. For the outsized creature, the cat represents something "alien." In a strange reversal, the creature appears to view the cat-in-the-box as an *anomaly*—an enigma it cannot place within the human scheme of things. And this distraction disrupts and divides the alien's relentless pursuit. It equalizes the playing field and allows Ripley to fight fire with fire, using Jones as her model.

Ripley's final stand

With the deaths of Parker and Lambert, Ripley and Jones are alone on the *Nostromo*. Ripley activates the automatic self-destruct mechanism and, carrying Jones in his box, hurries toward the shuttle entrance. At one point she tries and fails to reverse the self-destruct order. She curses M-o-t-h-e-r. Her anger reflects her judgment that Mother was indifferent to her fate, that Mother remained obtuse and recalcitrant about providing vital information, that Mother herself was in the dark about her programmer's intent, and ultimately that Mother failed to protect her from harm. In this moment, she separates from Mother just as the shuttle is separating from the mother ship, and fully comes into her own.

There is a key shot in the screenplay when Ripley stares down the creature through a glass partition. This gaze shows that, while fearful, Ripley is not intimidated. If the alien represents both the idea of femininity as anomaly and its mirror image: an aberrant female life form, then Ripley can look it in the face. What she sees there is disturbing but not destabilizing. In part this follows from the simple fact of "facing" the alien. For in the instant she sees the alien for what it is, the alien, in its turn, sees Ripley for who and what she is: a formidable woman warrior. She recognizes that the alien's metamorphosis reflects her own womanhood as a process of cease-less becoming, and vice versa; both beings recognize that no single static image can represent the reality of being a woman.

And perhaps for this very reason, Ridley Scott opted to not film this shot. He wanted to avoid having the alien look like an awkward man inside a monster suit. Instead, he adopted a two-pronged approach. On the one hand, he filmed the creature in a montage of profiles and odd angled shots that never reveal its face. On the other hand, his focus on Ripley's face and eyes suggests her riveted attention on the alien. Those eyes are always strain-ing, scanning, and surveying. In close-up, they loom large and steadfast, *and they never blink*. It is a measure of Sigourney Weaver's dedication to her role that she maintains her mental focus under the glare of lights. Scott intensifies the effect by flashing a light on and off her face like a stroboscope, disrupting the viewer's attempt to "capture" her image, and creating the illu-sion of constant motion.

In counterpoint to her mobile gaze, Ripley inhabits her body in such a manner that she is never *displaying* herself. In fact, when Ripley discards her clothes in anticipation of donning a spacesuit, she does so without attracting the slightest prurient attention. And yet we are bowled over by her beauty. That beauty is part and parcel of who she is; she has no need to advertise or promote it. In this respect she sets herself apart from the pin-ups visible on the wall during her battle with Ash. In the first place, she doesn't *lure* the viewer; instead of pulling him in or "leading him on" she lets him be where he is in contemplation of her. In the second place, she will not allow herself to be encapsulated within a static image. And finally she has neither the means nor the inclination to conform to any man or woman's fantasy.

For these reasons she resists the lure of the alien, thwarts its attempts to immobilize her, and sees right through its hideous and fanciful outward appearance. She is fooled neither by its alleged "perfection" nor its surrepti-tious sexual allure.

Conclusion: Ripley's immunity

In *Alien*, Ridley Scott and his team evoke an atmosphere of ambiguity that never wavers. And it is this pervasive ambiguity that, in my view, highlights the theme of female sexuality. From its opening minutes, the film raises questions about the relationships between crew members and the nature of the alien entity. It implies that these two enigmas are somehow related.

It raises the question, for example, of an erotic charge between Ripley and Lambert but it deliberately deletes the scene that would have made a lesbian encounter explicit. By the same token, it deletes a sexual encounter between Ripley and Dallas that would have made Dallas' unstated craving for submission explicit. The other deleted scene where Dallas pleads with Ripley to put him out of his misery only confirms the supposition. In both cases, the explicit sexual content is repressed to the movie's subtext, adding to the "charged" quality of all the relationships among the crew.

In a similar vein, the crew speculates upon the alien's true nature. Is it organic or inorganic? Is it male, female, or hermaphroditic? Is it mortal or immortal? All of these questions take the form of: "Is it this or is it that?" No question of this type is given an answer. However, questions about its capabilities *are* answered, its susceptibility to fire, for example. Therefore what the film keeps ambiguous is the *definition* of the alien, a word or words that would reveal its true nature. But there is never ambiguity about the *reality* of the alien. Its indivisibility and integrity as a thing-in-itself is never in doubt.

Its indetermination is given cinematic form through its fluidity, motion, and transformation. The fluidity comes through in the emphasis on the creature's bodily fluids dripping from its mouth and having a corrosive effect on solid matter. On the literal level, the "fluids" suggest the exchange of bodily fluids during sexual intercourse and the perception that female arousal entails "wetness" and overflow. As metaphor, fluidity suggests the flexibility of role reversals in intimate relationships, the spilling over of emotionality beyond the boundaries of the person, and the free circulation of attributes between the partners. Yet its eddies, whirlpools, and maelstroms suggest sexual frenzies that threaten to "suck in" the unwary. Thus it presents identity not as a frozen specimen, cut, or "cross-section" susceptible to scientific observation, but rather as a free-flowing and never-ending process of transformation. Such constant shape-shifting dissuades us from identifying the alien too closely with any of its outward appearances—even a femme fatale from outer space.

Thus we conclude that the term "female sexuality"—like the reality to which it refers—is multidimensional. I include within the term, the woman's sexual organs, both external and internal, her more diffuse and widespread experience of pleasure, arousal, and orgasm, her ability to adopt male attributes without thereby effacing her womanhood, her tendency toward the non-compartmentalization of psychic functions and against hierarchical modes of organization, and, given a healthy body image, the savings of mental energy brought about by not having to constantly defend the integrity and intactness of an imaginary phallus.

Ripley comes to realize that a portion of her own sexuality is alien to her. On the basis of her overcharged reaction to the alien appendage falling on her shoulder, we may speculate that she feels a repugnance to the "other" sexuality in its raw form. Freud (1905d) and others have postulated that disgust constitutes a primal position against sexual excess. That excess can be gauged as closeness to the sexual object or as thrall and captivation to the drives. It is obvious that Ripley possesses a reservoir of mental discipline. I posit that this discipline arises from her refusal to submit to her drives in their raw form and her resolute imposition of self-restraint. In so doing, she does not eliminate her sexuality but instead directs it toward ferocity of purpose and sublimation of its potential energy. From another angle, Ripley respects the reality of her sexuality by not trying to make it into something else.

If we had to summarize Ripley's attitude toward the "alien" aspects of her sexuality, it would be "expulsion." Recall that she advocates "expulsion" as the only way of ridding the ship of the alien menace. And note also that the word has two meanings: to force out, or eject and to cut off from membership or relations. It is the latter definition that I emphasize here. For Ripley studiously avoids incorporating the alien entity within the network of human relations, constituting her world. There is one fundamental question she declines to ask: What is the nature of this alien being? However she *can* ask and answer questions about its effects upon her, and this is how she asserts her womanhood; this is how she separates from M-o-t-h-e-r's hold over her.

Finally, let us end by noting that Ripley and Ridley differ by only one letter. Sigourney, however, is the actor's own creation. Her attitude and his nuanced ambiguity both contribute to the making of a science fiction classic.

Part II

Portraits of Addiction in Hollywood Melodramas

Psychoanalytic Observations on the Depiction of Greed in Two Hollywood Movies: *The Maltese Falcon* and *Wall Street**

H ollywood films make good vehicles for the depiction of greed because—before she even enters a theatre, inserts a DVD, or opens a movie app—the viewer is already a voracious consumer of what the "dream factory" has to offer. A typical Hollywood film saturates the viewer with "high definition" experience,[1] running the gamut from "predigested" to "indigestible". But regardless of where a given film falls on this spectrum of "orality," the viewer may feel "occupied" or "consumed" by it, especially upon first viewing. Throughout its history, Hollywood has held the viewer captive in this way. During the depression, film companies fed their audiences on fantasies of having it all when people were literally starving. The studios pursued a similar strategy during the excesses of the 1980s when the gulf between rich and poor began to appear unbridgeable. At the same time, however, Hollywood held a mirror up to our collective propensity for ungovernable greed. Thus, even in movies which reveled in the excesses of the rich, viewers could catch a glimpse of greed's infantile roots and its foothold in the individual psyche.

---

*The chapter was originally published as 'Greed in Hollywood movies' in *Greed: Developmental, Cultural, and Clinical Realms* (2015), edited by Salman Akhtar, (pp. 107–128), Abingdon, UK: Routledge. Reproduced with permission of the Licensor through PLSclear.

In the first scene of *Greed*, the 1924 film by Erich von Stroheim, the main character emerges from the mouth of a California gold mine riding a cart filled to overflowing with the glistening ore. Although little remembered by the public, in part due to its being cut from an original eight hours down to a spare two, this film exerted strong influence on the international film world. The next generation of Hollywood directors all learned from it. This influence can be felt in the films of John Huston and even much later, in the half-dozen or so contemporary films set in Wall Street.

From these, I have selected two films for detailed discussion in this chapter: *The Maltese Falcon* (1941) and *Wall Street* (1987). In part, I select these films because they appeal to a mass audience. They are entertaining, engaging, and emotionally evocative. They are also prototypical. Each in its own way has spawned a whole genre, in the one case, film noir, and in the other, what we might call the Wall Street thriller.[2] But perhaps more important is the fact that both these films are structured as parables of greed. That is to say, they are stories with a "message" and that message is the power and consequent dangers inherent in greed. Yet both films also carry an unconscious subtext that makes them interesting from the psychoanalytic viewpoint. We can say, in this regard, that the "message" is at odds with the subtext since each movie expresses an attitude of ambivalence toward greed. And this ambivalence is, of course, reflected in both the group "mentality" (Bion, 1961) and the individual psyche.

Structurally speaking, these two films, although addressing greed from different angles, reveal striking parallels. In the guise of a parable or cautionary tale, both present what I call Greed with a capital G—Greed that goes beyond the limit of the merely venal (Wolman, 2014). Each in its own way depicts characters who are the personification of such large-scale greed. In *The Maltese Falcon* greed is divided equally among three characters. In *Wall Street* it is concentrated in the figure of Gordon Gekko—and by extension his "minions." The two films also create striking and unforgettable images of the object of greed. *The Maltese Falcon* gathers all the objects of greed into one: the Maltese Falcon itself. *Wall Street*, on the other hand, displays the full range of possible objects of greed: money of course, in all its forms, but also fashion, décor, and *objets d'art*. In the characters who personify greed and through its objects, the films highlight the important role of a *façade of legitimacy* in the portrayal of greed. In this respect we see the full range of seduction, deceit, and self-delusion at work.

And in each film there is one subject of greed who is initially tempted, seduced, and self-deluded by greed. In *The Maltese Falcon* that subject is Sam Spade, the detective; and in *Wall Street*, he is Bud Fox, the young stockbroker. Each must undergo a process that leads from entrapment to recognition of their active role in their own undoing. This in turn leads to the recovery of their subjectivity—of their being able to say in *words where they stand*—and of making an act of renunciation.

In each film greed is shown to be antithetical to human ties based on loyalty, respect, partnership, or collegiality. This severing of ties is represented in the psyche by an "abyss"—or in a felicitous choice of words—"poverty" of internalized object relationships. And by placing the subjects of greed on the edge of a void, the two films underscore the problematic nature of the object of greed. That object occupies a place which, for want of a better word, we would have to call "extra-psychic."[3] Our two films are perhaps most adept in portraying this "extra-psychic" position as a "collective" mentality overturning the individual's power of personal engagement.

The Maltese Falcon

Let us begin with *The Maltese Falcon*, written and directed by John Huston. The film is structured as a typical Hollywood genre film, in which the detective Sam Spade attempts to solve the murder of his partner, Miles Archer. However, it can also be taken as a parable or cautionary tale on the perils of greed. The two levels intersect since both Spade and Archer become affected, or shall we say "infected" by the greed that permeates the story. This greed leads directly to Archer's death, and almost lures Spade into making a fatal error, until he takes a principled stand near the end of the film. In his struggle with his own propensity for greed, Spade traverses a kind of journey of self-discovery in the course of the film.

But in the parable of greed—that is, in one particular reading of the film—Spade plays a secondary role. The leading characters in this little allegory are: Brigid O'Shaughnessy, Joel Cairo, and Kasper Gutman. Each in their own way reveals the "character", or rather the "caricature" of greed. It is via these three that the theme of *The Maltese Falcon* is introduced, around which much of the action revolves.

Let us begin with the character who introduces the falcon into the story: Joel Cairo. He initially refers to it as an "ornament" which "shall we say, is mislaid"; and—like the first communication in a psychoanalytic treatment—this word accumulates meaning in light of later events. Calling it an "ornament" is a clear effort to mislead the listener as to its value, especially its value to him—Joel Cairo. Even the words "shall we say" imply that "ornament" doesn't quite capture the word's true meaning. As an "ornament" the falcon slips into the background of the scene without drawing attention to itself. It merely adds to the exotic ambience of the film. In the psychoanalytic sense, the word is a euphemism and a displacement, whereby an object of minor importance substitutes for one of great personal significance (Freud, 1900a).

Cairo's statement that the bird is "shall we say, mislaid" is open to interpretation. In a stock room or antique shop, chock full of *objets d'art*, an inconspicuous black statuette of a bird could easily be mislaid. Perhaps it was moved to another room, or placed in storage. This meaning seems to imply that Cairo wants merely to return the bird to its rightful place or rightful owner. At one point, he even pretends to be the *agent* of this alleged rightful owner. But as we shall see, "mislaid" can also imply a displacement or diversion outside the network within which objects can be located and wherein their provenance may be verified and their authentication established. It is this latter possibility that perhaps underlies Cairo's obsession with finding the falcon. As a symptom, his obsession may conceal an unconscious fear that the bird is irretrievably lost and incapable of being found.

Yet in seeming contradiction to his façade of *politesse*, Cairo does a shocking about-face: casting aside all his smarmy stratagems, he abruptly pulls a gun on Spade and demands he reveal the location of the falcon (or information leading to said location). In this instant he shows his real motive: an all-consuming desire to possess the falcon at any cost; in other words, naked greed. We shall encounter this sudden "switch" from smooth surface to overpowering rage again in the figure of Gordon Gekko, the lead character of *Wall Street*.

Part of greed's façade is made up of rationalizations for its legitimacy. Kasper Gutman, the most articulate spokesman for greed, offers two such explanations. He first spins a quasi-mythical story about the bird's origins that obfuscates the question of a legitimate owner. According to this story, the falcon was removed from its chain of custody by an original act of piracy, causing it to be "mislaid" in perpetuity and ensuring that the legitimate transfer of ownership never took place. In the absence of a legitimate owner or a "rightful place," Gutman argues, ownership is based solely on the act of possession itself as if "possession is nine-tenths of the law." Hence the object is fair game to any and all fortune hunters.

In the second explanation, he argues that the desirability of the falcon is based on its unique and incomparable value. The word he uses is: "priceless." On the simplest level, he is saying that the falcon is worth a fortune—a fact that should guarantee its desirability. But the word "priceless" implies something more: the impossibility of setting a price or a specific valuation for the object in question. This means that no matter what price is offered, the falcon will always be worth that price plus "n"—where "n" is some indeterminate amount. Thus regardless of offering price, the value is still just out of reach. By the same token, "priceless" suggests that no other object exists in the world of *comparable value*. There is therefore no means of fixing a price based on the series of similar objects of value. And taking this line of thought one step further: there can be no possible medium of exchange by which the falcon can be bought or sold in the marketplace or be used in an exchange of gifts. In other words, there is no "currency" that will be accepted as the equivalent of the falcon for transactional purposes. Consequently, the falcon's "pricelessness" resides entirely in itself and not in its circulation as a commodity.

In light of these two rationalizations, Gutman gets to the heart of greed when he says: "If you lose a son, it is possible to get another, but there is only one falcon." This is a shocking statement. It turns on its head the usual scale of human value: a material object is incomparably more valuable than one's own child. Moreover, the material object is irreplaceable whereas the child is not. This amounts to a debasement of human beings and their replacement by "statuettes." On the one side, we have the network of kinship relations— the world of object relationships—and on the other, the ultimate "object"— a single point at which everything of value in the world is concentrated.

The three character's relationship to the object of greed is laid bare when they finally regain possession of the falcon. For this scene, the camera pans in and the viewer sees their avid faces in close-up. Gutman chips at the surface of the bird with a knife, but when the precious metal does not appear, he stabs it repeatedly and viciously as if engaged in an act of murder. He acts out the trio's rage and disappointment that this long sought-after object is in reality *nothing more than what it appears to be*. At the same time, Cairo's smooth façade is cracked open by his rage and disappointment in Gutman, whom he calls "a bloated imbecile" and a "fathead." Perhaps he sees in this act his own "unveiling" as a worthless object at odds with his bejeweled appearance. In any case, the word "bloated"—pictured in Gutman's bloated abdomen—seems to suggest, not a surfeit or fulfillment, but rather the utter vacuous-ness of the whole enterprise.

Brigid O'Shaughnessy and deceit

Perhaps the most striking facet of the three characters is their deceit. This trait corresponds to the outer coating of the falcon, which supposedly hides its true nature (Freud, 1913f). On the surface, deceit is the means of controlling information about the falcon, and by extension, the identity of the murderer. As we saw in the case of Joel Cairo, each character wants to disguise his *intent* and therefore his history and provenance, so to speak. And like Gutman, each wants to obfuscate the falcon's value—especially its value to them personally. And finally, each wants to veil their willingness to use violence to achieve their goal behind a superficial *politesse*.

All these elements are present in the character of Brigid O'Shaughnessy, but in her case the element of deceit is less overt and therefore more sinister. Brigid—an apparently unsophisticated, middle-class woman lacking the flamboyance of the two men—presents herself as a person in disarray, at "loose ends," whose thoughts, intentions, and emotions run "every which way." Her mind seems like the open suitcases lying on her bed in her tiny apartment, brimming over with clothes and beauty products.

This apparent disorganization is evident in her compulsive lying. Everything she says in the film is a lie and yet she lacks the will or knack to tell a plausible story and to iron out the inconsistencies between one lie and another.[4] Indeed, in conversation with Sam Spade, her attempts at self-justification are almost ludicrous in their transparency and yet she keeps on lying as if the very blatancy of her deceit somehow supports her credibility.

Thus the transparency of her lying often leads directly to the truth she is trying to hide. For example, her frequent attempts to divert suspicion away from herself are in fact unconscious confessions. We can hear the truth when she says, "now I have to make a confession," or when she asks Spade, "Am I to blame?" The answer to this question is of course, "Yes," for her entire scaffolding of lies leads directly to the truth that she murdered Spade's partner, Miles Archer.

Even her façade of disorganization is disingenuous. Her "self" is a hodge-podge of borrowings and improvisations. She is making herself up as she goes along. This patchwork "self" is thus pure fabrication. Yet it is true in so far as it reveals the hollowness at her core: she lacks any principle or ethical position that would impart a semblance of unity to the disparate parts. But her boldest conceit (or should we say deceit?) is that this same disarray disguises a single-mindedness of purpose that is frightening in its raw avidity.

The menace that Brigid represents for Sam Spade is manifest as a concealed weapon. The other two characters display their guns and Spade neatly disarms them both (Wilmer, Gutman's lackey, has *two* guns). The men are therefore shown up as impotent bumblers whose greed overtakes their ineptitude as individuals. Interestingly, it is Gutman who warns Spade of Brigid's dangerousness. That danger lies in her hidden gun—the same gun she used to murder Miles Archer. It is a concealed weapon, affording her the advantage of surprise and representing the singularity of her ruthless purpose—the concentration of all her energy at a single point. Thus she is indeed a formidable woman—a phallic woman associated with two eunuchs—one of the great "femme fatales" of film noir.[5]

Sam Spade as the subject of greed

Sam Spade is the only true "subject" in the film. As a person, he is far from admirable, but he does retain a fundamental honor and decency that ultimately allows him to step back from the precipice. This set of principles includes a work ethic conspicuously lacking in the other three "characters."

Yet he is a man rent by conflicts, many of which are depicted in his conflicted relationship with his partner, Miles Archer. Archer is a slightly older, more bloated, and more corrupt version of Spade himself. Both men are tempted by the lure of money and the easy temptation to bilk unwary clients. Their business exposes them to a corrupt world and they sometimes succumb to cynicism. Their greed is merely venal. But this very venality makes them vulnerable to greed on the grander scale represented by the three characters' quest for the Maltese Falcon.

Spade doesn't like his partner because in him he confronts his own more "venal" self. And he knows he is only better by a hair. He has been conducting an affair with Archer's wife, for example, which he half-justifies by the latter's long history of adultery. His distaste for Archer is precariously balanced against the principle that partnership means something beyond the personalities of the partners.

The same conflict between money and principle affects his attitude toward Brigid. Time and again we see Spade's reluctance, hesitation, and ambivalence whenever he catches her in a lie. He knows he is being manipulated but part of him doesn't seem to care. Even when he expresses his contempt for her, he lets her suck him in—lets her "play him for a sucker"—and his surrender appears complete when they become lovers.

It is only the falling-off of masks and the unveiling of the falcon's true nature near the film's climax that finally breaks the seductive spell. Spade now confronts Brigid with his intention to "inform" on her to the police. In so doing, he renounces his bond with her. In their last exchange, he reviews all the possible justifications for his act: his original code of honor and his calculation that their shared knowledge of the crime makes each potentially lethal to the other. But in the end, Spade finds the most persuasive reason in his epiphany that despite all the barriers of scruple, common sense, and self-interest, he still wants her and the consequences be damned. He knows he can never rid himself of this desire and he also knows that it will come to dominate him as an individual, robbing him of his freedom as a human subject. And in fully articulating this drive—that is in stating clearly where he stands in relation to it—he achieves some measure of separation (Lacan, 1953).

And by speaking these words that represent him—that say who he is— he becomes the "subject of greed" as opposed to the others who are "objects of greed." As a "subject of greed" he recognizes that he is "subject to greed"; that he is conflicted over it, but not submerged in it. His words open up a subjective space for intangibles such as "the stuff that dreams are made of."[6] Consequently, he is able to step away from the false quest for the falcon, while the others are only momentarily stymied. Even if they should kill each other off, others will take their place just as they have in the past every time the bird changed hands. Hence with barely a pause, they will again take up the pursuit, still hopeful, and ever ready to hurtle down the next blind alley.

Wall Street

The 1987 film written and directed by Oliver Stone is a more overt—some would say cruder—parable of greed than *The Maltese Falcon*. The action follows the machinations of greed's chief proponent, Gordon Gekko, as he lies, cheats, and steals his way toward the big payoff. With Gekko, it is not so much the money itself that motivates him as the opportunity to create something big out of nothing and to do it all in one stroke, so to speak. Each of his "deals" is in fact an act of piracy masquerading as a business transaction.

In pursuing his aims he surrounds himself with enablers who do his bidding in the hope of riding his coat-tails to riches of their own. Gekko thus personifies the greed that already permeates the entire Wall Street milieu and that is visualized in the opening scene of people crushed together into an anonymous mass, "none of them acknowledging each other."

Yet unlike the three grotesques in the earlier film, Gordon Gekko is presented as a charismatic and in some ways sympathetic figure. In the screenplay's stage notes (imsdb.com),[7] Gekko has "genuine charm", projects "calm and confidence at the center", and "obviously loves what he does". His enthusiasm and energy are infectious. His attitude seems to be one of unconflicted enjoyment. In his gleeful avidity he grants the moviegoer a powerful vicarious satisfaction. They are similarly won over by his openness about aggressive aims ("let's go in for the kill") and primitive drives ("I'll eat his lunch for him"). And perhaps for this reason, we as viewers do not fully enjoy his final comeuppance as we do, for example, in Elia Kazan's *On the Waterfront* (1954), when the corrupt union official played by L. J. Cobb is arrested, while shouting "I'll be back, I'll be back." With Gekko, I submit, we are more likely to think of his actions as "irrational exuberance" gone wild, as opposed to evil incarnate.

Gordon Gekko as apologist for greed

However, we must observe Gekko's actions and most importantly listen to his actual words to gain a clearer idea of what he is about. Gekko is an accomplished and voluble talker. He is always shown talking to his assistants, talking on the phone, carrying on several conversations at once and seemingly talking to himself when deprived of an audience. In his speech he is glib, entertaining, and witty. One has the impression of being in the presence of a gifted inspirational speaker, say, or pitchman. We might characterize his style as modern day sophistry. The current definition of sophistry is: "the use of reasoning or arguments that sound correct but are actually false" or "subtly deceptive reasoning or argumentation."[8] Hence we must resist being persuaded by his style alone, and direct our attention to substance.

Gekko is a brilliant coiner of aphoristic sayings or "sound bites", the most famous of which is: "greed is good." These sayings emit an aura of profound wisdom. Let us examine a few of them, starting with: "I only bet on sure things." What does this mean? Well, it projects supreme confidence, which is both infectious and reassuring. The message is: "I can't lose," and by extension: "You can't lose." And to back this up, he quotes Sun Tzu (2002) on *The Art of War*: "every battle is won before it is ever fought." This lends his own words the semblance of authority and tradition. But in a volatile environment like Wall Street—or the churning forces vying for contention within the mind—is anything really that certain except for death and taxes? And don't you sometimes have to actually fight your own battles? Do not all important enterprises involve risk?[9]

Another zinger is: "If you're not inside, you're outside." That is, if you're not standing within the charmed circle, then you are barred from their secret knowledge. Thus, according to this logic, if you participate in "insider trading"—a crime—you are merely sharing what everyone on the "inside" already knows. Of course the unconscious significance of this remark is not too hard to guess: Gekko has, and always will, see himself as an outsider—as a child reduced to poverty, for example. On a deeper level, we can hazard that Gekko has made the *outside* world of Wall Street with its atmosphere of frenetic activity the replacement for his internal world, for which we see little evidence in the film. The Wall Street milieu is thus the only home within which he can exist.

And if being the ultimate insider helps us grasp G.G.'s self-concept, other remarks reflect his attitude toward money and wealth. One throwaway line is: "Money is better than sex." By money he means "the big score." So from the psychoanalytic perspective, he is saying simply that "money *is* sex." And again, it is not just money per se, but rather the supplementary bump or kick you get with a sudden and instantaneous gain that makes it sexual. This kind of transaction may seem more exciting than ordinary sex with a partner and it certainly may serve as a *substitute*. Indeed, it's virtually autoerotic, since you don't have to worry about pleasing others.

In the same vein, we have the idea that in the Wall Street game, you're either a major player or you are nothing. Small amounts of money and well-earned salaries are mocked. Gekko is imbued with the characteristic all or nothing logic of big-time greed (Boris, 1986). You play this game for keeps. You either come away with untold riches or absolute zero. And the incredible thing is, you do this without taking any risk. Thus his own principles lead to a contradiction, since by accepting "nothing" as a possibility, you actually risk everything.

From here we are led to greed's quintessential motto: "greed is good." This remark can be found in G.G.'s presentation before the shareholders of a large paper manufacturer. His aim is very specific: to persuade the shareholders to accept his bid to buy their shares and thus take over the company. It is the only time in the film that Gekko delivers a formal speech. Let us then take note of the way that Michael Douglas speaks the line: "The point is ... that ... greed ... for lack of a better word ... is good."[10] Now on one level these pauses and hesitations keep the listener in suspense so that the final word imparts a surprising meaning. Up until that point in the line, G.G. seems to be fumbling for the right word. It is as if greed were an entity that should not be verbalized in polite company, or going a step further, simply cannot be named at all, as if greed was simply too big to be reduced to a single word. From this angle, the various pauses between "greed" and "good" serve to *separate* the two words. The unconscious message may then be: greed is *not* good. It is not good because it stands alone as a thing in itself and cannot be limited by any attributive, whether good, bad, or indifferent.

Moreover we must consider the phrase: "greed is good" within the context of Gekko's entire apology for greed. The immediate context lies in the CEO's comments about "goods and services" being delivered and whether Gekko's buyout serves the public good. Thus Gekko's line raises the question, not just of whether greed is morally good, but the related questions of whether it promotes "goods" and services and serves the public "good." In his peroration, Gekko goes on to say: "Greed works, greed is right, greed clarifies, cuts through and captures the evolutionary spirit ... greed in all its forms, greed for life, money, love, knowledge."

But these theses fail to address the CEO's questions. Each is stated in an intransitive mode: Greed works—in what way? Greed is right—right as opposed to left? Right versus wrong? Everybody's inalienable right? And what exactly does greed clarify? Does it cut through the chaff leaving us only the essential wheat? And what is the so-called evolutionary spirit? Are we talking about Darwinian survival of the fittest? A gradual progressive trend? All these arguments raise questions they do not, and cannot, answer. Greed is too big to fit any argument or category. Even its forms expand outward from money to knowledge, love, and ultimately life itself. Only this last categorization strikes home: one definition of greed holds that greed is the demand for life at all costs and the refusal to pay death is its price (Freud, 1920g).

In this way, Gekko poses as the champion and savior of capitalism. He appears to advocate efficiency, investment, liberation, and even American nationalism. He depicts an environment where everybody wins. But the means to accomplish these laudatory aims are dubious. In fact, according to him, the only way to "create value" is to buy stock and have it go up. But can this be the *only* way? It raises the question whether Gekko's aim is to create anything at all. In fact, he says later that "money isn't lost or made, it's simply transferred from one perception to another" (*sic*). Moreover, trading is a "zero-sum game" where for every winner there is a loser. In one of his final epigrams he states: "I create nothing; I own." These statements contradict the idea that he "creates value" or that "everybody wins."

My point is that none of Gekko's words stand up to scrutiny. Together they make up the elements of a false persona (Winnicott, 1960a). That persona with its multiple sophistries resembles the interior of Bud Fox's apartment designed by G.G.'s decorator-in-chief and former girlfriend, Darien. It contains a neo-classical mural, "faux Etruscan pots," a Pompeii-like coffee table, a pseudo-Adirondack chair, a "gothic" oak refectory table, along with imitation rare woods, marbles and frescoes, and other forms of *trompe l'œils*, including pseudo-brick and crown molding. In other words, it is all sleight of hand. Gekko's seductive words offer no handhold to grasp or define the greed he embodies.

Gordon Gekko and the fathers

The character of Gordon Gekko is sharpened by contrast with the other fathers presented in the film, who are important characters in their own right. This contrast applies especially to the question of where the characters stand with regard to fatherhood and their ability to adopt a paternal role. These fathers occupy various positions on the spectrum of fatherhood from traditional parents, to anti-traditional moguls, to guardians of the law. The figure of Carl Fox—father of Bud Fox, the other principal character—for example, is depicted as Gekko's antithesis. Carl is the president of the maintenance workers union for Bluestar Airlines. His position on money is noteworthy: "Money is something you need in case you don't die tomorrow." It is therefore not something you need to accumulate for the long term. Ideally, you would die without a penny but with no outstanding debt. Interestingly, Carl's rejection of greed is intertwined with recognition of his own mortality. Indeed, he lives his life as if his death were imminent, as evidenced by his chain smoking.

In a brief disquisition, Carl considers the perils of money. There is something about its possession that dictates that you can never have *just* enough. Either you have too much and you worry about losing it; or you have too little and you worry about having more. That ideal point where you have *just* enough simply doesn't exist. Thus, for Carl, "money's one giant pain in the ass." In articulating what we may call the "anti-greed" mentality, Carl exposes the idea that money only has value in its wide circulation, to the union membership, say, and not in its accumulation in a bank or in the rich man's pocket.[11]

It would be a mistake, however, to view Carl's self-effacement with regard to money as a sign of impotence. For Carl has proved himself an effective and dedicated union leader who fights for his members. Nor is he strictly anti-management either, since he understands and accommodates to the airline's need to improve its business. His refusal of self-aggrandizement goes hand in hand with commitment to others. In general he represents a path that gives weight to traditional values even when they seem outmoded and anachronistic.

We find a slightly different but analogous approach to tradition in the figure of Lou Mannheim, Bud Fox's older colleague at the brokerage firm where they both work. Lou espouses his financial credo in the first scene set in their workplace: "Stick to the fundamentals ... good things sometimes ... take time." In his brilliant reading of the line, the actor, Hal Holbrook, inserts the two pauses that act like counterparts to the pauses in Gekko's credo. In Holbrook's reading, however, they add the dimension of time to the words themselves. And the reference to time fits with Carl's invocation of death. And also like Carl, Lou is advocating a policy of long-term investment in "science, research, and jobs."

For individuals like Lou, the purpose of business is productivity and creativity for all. In the paternal metaphor, this would be like begetting and raising numerous children. When Lou inveighs against the Gordon Gekkos of this world, he asks: "What's being created? Nothing. No substance behind it." Indeed, greed creates nothing, as we know by Gekko's own admission that he creates "nothing." Mannheim's critique of greed implies that its underlying nihilism is hidden behind a façade of trickery, "shortcuts," and sleight of hand.

Lou and Carl represent different versions of traditional fathers. But as we have noted, despite their outmodishness, they inhabit their roles fully. Both men know where they stand and say where they stand. Both men display confidence, firmness, and assertiveness in the ways they conduct themselves. However, they are not in themselves what would be called "power-players." If they have a flaw, it is that of being too risk adverse.

However, that cannot be said of Sir Lawrence Wildman, Gordon Gekko's chief rival. Wildman holds our interest because he and Gekko are so much alike. Both are men who have risen up from poverty to great wealth. Both compete in the cutthroat arena of leveraged buyouts and corporate take-overs. Both stand as counterparts and equals, despite Wildman's evident lack of charm or glibness.

So the question becomes: What really differentiates these two men whose attitude toward money and acquisitiveness is not really all that different? The difference is small but consequential. On one level, it is a difference in names. Gekko's name connotes bestiality,[12] a code word for greed; the name Wildman suggests pushing the boundary of the human without going beyond it. And this hints at the key difference: Wildman will sometimes aggrandize himself at the expense of others but *he will not break the law*. That is, he will stop short of insider trading. His allegiance to the law makes him an establishment figure, and so it is not surprising that Gekko resents him for his title "Sir." That title merely recognizes Wildman's unbroken link with tradition (at least in British society), and hence, the chain of fathers.

And this small but definitive difference brings us to the last in the series of fathers: the senior investigator who ultimately indicts Gordon Gekko and Bud Fox for securities fraud. His paternal position is shown by his seniority to the junior investigator who first uncovers the evidence. Both are por-trayed as faceless enforcers of the law. It is not even clear in the film which government agency they represent (SEC? FBI? Stockwatch?). Their sole identifying feature is their name tags. The name tag marks them as govern-ment officials and guardians of the social order. It is thus a kind of differ-ential for that aspect of fatherhood that purely and simply upholds the law.

Bud Fox's fall and redemption

In counterpoint to Gordon's Gekko's rise and fall, *Wall Street* chronicles the temptation, seduction, and restitution of Bud Fox. The film allows us to mark the various positions Fox occupies on this journey. And what is help-ful in our investigation of greed is that each of these positions is *clearly stated in words*. This factor makes Fox's psyche and the turmoil therein accessible to psychoanalytic listening.

First we ask ourselves what conditions make Fox susceptible to G.G.'s seductiveness. The camera's view of Bud's tiny apartment provides a clue. It is filled to capacity with books, papers, and stock market periodicals, all strewn about every which way, and leaving no room for anything else. In particular, the screenplay notes, there is "no semblance of a personal life."[13] Thus at the start of the film, Bud has already chosen to dedicate himself exclusively to monetary success. Moreover, if we take the apartment as a snapshot of Bud's psyche, then he has temporarily squeezed out the thoughts, fantasies, and emotions that constitute a rich internal life.

Nevertheless, Bud elicits our sympathy because his conflicts are so transparent. He reveals his psychic position at the start of the film in two throwaway lines spoken to his colleagues at work: "Doing any better would be a sin," and later, "Doing any better and I'd be guilty." So what does he feel guilty about? He feels guilty about his debt to his father who has loaned him money for college tuition and living expenses. This guilt is thrown into high gear when he is "stiffed" by a customer who demands that he cover a 7,000 dollar loss that was not Bud's fault. Bud's self-serving boss at the office tells him somebody's got to pay and "it ain't going to be me." Thus Bud feels he is being forced to pay what by rights should be *his father's debt*. This takes us right to the heart of oedipal guilt: it is not so much what we actually owe the father, among whose gifts is our very existence, but rather the father's own debts, as if the sins of the father must be borne by the sons.

It is therefore significant that the first stage in Bud's seduction by Gordon Gekko is the young man's betrayal of his father's values in revealing inside information about Bluestar Airlines. From this first step, it is a slippery slope downwards, to Bud spying on Sir Lawrence Wildman to obtain information about his buyout of Anacott Steel, to his buying a waste disposal company for access to their confidential files, to himself taking over the reins of Bluestar Airlines. We could, of course, point out that he takes each of these steps in reaction to Gekko's blatant efforts at seduction: dangling before him the chance of a "big score," giving him a million dollars to "play with,"[14] plying him with women (Lisa, Darien), and finally making him CEO of the very airline his father works for. But we would argue that it is Bud who takes the first step, and who therefore makes all the succeeding steps possible.

We can see the subtle interchange between Gordon and Bud in the way the older man addresses him. At their first meeting, Bud introduces himself with the words: "How do you do Mr. Gekko, I'm Bud Fox," to which G.G. responds: "So you say." Note that while Bud addresses G.G. as "Mr. Gekko", almost no one in the film actually calls him that. Moreover, Gekko seems to deflect or to discredit Bud's name. It is almost as if he were implying that

Bud is someone or something other than Bud Fox. And after this moment, Gekko mostly addresses Bud as "sport" or sometimes with "ironic" names like "Kemosabe," but not "Bud Fox." Nor does Bud attempt to correct him on this point.

And once fully in Gekko's clutches, Bud signs a legal document protecting G.G. from any accountability for actions taken on his behalf. Thus in the stroke of a pen, Bud effectively crosses out his own name and makes himself a pure extension of Gordon Gekko's greedy agenda. He is now so utterly "taken in" by his "mentor," he thinks "I can't lose and I can't get hurt." Such naïvety may seem exaggerated, but its obviousness is exactly the point. The change is structural: once you relinquish your right to speak, you fall into the position of the object—in this case the object of gross manipulation.[15]

And Bud Fox openly acknowledges this "fall" when he admits to Gordon: "All right Mr. Gekko, you've got me." That is, I am no longer my own man; you possess me—you *own* me, thus making me the object of greed. He comes to this realization in part through his encounters with Darien, his new girlfriend. Darien has also been seduced by Gordon literally (unbeknownst to Bud) and figuratively. As his decorator, she provides beautiful objects for her "clients" whose value resides in their "possession" rather than their utility or their capacity to evoke a human response in the viewer. When Darien transforms Bud's apartment into a veritable display case for such objects, Bud begins to suspect that there is no space in which he can be a person in his own right. He has become like the expensive vase on the table. His father later articulates this insight when he observes that: "It's like you've been standing in the display window of Macy's."[16] This in turn allows him to see Darien as his exact counterpart. Looking directly into her face, he says: "I'm looking in the mirror and I sure don't like what I see."

But it is only in the face of Gekko's egregious betrayal that Bud can begin to act as an independent agent. He is betrayed by Gekko when the latter decides to "liquidate" Bluestar Airlines, which would destroy everything his father has worked for all his adult life. This act of betrayal is itself complex and impacts Bud on many levels. But it has one salutary effect: it shows Bud that the decision to "liquidate" the airline has been made without his consent or participation as the titular head of the airline. In this moment he sees—as if looking in a mirror—what is in effect his own castration—his profound impotence—his being the "prick in Gekko's back pocket."

There is but one further step before Bud recovers his ability to speak and think for himself. He must first undergo the *devastating loss of the object*. He initiates this change through a piece of acting out. Returning to his apartment, he breaks a vase, rips a curtain off a window, upends a painting, and overturns a chair. In this "selected but not frenzied damage," he enacts a transition from entrapment inside these decorative objects toward full subjectivity. Everything hinges on the word-play between "turning around" and "turning upside down." He was deluded into thinking that he and Gordon were going to turn Bluestar Airlines around; instead, Gekko has turned it "upside down." So now, in "upending" and "overturning" objects, he begins to "turn the tables on G.G." Yet in so doing he must "shatter the image"—of him and Darien in their mirror relation to Gekko—and face "total loss."

From this moment, Bud recovers his powers of speech and hence his capacity to have a say in his own fate. He then proceeds to confront and question his former protector-turned-adversary. They have a more honest debate which lays bare Gordon's domination by the object of greed. Gordon is such a complete apologist for greed that he never seems to be speaking on behalf of a person named Gordon Gekko. Nevertheless, there is poignancy in the last confrontation between the two men, the one wearing a "wire," the other pummeling Bud with his fists.[17] No matter how selfish and self-deluded, Gordon's thwarted love and hate toward his surrogate son retains an authenticity missing elsewhere in the film. In him we bear witness to something which is quintessentially human and at the same time antithetical to the ties that bind us to others and to our own words.

All these elements of his reconstitution finally coalesce in Bud's oft-quoted answer to Gordon's question: "Why?" Bud says: "I guess I realized I'm just Bud Fox. And as much as I wanted to be G.G. ... I'll always be Bud Fox." In the light of our discussion, we would claim that he speaks in his own name and will continue to do so. But this is not simply, or even mainly, an act of self-assertion. Rather it is a declaration of commitment to his word. And we know that commitment binds as much, or more so, than it liberates. Hence, his name and word now exact a steep price—the price Bud, in recognizing his debt to others, must now pay by going to prison.

Lou Mannheim, Bud's true Wall Street mentor, beautifully sums up Bud's redemption in these words: "Man looks in the abyss, there's nothing staring back at him. At that time a man finds his character ... and that is what keeps him out of the abyss". This final word universalizes the confrontation with greed. The "nothing" staring back is the extra-psychic object of greed. Man's "character"—and he is referring to Bud's character—is his name and everything a name implies in the way of ethical principle. In a certain sense, *Wall Street* is the name for this abyss which threatens the integrity of all of us as individuals.

Conclusions

In an article about the screen kiss, A. O. Scott (2014), the film critic for *The New York Times*, writes: "movies have always been about sex and have always provided, under cover of harmless amusement, the tools of sexual initiation." In that same article, the author quotes Freud (1916–1917) as follows: "even a kiss can claim to be described as a perverse act." In other words, even a relatively innocent and seemingly conventional screen kiss always conveys an undercurrent of repressed sexuality.

I cite this idea in order to suggest that in our two films, greed is associated with sexuality. Both films under discussion are replete with sexuality, both muted and overt. In *The Maltese Falcon*, sexuality is implied in Spade's affairs with his partner's wife and with Brigid O'Shaughnessy. There is also an implied eroticism in his relationship with his secretary. In *Wall Street* sexuality is ubiquitous. It seems as if all the men are flirting with all the women. There are three explicit sexual scenes involving Bud Fox: an unnamed woman shown nude (in his apartment), Lisa (in the car), and Darien (again in his apartment).

The link between greed and sexuality is provided by Gordon Gekko in his phrase "greed for life." Such "greed for life" is presented as part of a series of potential objects of greed that also includes money," "love," and "knowledge." The point is that there is a relatively loose connection between greed and its object, just as pertains in infantile sexuality (Freud, 1905d). Thus greed is always ready to jump from one object to another. In *The Maltese Falcon*, the repressed object may be the homoeroticism of Joel Cairo and Kasper Gutman. In *Wall Street*, the "possession" of women makes of them objects of both sex and greed. And in the male-dominated sexuality of the film, the "many" substitute for the impossible "one" of the mother (Freud, 1910h).

And on the level of meaning, "greed for life" suggests the rampant nature of human sexuality. It connotes the oral craving, the anal obsession with accumulation and collecting, and the phallic monopolization of power and potency. In this regard, Gordon Gekko is an "equal opportunity" proponent of every psychosexual stage, along with the requisite aggressive component. "Greed for life" is a rallying cry for sexual satisfaction at any cost, on every level, and with every possible polymorphously perverse aim and object. No wonder that greed brooks no limits and that it defies every "rational" principle of self-regulation (including the pleasure–pain principle)

(Freud, 1920g). And finally, there is in the phrase "greed for life" an uncon-scious subtext: greed for death. This is an inevitable consequence of greed's obliviousness to the instinct for self-preservation. As in the case of infantile orality, for example, the drive for satisfaction is greater than the lesser aim of individual survival. Moreover, if we picture "greed for life" as the avid consumption of every satisfaction afforded by human existence, then that craving must eventually be directed *at the roots of life itself*, in a kind of cli-mactic self-immolation, an orgy of self-destruction.

Returning to our two films, we can review structural parallels in the way greed and its associated psychosexual components is portrayed, despite dif-ferences in milieu, era, and character. Concerning the object, both films attempt to demonstrate that the object of greed is impossible to attain. There is no single object and no finite quantity of objects that can truly satisfy greed or bring any sense of psychic closure to the individual dominated by greed. In addition, the objects of greed are almost exclusively *material objects*. In the earlier film, it is a black, matte statuette. In the more recent film, the most cinematic representations of objects are the various decorative pieces and the paintings hanging on the walls of Bud Fox's apartment. The material environment within which greed prospers is of necessity devoid of "intangibles" such as dreams, reverie, and ideals ("the stuff that dreams are made of"). It subsists, we maintain, in an extra-psychic dimension that displaces the rich internal world, grounded in networks of connections.

In relation to the object of greed, both films present a subject of greed who is initially tempted and seduced by the object and then himself reduced to the status of object. He later regains his subjectivity in the act of renounc-ing the object. In the end somebody has to pay for the excesses wrought by greed in the course of the film.

Each man is able to reconstitute himself as subject of speech by re-endorsing some law or principle. For Spade that principle is minimally rep-resented by the word "partner." What saves him from falling into the abyss of greed is his commitment to honor his partnership with Miles Archer by solving his murder. In so doing, he voluntarily binds himself to the very principle of partnership, despite his problematic and contradictory rela-tionship with his actual partner. Bud Fox, on the other hand, ultimately endorses the more expansive and general principle of paternity in all its guises: revering the father, obeying the law, conserving the historical links between fathers and sons, respecting tradition, fostering mentorship, and "paying one's dues" (Lacan, 1953).

Neither film, however, has much to say about the mother's role in the genesis of greed. And this brings to the fore the major question that is not addressed by the films: maternal greed, feminine greed, and the link between greed and female sexuality. Both films take an almost exclusively male perspective on greed, relegating most of the female characters to the status of objects. In *The Maltese Falcon*, only Brigid O'Shaughnessy manages to break free of the strictures placed on the women in the film, and to reveal her heretofore disguised voraciousness. In *Wall Street*, the women are presented as sexual objects and denied an authentic voice.

For what it's worth, during Darien's (Bud Fox's main love interest) scenes with Bud, I had the association: "they're not allowing her to show any teeth!" Then later a second look revealed a painting on the wall of four grotesque figures with huge barred teeth. For me, this fleeting image hints at what is repressed in the films: the insatiable maternal figure.

Notes

1. See McLuhan (1964), for example, especially the chapter: "Media hot and cold", pp. 36–45.
2. Examples of film noir are too numerous to mention but one fine example is *Double Indemnity* (1944), which also features greed as a subtext. Examples of the Wall Street genre include: *Boiler Room* (2000), *Wall Street: Money Never Sleeps* (2010), and *The Wolf of Wall Street* (2013).
3. We say "extra-psychic" because "external objects" are "psychical" since they carry a charge of libidinal investment. Alternatively, we might say that the object of greed is represented in the psyche by a void and in the external world by a series of material objects.
4. In this regard, see Bion's discussion of lies and truth in "Attention and interpretation" (1978).
5. For a Lacanian discussion of "femmes fatales", see Žižek (1991).
6. Huston borrows this line from Shakespeare's *The Tempest*. It is not present in the original screenplay.
7. Dailyscript.com and imsdb.com are free websites with access to the screenplays of both films.
8. All definitions are sourced from Dictionary.com
9. Note that these questions only occur to us after the finale or upon a second viewing.
10. This is an example of the "big lie." See Wikipedia.com for a definition.

11. For this reason he is unstintingly generous to his son, Bud. See Akhtar (2012).
12. Wall Street is filled with animal imagery: Gekko–Fox–dog–tiger. There is even a reference to "falcons."
13. Compare with Brigid O'Shaughnessy's apartment in *The Maltese Falcon*.
14. This bribe is but one example of Gekko's "generosity" for purposes of manipulation (Akhtar, 2012).
15. In unconscious phantasy, the breast over which the child claims absolute rights.
16. Interestingly, this line was deleted from the screenplay during the filming.
17. Here again we witness greed's sudden switch to rage, spite, and resentment.

CHAPTER FIVE

The Psychic Underpinning of Alcoholism as Portrayed in Three Hollywood Movies: *The Lost Weekend, Days of Wine and Roses*, and *Leaving Las Vegas*

Much like a patient's first dream told to her psychoanalyst, the opening shot of Billy Wilder's *The Lost Weekend* (1945) presents a striking image that introduces the movie's theme and prepares the viewer for what she is about to witness. The camera pans right, from the New York City skyline to an apartment building, and then "narrows its interest" to a bedroom window. From the exterior wall, we see a bottle of whiskey hanging from a length of string attached to an awning cleat. The bottle is "hanging by a thread," so to speak, and the danger of falling is ever-present. And from its position outside the building, the camera sees what everybody sees: a bottle hanging out there like a sore thumb. It literally has no place to hide—nothing to hide under or behind—no walls, ceilings, or floors—no "inner sanctums" to withdraw into. Indeed, the bottle hanging in outer space seems to defy *the very idea of interiority*.

Thus the bottle is the object of a universal gaze. And since its sinuous shape resembles a female body, it conveys the idea of a woman being forced outside without her clothes, along with her associated feelings of shame and humiliation. Moreover, its perceived "exposure" suggests the image of a corpse—male or female—and the universal impulse to cover the body. Additionally, the excrescence dangling outside the building reminds us of the migration of the testicles to their normal position outside the body. And we can add that infants are also thrust outside naked into the glare of adult scrutiny.

Indeed, with a slight jarring of the imagination, we might envision the moment of birth, when the infant is still hanging by the umbilical cord and right before she is "caught" by the mother. Even normal births are pre-mature on a number of levels, but in this opening shot, the traumatic moment is the sudden impingement of the outside world. In a similar vein, the "hanging bottle" evokes the infant thrust outside the protection of the mother's "holding" function (Winnicott, 1960b). For the securely attached infant, the mother's holding function provides covering (clothing), firm handling (a sac or snuggly for being carried), and of course a "safety net" which prevents falling.

And this is where the potential fate of the bottle meets that of the film's protagonist, Don Birnam, played by Ray Milland. For we soon learn that the bottle belongs to Don and that he is engaged in a desperate attempt to hide it from the critical gaze of his brother, Wick and girlfriend, Helen. Moments after lowering the bottle, his ruse is exposed when a casual flick of a cigarette butt draws Wick and Helen's gaze to the string snaking out the window. Thus the bottle-on-a-string epitomizes Don's point of greatest vulnerability. It suggests the fragility of his public persona (ego) and the uncertainty of his fate. Indeed, it exhibits his position at the start of the film: poised equally between a fall into the abyss and a hand-over-hand stepping back from the precipice.

The three films

In a sense, the hanging bottle stands at the intersection or overlap of the three films under consideration here: *The Lost Weekend* (1945), *Days of Wine and Roses* (1962), and *Leaving Las Vegas* (1995). These three films are interrelated in theme and storyline. In all three, the image of the bottle is paramount. Each film follows the narrative of a precipitous fall into a personal hell, followed by a wrenching and painful resurrection.

The most immediate turning point in all three films is the choice between life and death. Death is implied by the bottle's "hanging" and by its precarious position over the abyss. Moreover, lowering the bottle out the window invokes suicide by defenestration. Towards the end of *The Lost Weekend*, Don explicitly links death to the "snapping" of the string, when he remarks: "You can go just like that", snapping his fingers twice to empha-size the point. We might even say that Don "snaps" the moment he decides to shoot himself with a handgun. His death is staved off only at the last moment by Helen's heroic efforts. In *Days of Wine and Roses*, one member of the alcoholic couple, Joe, is saved; the other, Kirsten, presumably lost. And in *Leaving Las Vegas*, death is like a runaway train that finally collides with a wall. It leaves us feeling stunned by the lack of recourse or ameliora-tion. This shocking outcome reminds us that the alcoholic is separated from death by only a hair's breadth—or the fragility of a string.

What is interesting for us as critical viewers and psychoanalysts is the tension between these outcomes and the traditional Hollywood require-ment of a happy ending. We know, for example, that Billy Wilder wanted to end *The Lost Weekend* at the moment when Don snaps his fingers. A sud-den cut or fade-to-black in this instant would have replicated cinematically the "snapping" of the cord. But, even when forced to tack on a happy end-ing, the director leaves us feeling that Don has survived a very close call, the resulting outcome no more than a reprieve. *Days of Wine and Roses* on the other hand, effects a compromise between outcomes: Joe's salvation balanced against Kirsten's decline. Although never spelled-out, death is implied by her downward path. In this respect, *Leaving Las Vegas* is a direct slap in the face to the Hollywood establishment. It is as though Mike Figgis, having seen and studied *The Lost Weekend*, decided to shove death in our face as a correction to the earlier failure of nerve. Thus the three outcomes may be summarized as: reprieve, recovery (psychic and physical survival), and resignation (death).

These three films seem unanimous in their depiction of "the bottle" as the prototypical alcoholic object. In the films, it dominates the lead charac-ters' personalities, determines their relationships with others, depletes their psychic worlds, and affects their ability to mentally process primitive mental states. From this perspective, we can examine its placement among other objects, between persons, and along the border of psychical space. In each film, the bottle is set against a prototypical symbolic object like a portable typewriter or literary digest.

A fundamental problem posed by the films is the difficulty in locating the object. Does it inhabit psychic space, so-called "external reality," a strange hybrid of the two, or a zone which has somehow been turned "inside out"? A second problem concerns relationship networks. It would appear, for example, that these films challenge the assumption that the alcoholic lives in isolation from others. In fact, we shall argue that "the bottle" facilitates the formation of "threesomes" and "twosomes." But if the bottle appears to act as catalyst for these relationships, its constant demand for exclusivity strains, frays, and ultimately severs object ties. Thus the "threesomes" tend to collapse into "twosomes," which in turn decay into isolates, and finally, a kind of intoxicated self-immolation.

This final outcome raises the question of the alcoholic's subjectivity and by extension, our own subjective position as psychoanalytic viewers of these films. The protagonists of the films are engaged in a prolonged struggle to preserve some shred of their individual dignity and freedom of choice. Yet on the relationship between their raw experience and its formulation in words, they remain undecided. At times they appear to view their plight as if it were an "objective" thing hanging out the side of a building for all to see.

I therefore do not claim that the ideas set forth here are anything more than an exploration of the effect these films may have on the viewer's mind. None of the films offer a definitive answer to the question of alcoholism. Yet they do reveal the psychic complexity of a condition often regarded as mainly physiological. In this respect, our subjectivity can serve as a corrective to the idea of a pure and lethal objectivity. Viewed exclusively from the outside, suicide presents itself as a rational solution to an impasse. It is important to approach "the bottle" from the inside, even if that "inside" seems to have shrunk down to a larval vestige.

Our foray into the world of these films will explore these questions. From there we proceed to the topic of cures and remedies and finally to the thorny issue of Don, Joe, Ben, or Kirsten's receptivity to psychoanalysis.

The alcoholic's object world

Before reviewing the variety of objects in the films, we must take up the following question: Why is the alcoholic's primary object the bottle and not the alcohol itself? This issue is addressed visually in *The Lost Weekend* when the camera closes in on the liquid contents of the glass. Suddenly that liquid fills the entire frame, producing a womblike, "oceanic", feeling. Thus we have, not an object, but the state of oblivion produced by the object. The relationship between this undifferentiated field and the object is one of containment. The bottle "contains" the alcohol, on the one hand, preventing it from overflowing or inundating the alcoholic's world, and on the other hand, maintaining and sustaining its own essence, ensuring the absolute purity and uniformity of the precious elixir.

In *Leaving Las Vegas*, its new incarnation is a silver-plated hip flask. Taken together, the two versions emphasize the plasticity of the bottle's shape, while always preserving its function as a container. Noteworthy in the hip flask is the bottle's portability and use as a "transitional object" between one place or temporal zone and another (car trips, for example). Also the flattened design of the hip flask allows it to fit any pocket and mold to the curve of the hip, like a kind of somatic "adjunct." In this vein, it's protean shape may remind us of an auxiliary bladder or, when lengthened, a prosthesis—the alcoholic's wooden leg.

From a cinematic point of view, the bottle can be visualized in relation to a variety of other objects. Early on, for example, the films establish a relationship between the bottle and other oral objects, but not that of simple equivalence. In the opening scenes, Helen (Don's girlfriend), gives Don a little gift package containing two amusing books, cigarettes, and chewing gum. These are meant to help him cope with the lack of alcohol on their planned long weekend in the country. Yet Don secretly scorns these poor substitutes. Surprisingly, he detests such healthy fluids as "sweet cider, buttermilk, and cold spring water" treating these items with mock disgust. But more surprising still, he dislikes the taste of alcoholic beverages. When buying liquor he always chooses the cheapest rye whiskey. The range and variety of alcoholic drinks leave him cold. In the *Days of Wine and Roses*, Kirsten's initial infatuation with alcohol is tied to her love of sweet things. In the film, drinking starts out as an oral craving for chocolate, milk, and Brandy Alexanders, but ends up with cheap gin devoid of the sweetness that initially attracted her. Thus while the films imply a kind of indirect relation to the oral object, "the bottle" is located outside the "set" of oral objects.

In particular, the films show an antithetical relationship between the bottle and its immediate counterpart: the portable typewriter, or more generally, the symbolic object. In *The Lost Weekend*'s opening scene, the typewriter is a kind of decoy or proxy for the bottle, which Don wants to hide. Thus when the bottle is lowered outside the building, that is, outside of the place which people inhabit, the typewriter remains inside the apartment, within a matrix of ordinary and symbolic objects. You might see it on the desk near a lamp, next to a paperweight, dictionary, or thesaurus. The works of literature lining Don's apartment—including volumes of Shakespeare—evoke the world of literature and poetry. And as an ordinary, utilitarian object, the typewriter may be exchanged with other related objects, thus traveling from one place to another in the social network.

The convergence of the two objects occurs when Don carries the type-writer up Third Avenue, on his way to a pawnshop. He intends to pawn it for cash with which to buy another bottle. In transit, however, the type-writer seems to become heavier and heavier. Moreover, Don is thwarted in his attempt to find a pawnshop, first by the fact that most of these shops are closed, due to it being a Saturday and also Yom Kippur, and later by his collapse down a flight of stairs. Right before his fall down the stairs, he is distracted by a little girl running, and is literally "unbalanced" by hav-ing to switch the typewriter from one hand to another. After his fall, Nat, the bartender, picks up the machine and in effect becomes its custodian. Toward the end of the film, he returns the typewriter to Don and Helen, having protected it from being reduced to another bottle.

In these key scenes of the movie, there is an elegant interchange between the two objects. During Don's arduous "Via Dolorosa" up Third Avenue, the typewriter seems to actively resist Don's intent to exchange it for a bottle. Its increasing "weightiness" suggests the typewriter's "potential" as a symbolic force in Don's life and mind. Alternatively, we can think of the bottle's sheer weight as an *a-symbolic and obtrusive materiality*, which makes Don sus-ceptible to falling or collapse.

This war between the typewriter and the bottle calls to mind an earlier exchange that brought about Don's first meeting with Helen, his girlfriend. In that inadvertent meeting, Don and Helen meet because of a glitch at the cloakroom of the Metropolitan Opera. Due to a mistake, Don ends up with Helen's leopard skin coat, while she holds his shapeless grey raincoat. Examining the leopard-skin coat, Don notices the embroidered words of the maker, the place of origin (Toledo, Ohio) and her initials: Helen St. J. Thus the symbolism of Helen's coat resides both in its animistic imagery and the words and letters imprinted within it. Once the two have given back the coats and are walking away from each other, Don's bag falls to the street causing the liquor bottle to shatter. Its sudden drop actualizes the potential fall of the bottle hanging out the window, and foreshadows Don's actual fall down the stairs, and later, into the depths of alcoholic despair.

In the *Days of Wine and Roses*, we see the same contest between a pri-mary symbolic object and the bottle. In this case, the symbolic object is a book, *The World Library of Great Literature*. This book has been a mainstay of Kirsten's psychic life. Her future husband, Joe, calls it her "Pilgrim's Prog-ress." It is a kind of digest or distillate of literature and poetry arranged in alphabetical order. Each volume is identified by its first and last entry, as in

Ja to La, which Kirsten pronounces "jaylay," in a funny neologism. And as in the example of the leopard-skin coat, the material is arranged like the objects in the opera cloakroom and the monogram on the coat's lining. The contrast between this "book of books" and the bottle emerges later during a crucial scene in which Joe trashes his father-in-law's greenhouse. He had hidden a bottle in a potted plant, whose location is marked with three numbered coordinates for, respectively, table, row, and position. Joe loses track of the "address," and in fact of the entire combinatory that produces the address. In effect he finds the bottle only by destroying the entire arrangement of plants, thus forcing the bottle to appear "extra-systemically" in the place where the system fails.

In a similar vein, *Leaving Las Vegas* shows Ben, the alcoholic lead, stuffing a variety of symbolic objects into king-size garbage bags. These objects include, first, kitchen utensils, clothing, books, and long-playing records. Then, in a more definitive act of destruction, he burns "a water color, a poem to his wife, a polaroid of a naked woman, his medical records, his birth and marriage certificates, divorce papers, photo strips, post cards from Hawaii." In this series, we see the same two broad categories: objects that refer to his cultural and artistic sensibility (water color, poem, long-playing records) and other objects that "alphabetize" him within a symbolic grid (medical records, birth and marriage certificates, divorce papers). Other objects such as the clothes, kitchen utensils, Polaroid, and postcards are ordinary souvenirs of a past life.

However, the long-playing records are loaded with symbolism that encompasses all three categories. Ben's huge record collection testifies to a love of music and the important role music plays, or has played, in his life. The film's soundtrack may be heard as a playlist from his vast collection. Also note the repetition of the word "record" in "record album" and "medical records." Indeed, all these objects serve as "records" of his past life.

Interestingly, the director decided not to include these objects in the actual film. Instead, he had the inspiration to substitute a single image: a framed photo of Ben, his wife, and standing in the foreground, his son. The picture makes his son the focal point. Hence in making this substitution, Mike Figgis, the director, lets the frame of the picture allude to both cultural artifacts (paintings) and "records" (official portraits). Moreover, he might have been making a pun on the word "album" in "photo album" and "record album." But be this as it may, the heart of the image is the child. The child incarnates the idea of loss, which is both unfathomable and incalculable.

Ben has, in effect, expunged his "records," severed his ties, and expelled his objects. And in their place, there is only "the bottle."

Threesomes

In the films, the bottle acts as a focal point for the formation and dissolution of threesomes. We see this configuration at the beginning of *The Lost Weekend*, in the interrelationships between Don, his brother Wick, and his girlfriend, Helen. In the first scenes, the three are already planning a weekend in the country with the aim of boosting Don's efforts at recovery. In this triangle, Wick and Helen form a parental couple, while Don plays the passive, pouting child. Wick and Helen are active collaborators, hence, partners. Don, however, has not taken on the weekend as his own project.

This triad reconfigures itself around Helen's two free concert tickets. Helen, Wick, and Don discuss the idea of taking a later train so that Helen can attend the matinee with Don. But Don surprises them by proposing that Wick should accompany Helen in his stead. For a few minutes, Wick and Don seem to be vying with each other over who should attend the concert with Helen. Helen confirms that the second ticket is essentially an empty seat that can be filled by Don, Wick, or "a South American millionaire." Don succeeds in convincing them that he needs time to mentally prepare for the weekend, and that, therefore, Wick should go.

Thus in the reconfiguration, Don *cedes his place* to Wick. In this way, he reaffirms Helen and Wick as the parental couple, with him in the place of child. Thus, he gives up his status as Helen's adult partner. As the "child," he draws Helen and Wick into a triangle whose focal point is "the bottle." They spend time and energy trying to thwart Don's access to bottles by cutting off his money and searching his apartment with the thoroughness of "a fine-tooth comb." In this configuration, therefore, Don's interests become so aligned with "the bottle," we can think of the latter as his stand-in.

At about the midpoint of the film, the inherent tension and sense of futility in the threesome is resolved more definitively. Wick initiates the change by speaking frankly to Helen. He tells her he is fed up. He will no longer act as Don's keeper. As Helen's ally and friend, Wick begs her to "give yourself a chance." What he means is: don't get so enmeshed in Don's problem that you give up your own life—your career, your chance for happiness, a child of your own. Helen refuses this offer. She decides to commit herself to Don at the moment Wick opts for separation.

What remains is a reversal of the original threesome. Wick exits the trio leaving the field open for Helen and Don. The earlier partnership between Wick and Helen is now dissolved. They are in effect divorced. Whereas before, Don appeared to exit the trio, now it is Wick, leaving Helen free to switch her alliance. Consequently, Don and Helen—in an act of mutual self-sacrifice—form a tightly bonded alliance with "the bottle" as the third party. In the words of Joe in the *Days of Wine and Roses*, their love has become a "threesome" composed of himself, Kirsten, and the bottle.

The triad of prostitute, john, and pimp

All three films feature a particular variant of the love triangle: the prostitute, her john, and her handler/pimp. In *The Lost Weekend*, this motif emerges as a subplot to the main action. In *Days of Wine and Roses*, it is less explicit, but surfaces as a potential alternative to Joe and Kirsten's marriage. And in *Leaving Las Vegas*, it moves to the foreground as the film's primary relationship and plot device.

In *The Lost Weekend*, the prostitute scenario is set in Don's favorite bar. The scene opens with Don talking with Nat, a bartender that he likes. When Gloria, a prostitute, walks in, Don begins a flirtation with her. In their conversation, Don is the exalted knight deigning to speak to a commoner. But the elephant in the room is the "john" whom Gloria expects to meet shortly at the bar. However, Gloria ups the ante by sending away the john amid talk of her being "engaged" to Don. At this point Nat enters the conversation, objecting to Don's lies and defending the two women in Don's life: Gloria (low class) and Helen (high class).

This little drama starts with two object positions: a degraded object (the prostitute) and an exalted object (the knight). At first the degraded object is Gloria. She is both low-class and a prostitute. But the anonymous "john" or "mark" is also degraded. He is divested of all his personal qualities the moment he walks in the door. The moment of his complete degradation comes when Gloria sends him away—that is, denies him even the lowly status of a "john." In the moment of being discarded, the "john" finds himself a mere excrescence in the scene, excluded from participation.

At the start of the flirtation, Don plays the role of the exalted object. He is exalted in his own eyes and in Gloria's. But at the moment when she rejects the "john" *she* rises to the level of the exalted object. In her mind, Don's mocking attention raises her to his level and lends her a measure of class. In this fantasy, she is at the very least, a prostitute of a higher class, and, at most, a legitimate object of love.

Nat's changing status in the scene is also noteworthy. Because of his ongoing relationship with Gloria, which pre-dates the scene, he can be viewed as her "handler." He is her mentor and to an extent, her enabler. After all, he permits her to meet her "johns" in the bar so long as she is discreet. Perhaps he even gets a kickback from her earnings. He certainly has a proprietary interest in Gloria. In this role he is not very different from a pimp. Once he sees where Don is going with the flirtation, he intervenes as Gloria's protector. In this about-face, he is now the exalted object, while Don is exposed as an exploiter of women.

What we see is first, the complexity and fluidity of the various roles. That of "handler," for example, encompasses "pimp," "enabler," "mentor," and "protector." Moreover, Nat's pivot to the woman's protector involves a shift from object to subject. Nat has always been a "subject" in his conversations with Don. He is never someone who just allows himself to be used by his progressively more inebriated customer. At various points in Don's monologue, he speaks his mind, even if this contradicts Don's fantasy that he and Nat are always in agreement. Thus when Nat takes up the cause of the women he accomplishes two things. He deliberately links the two women in Don's life and implies that they are linked *psychically* for him. And in speaking on their behalf, he demands they be treated as human beings in their own right. Indeed, by creating the subjective trio of Gloria, Helen, and Nat, he suggests that all the participants in the prostitution scenario retain the potential to break free of their object positions.

Later in the film we are witness to a similar reconfiguration of Don and Gloria's relationship. At this point in the story Don cares only about his next drink. He knocks on Gloria's door and begs her for money. Gloria knows that he stood her up for their "date" and that he probably never intended to keep his word. Her image of him as an exalted figure is tarnished. She sees him for what he is: a miserable, pathetic drunk. He is no different from any other "john" who craves satisfaction at any cost. Yet she is touched when he kisses her. She relents and gives him five or ten dollars. Thus in the moment, *she becomes his patroness, he, the one prostituting himself.* Is her giving him the money an act of love, or at the very least, a noble gesture? Don responds in kind when he kisses her hand, and then, in reply to her remark: "You do like me a little, don't you?" says, "Why, Gloria, natch." In this last phrase he mimics Gloria's "low-class" habit of shortening words. At this point, both

Don and Gloria have in a certain way become debased objects for each other. Don, of course, debases himself in exhibiting his pathetic fall from grace and in asking for money. Gloria debases herself by choosing to ignore Don's betrayal. *And yet their mutual abasement in so far as it brings the pair together in a moment of selflessness, conveys an air of nobility and sanctity.*

These themes of debasement, selflessness, and bondage become more explicit in Sera's backstory in *Leaving Las Vegas*. In the early scenes, which establish background, we see her working as a prostitute under the watchful eye of her pimp, Yuri. We understand that their relationship is both protective (Yuri provides money) and abusive (the visible scars on Sera's buttocks). When Sera looks at Yuri directly, he hits her. And in this action, he reveals his underlying vulnerability to Sera in contrast to his overt domination of her. Already, we have hints that Yuri is a compulsive gambler who is in way over his head. The film makes clear that his murder at the hands of local gangsters is all but inevitable.

Yuri's dependency on Sera is in part a matter of money: if she does not bring in a lot of cash soon, he will not be able to pay his debt to the gangsters. But Sera only nets $500 that night (she had been distracted by being with Ben). When Yuri hits her out of desperation, Sera reminds him of his own rule: never mark the face. Hence even this seemingly out-of-control relationship still pushes up against a limit. At this point, Sera gives Yuri the knife and bends over, exposing her buttocks to him—in effect inviting him to hurt her. In this moment, she puts the entire relationship to the test. She needs to know just where the limit is. And she finds it, because Yuri retreats, saying: "You go too far." Yuri then recovers, by reminding her that: "I could kill you." This too would be "going too far." Thus Sera pushes the envelope to the edge of death (her death) itself, and in so doing re-establishes her credibility in Yuri's eyes.

Yuri is mollified and, for the moment, pacified. Sera stages an enactment similar to the child pushing herself to the edge of death in order to test the parent's love. So it would seem that Yuri does care—at least *in extremis*. He will not kill her. And *in the twisted logic of their relationship, this means he loves her*, and that he will protect her. Indeed, Yuri proves his love for her the following night. By this time, Yuri has become convinced that he is about to be killed by the mobsters to whom he owes money. He tells Sera to go away and never come back. Yet in this apparent rejection, he in effect saves her life. If she were merely an object of expedience for him, he wouldn't have bothered. Or perhaps he just wanted to end his life with a noble gesture?

But whatever his reasons, by severing his bonds to Sera, he reveals the nature of the relationship: bondage. On the superficial level, such bondage entails playing the submissive in a sadomasochistic ritual. But it also encompasses the bonds of dependency that hold the pair together. For Sera, it means placing herself in the object/abject position for Yuri (the face, the buttocks) and casting aside her personal dignity. Yet Yuri is never the absolute master. In baring her buttocks to Yuri in a moment of absolute self-abasement, when she appears to cede any claim to independent action, Sera proves that she occupies a place in Yuri's life and mind. The same ties that bind her bind him. Indeed, Yuri needs her to survive—not just for the money—but because her survival "carries a torch for"—keeps some remnant of Yuri's psyche alive in the face of his death.

The alcoholic couple

The "bondage" between Yuri and Sera hints at the tenacious bonds joining the alcoholic with his partner. Let us therefore examine the details of this partnership in each of the three films. In *The Lost Weekend*, for example, Don and Helen are drawn together in stages. Thrown together by a glitch at the opera cloakroom, Helen and Don seem on the verge of parting ways. Yet just as Don is walking away from Helen, his pint bottle of whiskey falls to the ground and shatters. And in this bungled action he reveals his unspoken desire to expose himself to Helen. What is now patently visible is the fact that he is an alcoholic. He is saying in effect, this is who I am; this is what defines me, so where do you stand on this? Is this a deal breaker for you?

Crucial to the future of their relationship is Helen's response: she does not overreact, she does not judge, and she certainly does not reject Don as a partner out of hand. Indeed, we can speculate that this flaw in Don is exactly what attracts Helen to him. Be that as it may, her response "breaks the ice/glass" between them, and strikes an initial bargain. The presence of the bottle is not a deal breaker for Helen; yet the exclusion of the bottle *would be* a deal breaker for Don. The bottle is a necessary third party in their relationship, a foundational element that bonds one to the other. In confirmation of their successful bargain, Don accepts Helen's offer to attend a cocktail party with her.

The second stage is set in motion by Wick's withdrawal from the trio. In ceasing to be Don's caretaker, Wick in effect defines the choice Helen will have to make. On the one hand, she can "give herself a chance," in other words, speak her mind, say what she wants, and question her partner's decisions. Or she can, "throw herself away" (the quotes are mine) by re-dedicating herself to Don at the expense of herself. Without reservations or hesitation, she chooses the latter.

It is near the end of *The Lost Weekend* that we see just how far Helen is willing to go in shoring up Don's existence. In a late scene, Helen enters Don's apartment only to find him in a suicidal state. We know as viewers that Don has pawned Helen's leopard-skin coat for a gun, which he has hidden in the apartment. Upon entering the apartment, she must confront the fact that Don has casually and unthinkingly discarded her leopard-skin coat. The coat is Helen's most prized object, the thing she values most in the world. She is dismayed by Don's cavalier treatment of it on three levels: one, the coat represents the emotional investment she has made in Don; two, it is "the thing which brought us together"; and three, it's presence hanging in Don's apartment would have reserved for her a symbolic place in Don's inner world.

Helen realizes that she must be ready to sacrifice her "coat" so that Don might live. And in this acutely focused frame of mind, she sees the gun in Don's shaving mirror, hidden in the hollow of his washbasin. We might say that she sees the gun because she recognizes the willingness to die in herself as well as in Don. And it is here and now that she places all her cards on the table: she exhorts Don to fill his glass from the bottle and to drink. Seeing that Don stands on the knife's edge between the bottle and the gun, she chooses the bottle. In the end, she usurps the bottle's position in Don's life: the omnipresent and available source of life and his bastion against both physical and psychic death.

Seguing to the next film, we find the closest parallel to Helen and Don's pact in *Leaving Las Vegas*. Indeed, that film is even more explicit about the terms of Sera and Ben's partnership. In their first meeting, Ben sees that she is a prostitute, and offers to pay for her time. His offer seems to imply he is not bargaining for her sexual services, at least not directly. Agreeing that they both tend to "fade in and out," Ben suggests that they "synchronize" their "spells" or "stagger" them. Both techniques would seemingly elimi-nate breaks or holes in time. Thus Ben hopes to attain some semblance of spatial–temporal continuity through being with Sera. He wants at least one of them to be "present"—mainly Sera—at all times.

Hearing these words, Sera tests the waters regarding their sexual rela-tionship. She outlines in crude detail the sexual services available to him.

Ben is hardly surprised by her frankness, not only because she is a prostitute, but because he too views his sexuality in crude terms. In seducing a woman at a bar, for example, he in effect rams his sexual intent down her throat, thus souring her initial attraction into disgust. When it comes to sex, Ben denigrates sexual desire, which thrives on postponement. Only the sexual "thing" itself interests him. Yet Ben tells Sera that he doesn't want this "thing"—the elephant in the room in any relationship with a prostitute—to define their relationship. He says it isn't important that he "come." Indeed, he declares Sera free to be herself: she can do nothing at all or she can "talk or listen."

Why does Ben make this concession to Sera? After all, in all his other relationships with women, most of which are one-night stands, and which happen when he is intoxicated, he only wants one "thing." But note that Ben doesn't rule out a sexual aspect to their relationship; he just doesn't want sex to be the only object. This is important to Ben—and it will become important to Sera—because their relationship must be distinguished from her working life as a prostitute, which both assume will continue as before. Ben doesn't want Sera to be just another whore; she in turn, doesn't want him to be just another "john."

And this brings us to the crux of their initial arrangement: Ben's admission that he is a drunk. This corresponds to the moment when Don lets slip the bottle. Ben takes it a step further when he shockingly confesses his plan to drink himself to death in the space of about one month. For Ben, his drinking and his death trip are basic assumptions of any relationship between them. Sera must accept his drinking unconditionally, and must seal that acceptance by drinking with him. Hence the only deal breaker would be if Sera rejected Ben's drinking and did not admit the bottle as a fixture of their life as a couple.

With these preliminaries out of the way, Sera accepts Ben's invitation to dinner. She asks him if he is "serious" and he replies: "I think you know I'm serious." At dinner, Sera asks Ben a fundamental question: "Why are you a drunk?" Ben's response is twofold. The fact that Sera asks this question means she is treating Ben as a potential partner. But if the question itself is that important to Sera, it might be another deal breaker, because Ben has no intention of answering it. Nor will he answer related questions of causality such as, "Why are you drinking yourself to death?" The most Ben will ever say is that, "I just know I want to." In order for the relationship to have a chance, Sera must accept his drinking and his death wish at face value. Thus this dinner might be their "first date" or their "last."

In the end, Sera decides not to challenge him on this issue. Like Helen in *The Lost Weekend*, she decides to dedicate herself to Ben. She makes this choice because helping Ben is a "bonus for being alive." However, we could equally say the reverse: "Being alive is a bonus for being good." That is, by playing the part of a good person—one who isn't sadistic, manipulative, or exploitive—she preserves the good object within her. In other words, by doing no harm, by not destroying, she *implicitly creates*. Whatever her motives, however, in deciding to do good by helping Ben—or to stay psychically alive by helping Ben—she makes an ethical choice.

Interestingly, it is Ben who questions her on this issue. He asks (at a slightly later point): How can you be so good? Are you really an angel out of one of my drunk fantasies? He is really asking her, are you too good to be true? These questions are troubling to Sera in light of her continuing to work as a prostitute. And she mostly evades them just as Ben evaded questions regarding his drinking. Yet how can she avoid the contradiction, to say nothing of the emotional disconnect, between being an "angel" during the day and a "whore" by night? Perhaps the hardest question is whether she may be unconsciously exploiting Ben's weakness for her own advantage (using him to enhance her own self-esteem?). She half-acknowledges that she could be "using" Ben, but she mainly stays reticent on this subject.

Nevertheless, Ben's questions raise the question of what it means for Sera to be an "angel" in Ben's life. Being an angel seems to convey more than just being saintly or impossibly good, à la Helen *St.* James, for example. Perhaps it is simply the "manifestation" or hallucination of Ben's drunken fantasy. But against this interpretation is the fact that Sera is enabling Ben's death by doing nothing to stop it. By offering no resistance to it, she in effect, hastens it. Thus this "angel" could be a destroyer, an "angel of death," as it were. In colluding with Ben's death drive, Sera destroys the object who embodies her own self-destructiveness (as, for example, enacted in her tryst with the three college boys), and in so doing, paradoxically ensures her own survival.

Monad: the alcoholic on his own

Whether in partnerships, trios, or groups, the three films portray the alcoholic as a man (with one exception) who needs the company of others.

In the majority of scenes, we observe him in social or public settings such as bars, social gatherings, or city streets. Two work at jobs that require intensive social networking. Joe works in "public relations" and is expected to shape his client's public image with the right kind of social connections. Ben works as a talent agent in Los Angeles, as we observe in an early scene set in a restaurant. At this point, his drinking has already made him a pariah, and yet he still persists in trying to "network" with former colleagues, one of whom he asks for a loan.

On the surface, it would seem that Don's vocation as writer is more solitary. But for Don, writing is largely a "making public"—an act of publication, if you will. We have no evidence from *The Lost Weekend* that writing is in any sense a private pursuit for Don, nothing about him keeping a journal or even writing letters to his friends. No, in his case, the entire enterprise is performed in the public eye. Indeed, he cannot write even a single paragraph without feeling invaded and paralyzed by the gaze of others.

Joe, in *Days of Wine and Roses*, expresses anxiety about his public persona in the opening scene of the television play (*Playhouse 90*), when he gives his first talk to fellow-members of Alcoholics Anonymous (AA). In this scene, he wears an old sports coat while constantly fiddling with the missing middle button. The coat itself draws attention to his public appearance just as did Helen's leopard-skin coat and Ben's new sports shirt. Joe's fiddling with the buttonhole suggests the outfit is being held together by a thread. And just as a button holds the ensemble together, its absence implies the loss of a symbolic "coupler," which might have anchored his sense of self from the "inside." Hence he fears becoming literally and figuratively "undone".

This dread of coming apart is especially acute when Don, Joe, or Ben, is alone in his apartment. To compensate for the lack of an internal "coupler," each man obsessively hides bottles throughout their personal space, or in Joe's case, the space of his father-in-law's greenhouse. This network of bottles provides each with an antidote for being lost in the claustrophobic space of his own apartment. It lays out an alternative to intra-psychic space that is *contained around and within the bottle*. As such, it offers the drinker access to fantasy and related mental states that cannot be sustained in the chaos of his mind. For the alcoholic, this object functions to "bottle" intangible, fleeting, and otherwise subjective processes in a concrete and readily accessible form. According to Don, it must always be there, ready to hand, and available, even if it is not used.

Las Vegas

In *Leaving Las Vegas*, the contained space inside the bottle is expanded into a macrocosm. Mike Figgis, the director, uses this space to reflect the alcoholic's world. He shows convincingly that it is a space seemingly without *geography*. As we follow Ben and Sera in their meanderings, one casino is much like another. The casino floor, for example, is always depicted as a large, open space without defined sections. Within every casino there is always a bar a few steps away, which is indistinguishable from all the others. Moreover, the entire city is presented as a closed space, cut off from the outside world and therefore disconnected from other locales.

But the city's most important asset is the superposition of exterior and interior space. By now, we are all familiar with the slogan: "Whatever happens in Vegas, stays in Vegas." In other words, whatever you do in public, remains private. And whatever you fantasize doing in private, you can safely publicize. And since the entire public/private space is enclosed within itself and closed-off to the world—much like the space inside a bottle—it offers every inhabitant of this privileged zone the perfect place in which to hide.

Thus we can understand Ben's flight to Las Vegas from his former life in Los Angeles as the ideal solution (in fantasy) to the alcoholic's fundamental vulnerability. Indeed, we can easily imagine Don, Joe, and Kirsten jumping at the chance to spend a "lost weekend" there. All would revel in a place where you can't get lost, where time doesn't matter, and where bottles are always within reach. It is, in sum, "the bottle" writ large.

The reduction to nothing: the alcoholic's zero point

En route to "the bottom," the alcoholic undergoes an experience of acute horror. The dictionary defines "horror" as "an overwhelming and painful feeling caused by something shocking, terrifying, or revolting." Alone with the bottle while Wick and Helen are attending the concert, Don's face captures this affect in close-up. In that shot we audience members become privy to an intensely private look, which is one part gleeful anticipation, one part ecstasy, one part crude satisfaction, and one part self-disgust. This look reaches its apotheosis later in the film, again when Don sits alone in his apartment. This time Don, in the throes of the DTs, hallucinates a little mouse emerging from a hole in the wall, followed by a bat swooping down on the helpless creature and biting it. Seeing the gushing blood,

Don lets loose a blood-curdling scream. The gushing of blood and the scream express the sense of psychic devastation and helplessness in the face of catastrophic turmoil.

This moment in the film—and its counterpart in the other two films—more than any other, invokes the role of unconscious fantasy. We would suggest that the little mouse emerging from a hole in the wall depicts the premature and traumatic birth of an infant who is born blind, naked, and barely viable. Keep in mind that a lost child haunts the minds of all the main characters, in Helen's sacrifice of motherhood, in Ben's abandoned son, and Joe and Kirsten's daughter having been literally pulled from the breast. The idea of birth as a bloody operation suggests difficult births, such as placenta previa and Cesarean births. And it portends failed births such as abortions, stillbirths, and miscarriages. Thus in the moment of horror, the drinker lives out the fantasy of being aborted at the moment of birth.

The movements of birth are indicated in the participant's extreme agitation. All three films stage the DTs. The ordeal reaches a "climax" in Ben's powerful orgasm undergone at the moment of death. Since to the child, coupling is the process of making babies, we can say that this viscerally disturbing image links the birth trauma with death (without the reassuring interval between beginning and end). Mike Figgis visualizes the event in four convulsive yet alternating movements: the back-and-forth of sexual intercourse, the aforementioned shakes of the DTs, the tremors of orgasm, and finally the "death rattle."

It is therefore not surprising that in moments of clarity the characters described their downfall in similarly graphic terms. Ben misreads a hotel sign, "The Whole Year Inn" as "the hole you're in." Don describes the downward spiral as follows: "You're on a merry-go-round. You've got to ride it round and round until it wears itself out." Joe sees himself on the brink of drowning. He says: "I've got hold of something to keep me from going under, and I'm not going to let go."

And at the end of the whirlpool aka traumatic birth, they are left on the ground, spent, depleted, "used-up," "exhausted," discarded, like empty bottles whose contents have been spilled.

The possibility of recovery

Once the alcoholic has suffered the horrific descent into the DTs, the films offer the possibility of recovery. In addressing this issue, each film offers a different path or paths. *The Lost Weekend*, for example, puts forward two pathways: the writing cure and the cure by love.

The writing cure is important because the source material for all three movies is based in part or whole upon works composed by alcoholic writers. We have already noted in this vein that the screenplay of *The Lost Weekend* was titled "the bottle," and embedded in the film is the planned novel of the same name. The plot of *The Lost Weekend* follows the history of this writing project from its inception as a planned weekend retreat, to Don's rejection of the idea, and finally—with the return of the typewriter into Don and Helen's possession—the re-dedication to the project. The other two films, while not highlighting this path, allude to it, in *Days of Wine and Roses*, by way of the "book" of AA and Kirsten's encyclopedia; and in *Leaving Las Vegas*, via Ben's abandoned trove of written documents (including detailed client files captured by the camera in an early shot of Ben's office).

Because the typewriter is securely anchored in the social and psychical network, it represents a point of access to the symbolic. It gives the alcoholic an opportunity to tell his story in his own way and on his own terms. Thus it gives private thought the means of articulation and a public face. The words stand out on the page for all to see. And if published (as all of the novels were), they take on a life of their own in society at large.

We see the love cure at work in *The Lost Weekend* when Don falls in love with Helen, and is consequently able to abstain from alcohol for six weeks. The film makes clear that Helen is "hopelessly" in love with Don from the beginning. She hopes that by loving Don unconditionally, she can keep him from drinking, or at least prevent his drinking from getting out of control. But when push comes to shove near the film's end, she makes a devil's wager that her love will at least keep Don alive even if it fails to stop his drinking.

This is where the illusionary aspect of the love cure shows its hand. The demand for a happy ending in *The Lost Weekend* forces Helen into the untenable position of acting *in loco parentis* for Don. She in effect assumes the role of his psychiatric nurse and mother rolled into one. Such a heroic gesture conveys the essence of the romantic illusion, to which Hollywood often succumbs. The romantic subtext is enhanced by the musical scores of all three films, which include arias from La traviata, "Days of Wine and Roses" by Henry Mancini and Johnny Mercer (1963), and Ben's favorite song, "Lonely Teardrops" (1958). The scores of all three films reinforce the idea of the grand gesture in the face of aching loss.

Thus the love cure involves a fight-to-the-death for the alcoholic's soul with no quarter given and no compromise possible, while the writing cure at least allows for a possible reconciliation between the two rivals for Don's love. Nevertheless, the very implausibility of Helen and Don's quest reminds us of his original vulnerability. We can feel moved and even exhilarated by Helen's brave gesture while acknowledging that the "love cure" will probably fail. Indeed, we can read Sera's love for Ben in *Leaving Las Vegas* as a caricature of the "love cure," one in which the "cure" is death.

One criterion of cure would be the rehabilitation of the alcoholic's ability to speak freely about himself (while sober). Let us therefore review the subjective capacity of the three men, given their known restrictions in this area and their decimated interior life.

The men do exercise their powers of speech in several important areas: they openly acknowledge that they are drunks and refuse to make excuses for themselves. Especially within the historical context of *The Lost Weekend* and *Days of Wine and Roses*, such an admission was atypical. The three men also acknowledge their tendency to lie and to rationalize their behavior. And in a third arena, they verbally commit themselves to an exclusive relationship with their love partners. A key aspect of this commitment is the exclusion of a particular limit: the demand to cut down or stop drinking.

But these few areas of verbal commitment reveal an underlying unwillingness to talk about other topics or to verbally engage with others (or with themselves). Although open about being alcoholic, they adamantly refuse to challenge themselves on this issue. They will not ponder the question: Why do I drink? Either they mock the question or they deem it unanswerable. This attitude applies to all other areas of their personal histories and reflects a basic incuriousness about themselves.

Similarly, none of the men seem capable of taking an ethical position and standing by it. At one point, Don pleads with Helen to leave him as a lost cause, but we don't get the impression he really means it. At this point he has given up on himself and apparently has nothing more to say. And in conversation with Kirsten, Joe expresses unease about his boss using him as an unofficial pimp and later, exploiting him to get his clients drunk. But Joe will not "quit," as did his predecessor over a matter of "personal integrity." Indeed, he concedes that he "always had a great line of bull," but never had "a mind of his own." Ben, for his part, never utters a word about abandoning his own child.

The psychoanalytic cure versus Alcoholics Anonymous

This brings us to a choice of pathways: Alcoholics Anonymous versus psychoanalysis/psychotherapy. Joe makes the life-altering decision to join Alcoholics Anonymous. In the few short months Joe has been a member, his personal life has been transformed. He has a new job. He takes responsibility for his daughter. He has a sponsor willing to act as a kind of life coach for him, as well as a built-in social network of fellow-alcoholics from every walk of life. He is even willing to reconcile with Kirsten provided she stops drinking. And of course he has been sober for four months.

But for him, the key element of AA is what he calls, "the book." He describes its effect as "snapping on a light in this long dark attic of mind." In his first conversation with Jim, his sponsor, he refers to it as a "secret formula." Thus the book illuminates a previously closed-off and disused portion of his mind. Almost immediately he accepts it as a kind of Bible—a comprehensive guide to life. It is filled with the slogans and sayings that have shaped the popular image of AA. Joe would no doubt agree that it offers him an effective replacement for a mind of his own. Repeating his own words: "I've got hold of something to keep me from going under, and I'm not going to let go…". Thus "the book" functions as an anchor or clamp that stands-in for the missing psychical coupler and relieves him of the burden of "a mind of his own." Hence the essence of the AA cure is the adoption of this more benign alternative.

Nevertheless, to its credit, *Days of Wine and Roses* depicts in some detail Kirsten's vehement rejection of the AA path. As viewers, we cannot help but feel sympathy for her willingness to make a stand amidst the detritus of a world that seems to have abandoned her. To understand her position, we must first distinguish her mindset from that of the men. Unlike her male counterparts, Kirsten possesses a rich and varied, not to say, lurid fantasy life. Looking out over the river with Joe, she pictures sea monsters lurking beneath the dark waters. She thinks of her apartment taken over by roaches, and in general, having to do battle against a tide of filth. In her unconscious the monsters, the dirt, and the vermin represent the return of her repressed sexuality. And her oral cravings follow a line of verbal associations: sweet–taste–chocolate–milk–Brandy Alexanders (or in the teleplay, vanilla extract)—gin. Note also the verbal assonance between "gin" and "Joe." Indeed, this sort of play-on-words might appeal to her, given her love of poetry. Unlike Joe's "book," Kirsten's compendium of literature doesn't tell her *how* to live, but rather adds resonance to the life she *is* living.

In addition, she maintains a conflicted yet vital relationship with her parents. Her father still holds an important, albeit conflicted, role in her life. She harbors complicated feelings about the loss of her mother, her parents' exclusive relationship, the effect of the mother's death on the father, and the latter's need to see her as an asexual child. Without getting into a full discussion of her psychodynamics, we can say that much, if not all, of her addictive behavior is directed toward her father. She confesses to Joe, for example, the wish to be murdered in order to get her father to talk to her. This fantasy reveals her deep desire to speak and to be heard. As much as she protests her father's rigid demands, it is his silence (and behind this, the silence of her mother) which is most difficult to bear.

But Kirsten will not be silent. We have seen that she wants to tell her story. And ultimately, her own story presents her with an ethical choice: her refusal to accept the AA way. For her there is a stark contrast between Joe's endorsement of the public sphere and her own advocacy of private life. In deciding to preserve her privacy, she opts for her subjective point of view. In so doing, she opposes her father's "holier than thou" attitude, and sets herself in the "place where people live." And in not wanting "to be degraded"— that is, forced to reveal herself—to figuratively "undress" in public, she saves part of herself from universal scrutiny. By taking this stance, she is saying: "I am something more than your smug definition of me." Or in other words, "I am not an alcoholic, I am Kirsten." And despite the hazards of such an approach, nobody can say that Kirsten lacks "a mind of her own."

We can posit that "the hazards of such an approach" apply to psychoanalysis/psychotherapy as "cure" or means to recovery. None of the three films mention psychotherapy as a possible remedy, and in part we can see why. The three men have, in aligning themselves with the bottle, effectively shut out any exploration of their inner life. Even if they were persuaded to try the couch, we can imagine them giving their analysts "a line of bull." Any chance of success would depend upon the treatment eliciting some interest or desire to know themselves. Kirsten, on the other hand, might well benefit from psychoanalysis. Yet we know that it can never promise a sober life in the way AA can and does. Indeed, her position that the possibility of "another drink" must remain on the table almost ensures that her drinking will get worse.

Indeed the clear message of all three films is that the alcoholic's life is at stake. How many therapists are willing to risk this? Can we visualize even in theory a successful psychoanalysis that results in death? I doubt it. But can we deny the alcoholic with a "mind of her own" the chance to live a fuller life? Thus the three films pose troubling questions that open out into a wider discussion of the psychoanalytic approach to addictions.

Coda: the object and its relations

The image of the alcoholic as an emotional isolate is refuted by these three films. Not only do Don, Joe, and Ben maintain ties to others, but each creates a powerful bond with one partner. Seen through the lens of these films, it is not so much a question of "object relationship" as that of a single object—"the bottle"—functioning as a catalyst which cements ties and holds psychical elements together.

More specifically, it helps the men manage their orientation in personal space. The films permit us to envision that space. Thus, when inside his apartment or, in one instance, a greenhouse, the alcoholic is unable to situate himself within a spatio-temporal grid. For our purposes, think of the grid as a network of holes so tiny it can hold and therefore prevent even the smallest of particles from "falling through the cracks." For the alcoholic, however, that grid—if it even exists—consists mainly of gaping holes. Thus to the extent he retains a rudimentary sense of "inside-ness," he experiences that space as filled with "pitfalls."

We have seen that the three men draw closest to the void when they are alone in their apartments, or other cinematic representations of interior space. By depicting the alcoholic "inside" a void, the films show us the (potential) void inside their minds. Each man attempts to cope with this danger, first by mentally "bottling" the void inside bottles, and then by hiding the bottles throughout interior space. In "bottling" the void each man confines it to a restricted, compressed space; in hiding the bottles he attempts to create a defensive perimeter surrounding the void. Indeed, he seeks the company of others for the same reason. Why—when he could just stay home and drink all the time—does he force himself to sit in bars? The bartender places a human limit on his drinking, by meting out drinks in shot glasses, thus slowing consumption, and by refusing to serve him (or bodily throwing him out).

The notion of "bottling the void" recalls Bion's (1962) interpretation of the bottle's container function. In this view, Don, Joe, or Ben attempts to protect the contents of his mind by expelling them into a "bottle." Paradoxically, as if through a mirror, "the bottle" sucks in psychic contents that have been extruded, scattered, and exposed in public space. As it happens, mathematicians have constructed such a "Klein" bottle (*sic*) by sewing together two Mobius strips (Wikipedia). In any case, relocating psychic contents permits sexual fantasy to exist in a latent state inside the bottle, as it were. In this way, the bottle preserves for the alcoholic the *possibility* of fantasy, and more broadly, the possibility of an "internalized world"—a mind of one's own.

Inevitably however, the bottle becomes the breaking point of any relationship. Keep in mind that most of the threesomes in the films—Don, Wick, and Helen; Yuri, Sera, and Ben; or Joe, Kirsten, and Jim—decompose into units of one and two. And even the apparently unbreakable twosomes, such as Joe and Kirsten, break apart over the bottle. Joe expresses astonishment that the heretofore solidity of their relationship could be severed so easily. And in each film, there is a pivotal moment when the alcoholic throws off all human ties in favor of "the bottle," becoming, at least temporarily, the very thing he most dreads: an emotional isolate.

The contradictory nature of the bottle emerges in its creation of an almost superhuman attachment that replaces and severs all other attachments. On the intra-psychic level, it is simultaneously inside and outside, like a Klein bottle. And in its quest for compactness, uniformity, and comprehensiveness, it concentrates its product while simultaneously reducing it to the lowest common denominator. It is both the elixir of life and the pure culture of the death drive. It is buried treasure and the garbage accumulated throughout one's personal history. In a sense the prostitute scenario, found in one form or another in all three films, serves as a primitive schema for "comprehending" this paradoxical nature. In this "alternative universe," the same object can be both "abject" or "exalted," "toxin," or "panacea."

In the end, the films leave us with unresolved and problematic questions which we cannot expect them to fully address, but which have implications for psychoanalytic theory and practice. These include the areas of love, sexuality, and individual subjectivity.

We have seen that all three films, playing on the conventions of the Hollywood romance, portray the alcoholic's primary relationship as a love affair. In all three cases, there is a moment of "falling in love." In all, the love between the lead characters holds together as a nearly unshakable bond. It is an absolutely exclusive love that brooks no rivals. Yet it is founded upon the illusion that such a relationship can exist. When Joe discovers, for example, that without the "bottle," the love between Kirsten and himself would founder, he is aghast. That illusory component is also present in Joe's idealization of Jim, his sponsor in AA, and his consequent overvaluation of the "book."

Perhaps the most problematic aspect of love in the three films is its association with the abandonment of a child. In *The Lost Weekend*, Don becomes Helen's surrogate "child"—compensation for the one she will never have. In *Leaving Las Vegas*, Ben's inexorable march toward death, with Sera by his side, is in some ways an atoning or re-enactment of his unresolved abandonment of his own child. But the most explicit and painful example comes from *Days of Wine and Roses*, when Joe—at his most infantile—demands that Kirsten interrupt and deprive their own daughter of the breast. In repudiating the child, the lovers repudiate the possibility of a lost object. In a love that seems to offer "everything," neither partner can acknowledge that at least one "thing" is unrecoverable.

But in contrast to the longed for certainty of love, the characters see their sexuality as a minefield. All the male characters—explicitly or covertly—proclaim their impotence in advance in order to forestall any challenge to their virility. Given the inflation of the public sphere in their lives, they certainly suffer from "performance anxiety". Yet it would be egregiously wrong to view them as asexual, just as it would be wrong to impute their sexual issues to the physiological effects of the alcohol alone. In all three films, the "bottle" serves as a kind of conduit to orgiastic displays of sexuality. Ben, for example, imagines the "bottle" as a kind of "fountain"—a fountain of youth, say—which literally overflows with life.

In one way, it appears as if they are dominated by the orgasm at the expense of sexual desire. We have seen in this regard that it is very difficult for the main characters to hold the "bottle" at a necessary distance for eliciting and sustaining desire. More problematic still is their capacity to view the bottle as just beyond their reach, hence unattainable. The bottle's complete accessibility and readiness to hand seems to rule this out. Yet without adequate barriers to complete satisfaction, the alcoholic's orgiastic tendencies are uncontainable. There is nothing to stop it from crossing the pain threshold and nothing to confine it to the male "organ." The films depict the alcoholic's fall from grace as a breaching of limits—the sudden bursting forth of all bodily fluids in a final common pathway, the confluence of semen and blood, of Eros and the death drive.

The advocate of subjectivity and the "talking cure" is represented in the films through a surrogate, the bartender. In *The Lost Weekend*, we can observe this character—Nate—playing a therapeutic role. He listens to Don without comment or judgment. He demands money for his services. Don esteems him as a "professional" who understands the lot of problem drinkers. For his part, Nate stands for limits on drinking. As noted, he admonishes Don to stop, refuses to serve him when he is too drunk, and then threatens to throw him out of the bar. And in the midst of Don's prostitute reverie, he makes a connection between Gloria and Helen, just when Don is intent on "splitting" them apart. Finally, he returns the typewriter to Don, providing the means for his "writing cure."

If Don, Joe, Ben, or Kirsten turned up in our consulting room, the therapeutic task would hinge on the patient saying to the analyst: "I am an alcoholic." We know that when he says this in the movies he is lying—lying by hiding something. The psychoanalyst will think, and perhaps say, "In telling me this what are you not saying?" or "Who says you are an alcoholic?" Hence without denying the fact of alcoholism, the psychoanalyst adds a note of ambiguity that belies the original certainty.

In the end, the treatment stands or falls on the possibility that "the bottle" will transmute into "the message inside the bottle."

Part III

Perverse Desire
in Mainstream Cinema

CHAPTER SIX

The S and M Cure in *Secretary*

C ritics have long been divided over how to categorize the movie *Secretary* (2002); and often their estimate of its worth follows from their choice of which genre fits it best (rogerebert.com). Some reviewers, for example, noting its focus on the on–again/off-again "relationship" between the two lead characters and their eventual arrival at the altar, dubbed it a romantic comedy. Others saw parallels with fairy tales such as *Cinderella, Snow White*, and *Little Red Riding Hood*, implied by the transformation of the female protagonist—Lee Holloway—from an awkward, dowdy-looking reject to femme fatale, clad briefly in a long blue cloak, and "awakened" from sleep by a first kiss late in the movie. Still others saw the film through the eyes of feminist ideology—either as a slap in the face to orthodox feminists—or a subversive plea for another kind of liberation with the motto: doms and submissives unite and come out of your closets! Yet others viewed such messages as cover for what they thought was at base a sophisticated piece of soft-core pornography. In this regard, the film contains several highly erotic scenes—erotic both for protagonist and viewer alike. Perhaps they wondered whether the film would have been nearly as popular if those scenes had been deleted. And this last gloss introduces a broader classification implied by the film's high degree of stylization, jarring color palette, and blurring of fantasy and "reality." Could the film make sense as pure fantasy, either as Lee Holloway's private imaginings or as an emerging cultural flirtation with S and M practice? In this light, *Secretary* is just another product of the "Hollywood dream factory."

But none of these various categorizations quite stands up to scrutiny. To see the movie as nothing more than a romantic comedy, we must confront the fact that it is never played for laughs. The two leads perform their roles without self-parody and without even a hint of irony. What humor there is arises from the apparent absurdity of their infantile games *as seen from an outside perspective*. Moreover, the lead character—Lee Holloway— tells us that she has been cutting herself since the seventh grade. Thus the game-like aspect of the interactions between Lee and Mr. Grey—her S and M partner—should not blind us to the fact that she suffers. Self-cutting is a deadly serious act for Lee, testing the very limits of her existence. So when she enters into a strange compact with Grey, she is putting her life on the line. And for this very reason, the element of "romance" is always problematic. The film purports to follow an initially tenuous and "restricted" sexual relationship as it slowly transforms, after a series of crises, into a passionate love affair, and finally marriage. But can love and sex be so easily reconciled? And more importantly, can love save this couple from drowning in their own dark abyss? And if they are dancing on the edge of that abyss, does it not require a degree of self-delusion to think that sexuality—especially in this particular form—can be so easily tamed? Like many of its Hollywood predecessors, *Secretary* uses the "happy ending" as a feint, at once pacifying the audiences' need for closure while subtly conveying that life will never be uncomplicated for the happy couple.

For these reasons, I view the movie as a classic Hollywood hybrid—a genre picture that defies inclusion in any one type, a fantasy that reveals itself *as* fantasy, and a disturbing dream whose façade reveals cracks and fissures through which we can discern a complex psychic reality. These cracks and fissures are easily overlooked, but they readily reveal themselves to slow motion examination. We see them as snags and glitches in the highly choreographed and largely silent *pas de deux* between two partners. These impasses prove to be every bit as important as the smooth progress of the dance. Indeed, the filmmakers deliberately straddle the fence between rigid orchestration and spontaneity; impossible fantasy and the bland ordinariness—not to say bleakness—of the characters' daily lives. In so doing it suggests that conventional definitions of love are too narrow and that we cannot rule out the possibility that this couple finds its own "cure" for its shared suffering.

In this chapter I shall attempt to describe the couple's negotiations through a series of crises that ultimately lead to a rapprochement. Throughout the exposition I will explore the role of the erotic encounters in the psyches of the protagonists. Does the highly ritualized format of the encounters help to stabilize inward chaos? Do the encounters fulfill the same function for both partners? To what extent may we speak of a sexual or erotic bond between them? What does this bond—if it exists—have to do with love? Is there perhaps a subterranean dimension that threatens to break out at various points, undercutting the smooth functioning of the sexual ritual? And yet alternatively, can their arrangement be integrated within societal norms? Will their marriage based on mutual affection and joint commitment be compatible with the erotic requirement of always pushing the envelope, of inevitably exceeding the pleasure principle (through the embrace of pain and suffering)? And, finally, is there such a thing as an S and M cure? Or is the couple's arrangement just a new form of *folie à deux*?

Lee Holloway and her family

Lee's story begins with her discharge from a psychiatric hospital she calls "The Institution." She is being discharged on the day of her "normal" sister's wedding. The rather arcane use of the word "institution" suggests the kindred institutions of marriage and the family. Therefore her family now takes over the institutional function formerly served by the hospital. An institution is a structure, and as a structure, one of its chief roles is regulation. In this respect Lee notes that the hospital imposed upon her a rigid and inflexible routine and that this framework was deeply reassuring to her. In the family, Lee's mother assumes the role of organizer and chaperone, watching her daughter like a hawk and keeping the kitchen knives locked up to prevent her from cutting herself. In addition, Joan Holloway encourages Lee's own attempts to find structure, such as looking for a job.

But such surveillance on the part of the mother is inimical to Lee's sense of independence. She cannot go anywhere without her mother looking over her shoulder. In order to impose order, the mother feels compelled to be intrusive and her role tends to eclipse her traditional nurturing role. Moreover, Lee's father is constantly subverting his wife's efforts. In the first scene with Burt, her father, at Lee's sister's wedding, he is visibly intoxicated and, as a result, excessively affectionate with Lee to the point of slobbering over her. Then he has to sit down when feeling sick. Lee feels a combination of love, pity, and disgust at her father's unrestrained excess.

In her dismay, Lee runs up to her bedroom and prepares to cut herself. But before we know this intention, she retrieves a mysterious package from under her bed, wrapped in a pillowcase adorned with hearts. At this point the object appears quite innocuous. Underneath the pillowcase is a box decorated with multicolored, iridescent figures, made of glass or plastic: winged insects, a butterfly, and a little fairy with gossamer wings. The figures make us think we are about to see playthings and mementos from an innocent girlhood.

And then—to our shock—we see what's really in the box: an assortment of cutting tools comprising a kind of torture kit. It includes: a razor, a short handled knife, a drill bit, scissors, an X-acto knife, a can opener, a dart, and a pointed chisel. Also included are Q-tips and tincture of iodine for dressing wounds. Now Lee's intent dawns on the viewer. But before recounting Lee's actions, let us pause for a moment to consider this special box and its contents. We note first that the box is hidden. Of course Lee wants to keep it hidden from her mother's scrutiny, given the latter's incursions into her private life. But we can also guess that it encapsulates the deepest core of her being. And since the "box" is a feminine symbol, we can amend that to: the deepest core of her being as a woman. But the box is also designed to deceive. Its façade gives a completely false impression of what's inside and moreover, its surface lures the viewer into a realm of gauzy fantasy that covers over a "painful" reality. Furthermore, the number of cutting tools exceeds the few she would need to do the job. Nestled in their box, the tools have taken on a fetish-like quality as if their mere association with the act of cutting holds an erotic charge. Similarly, their phallic association might derive from Lee's childhood view of the phallus as a knife-like organ.

But Lee surprises us by not using a cutting tool and instead grabbing a porcelain object and testing the sharpness of one of its projections against a flat white stone. She uses it to depress the skin of her upper thigh but before she can draw blood, the camera cuts away. In a pang of regret she bundles up her cutting tools and throws them in a bureau drawer.

The film cuts to Lee overhearing a desperate scene between her parents. She is in the kitchen brewing tea when she hears her mother screaming at her father for losing his job and being drunk all the time. He pushes his wife to the ground and in the process a piece of crockery shatters on the floor. Retrospectively, those jagged shards represent the sharp porcelain object. The film makes a direct connection between the object used for cutting and the chaotic breaking apart of the family structure. In utter confusion and disarray, Joan vainly struggles to restrain a father whose behavior has become ungovernable. Later in the film when her father leaves Lee "dangling" in limbo on the phone, she bangs the receiver repeatedly on her desk at his erratic behavior.

Lee again runs to her room, this time carrying the teapot. She pushes its hot edge against her thigh in the same general area as before. She burns herself, and with the sensation comes both relief and release, a half-smile forming on her face. On the most superficial level, the "relief" is relief from her distress over her parents fighting. In every case her impulse to cut is triggered by volatility between her parents. The erotic discharge, I would postulate, dissipates her sexual arousal at her parents fighting, as if fighting and sexual congress are interlaced in her mind. But it also reveals another aim: a kind of narcosis or anesthesia and a return to a womb-like serenity.

The film then cuts to Lee face up in her family's swimming pool buoyed by inflatables around her hands and feet, as if floating in tepid amniotic fluid. The reference to birth in this oft-repeated pool scene, becomes more specific when Lee tells us about the "accident"—the moment when her cutting crossed a line. She had been cutting herself since the seventh grade, but had always been careful not to draw blood. But one time in the kitchen, she cut herself with a piece of glass (a shard) when her mother was present and her father was fortifying himself with alcohol before going to work. In her haste, she cut "too deep" and started bleeding. She doesn't know how she could have "misjudged" the situation. Her parents and others obviously viewed her action as a suicidal gesture (at the least) and it led to her hospitalization at "The Institution."

Lee viewed her action as an accident because she never intended (consciously) to make herself bleed. However, given the perfunctory nature of her rationalization, we can assume that it was, and it wasn't, an accident. It was an accident in the sense that it restaged Lee's concern that her parent's volatility could very well lead to accidents. And among these possible accidents is Lee's very existence. Lee may have viewed her birth as an "accident" because she saw herself as an unwanted child. Specifically, Lee may feel that her mother's overprotectiveness compensates for having never been wanted in the first place. We could picture the situation as a primal scene fantasy of the parents' rough sex "accidentally going too far"—the equivalent of cutting "too deep." As noted, Lee, as a child, might have visualized sexual intercourse as a bloody act, of which menarche—the age at which she started cutting—and later defloration—serve as reminders.

And in light of this vivid imagery, we can posit that Lee's "accident" reflects her ongoing concern with boundaries within her family, and therefore with things "going too far and too deep." Thus her practice of superficial cutting aims to mark off or "underscore" such a boundary, as if drawing a line in the sand (skin). Yet the "accident" when she cut "too deep" stages the "accident" of her existence. In this act, therefore, Lee might have been crying out for recognition of her right to exist, crying out, in effect, I *am* that error, that mistake—the one who ended up as your problem child. In so doing, she addresses to her parents an urgent question: Do you want me dead or alive? Do you want me never to have been born or will you embrace your mistake? And because this question remains in suspense, Lee floats in a kind of limbo or inertia between life and death. The pain of her self-cutting offers her a transient feeling of aliveness, of life on the "cutting edge" so to speak, while also suggesting an underlying suicidal impulse. And because the question of her existence is unanswered, she cannot fully "own" or assume the "deep inward pain" lying at the core of her psyche.

At this stage, therefore, Lee is only looking for a structural support—something analogous to "The Institution"—that promises a measure of psychic stability. She chances upon such a prospect in a want ad for a secretary, and with her mother's encouragement, she goes for a job interview. This first encounter initiates—as I will try to demonstrate—an evolving erotic compact that succeeds brilliantly in providing both parties to the agreement with a measure of that stability. At the very least, it will provide them with a safety net that keeps the question of their existence moot for the moment and offers a fighting chance at psychic survival.

Stage one: overtures

Upon entering her prospective employer's office, Lee notices that the room is in a state of chaos, with books and papers strewn across the floor, the middle-aged former secretary in the act of leaving the premises. Because we will learn very little about Mr. Grey's past history, we rely on this scene to portray a man on the brink of internal chaos. We first see him peering at a snapshot of a blond woman—presumably his ex-wife—in an effort to hold on to some shred of his former life. He briefly checks his face in a mirror at the bottom of his desk drawer, in an attempt to regain his composure. Still, Lee must notice that he is slightly off balance. She asks: "Are you the lawyer?" After a pause for internal regrouping, Grey replies: "Oh, uh yes." Even his identity seems fragile. Noting his discomfiture, Lee offers to leave and come back later. Grey tells her to stay.

Once Grey realizes he is conducting a job interview, he begins with an odd question: "Are you pregnant?" He follows up with a series of other personal questions as if reading a questionnaire, but the first question effectively stands in for the others. Interestingly, Lee is not at all put off by the question and her face registers a half-smile—an augur of things to come—that contrasts with her typical deadpan expression. She answers the question calmly: "No."

This question seems "out of order" both in the sense of appropriateness and its occurrence at the wrong place in the interview. What can it mean for Grey to say it and for Lee to hear it? For both, it appears to form part of a standard job questionnaire. However, it might have been more suitable for the 1950s or 60s. In 2002, such a question would be taken as a clear sign of misogyny on Grey's part. Lee, however, seems unconcerned. And then on a purely pragmatic level, Grey might foresee Lee having to stop work if she were pregnant. Grey doesn't like disruptions of his daily routine. And given the recent defections from his ranks, he might want to ensure that he has Lee's full commitment, without the distractions of a husband, boyfriend, or baby. But given the "disorder" of the earlier scene, perhaps Grey wants to reorganize the office from scratch, and thereby rewrite the chaos of his life by eliminating the possibility of "accidents," spontaneous irruptions, and other untoward events.

At this early stage, however, Grey is satisfied with Lee's answers and qualifications (her award from typing class). He is willing to hire Lee on a provisional basis to see how things work out. He gives his assent indirectly by tripping a switch, releasing a watery mist on a beautiful pink orchid in a glass enclosure. Lee gasps in pleasure at its beauty. One can't help wondering if she wants to become Grey's "hothouse flower"—his precious object in a sheltered environment. Then Grey reads Lee's typing certificate and states her name: Lee Holloway. Thus he recognizes her as his new secretary. To seal the deal he files the snapshot of his ex-wife in the filing cabinet.

Typos

Before too long, however, a major glitch in the relationship occurs. One day at work, an enraged Grey confronts Lee at her desk with three typing errors in a letter she has just completed. He gives her a severe tongue-lashing. Lee feels chastened, but also surprised by the vehemence of his response. Lee tries again but then makes another typo. Grey responds: "You're wasting my time." She tries yet again, and this time shows her anxiety by "sniffling" and tapping her foot. But instead of merely reacting, she also does something deliberate: she takes out her sewing/cutting kit and cuts out a small rectangle of fabric from the hem of her skirt. On office stationery, she types a heading: a small sacrifice for Mr. Grey. Then she brings Grey the corrected letter, hoping he will proofread it. On her way out, Grey sees the notch in her skirt hem.

Let us pause here to consider the various permutations of Lee's actions. We first note that the director has already highlighted the importance of typing in three ways: in one of the opening shots we see a typewriter pounding away and in their first interview, Grey emphasizes that Lee will be using an old-fashioned typewriter and *not* a word processor, which would have been readily available in 2002. And for her part, Lee excels at typing, having earned top honors in her typing class. The fact that typing is dull and "boring" doesn't faze her in the least. At this stage, she wants nothing more in life than recognition as an expert typist. That recognition is documented in the certificate she presents to her boss at the first interview.

What is it about typing that so captivates Lee? First and foremost, typing is completely *rule governed*. There is no requirement for "editing" or "revising"—indeed such actions would, in themselves, be proscribed. Thus for Lee, typing offers an absolute and unvarying structure, one that provides a daily routine and that yields her a stable slot in the social structure. Thus, it not only offers her a structure, it places her *within* that structure. Hence typing offers a powerful prop to Lee's fragile sense of identity. As a corollary, typing has a lulling, soothing effect, much like a baby's pacifier or more broadly, the child's feeling of utter security when firmly held by the mother. In general, typing presents an ideal state of affairs in which all exchanges between people are completely scripted, or in Grey's own word: "prescribed." Typing's relationship with forms of writing—such as cuneiform—also come to mind, and I shall explain the relevance of this aspect shortly.

Now we can ask the more urgent question: What do typing, and more specifically a glitch in typing, signify in the relationship between the two principals? Why does Lee—an expert typist—make such glaring errors in the first place? Surely she was trained in typing class to proofread her own work. We must consider the possibility that the typos were intentional. This view is supported later in the film when, after stockpiling bottles of whiteout, Lee *consciously* makes a typo. If this explanation holds, then Lee is inserting a typo in order to communicate something to Grey. On some level she wants to get a rise out of him and provoke him to punish her, which interestingly would itself become part of a "scripted" scenario.

But Lee's deliberate action of cutting her skirt hem suggests another aim. Her use of the sewing kit makes an immediate connection between typing and cutting herself. What is the primary difference between typing on an old machine and typing on a computer? Only the machine makes an impression or "stamp" on the paper. Thus Lee's long-standing practice of marking or scratching herself with a sharp tool may function as a kind of writing on the skin, analogous to tattooing (often referred to as Ink). That is to say, the writing on the skin or the blank page is the equivalent of forcefully imposing a structure or "rule." At the most rudimentary level, scratching a line draws a boundary on the skin, whose expanse no longer offers sufficient delineation.

If we keep within the terms of this metaphor, then the glaring typos correspond to the "too deep" cuts. Recall that Lee was disturbed that her very careful practice of cutting herself should result in a "slip of the blade." Hence Lee may be staging for Grey's benefit, the "accident" of her own *being*. This is why—despite her longing for structure and routine—she makes sure that Grey knows that her being—those features that make Lee who she is—reside in the typos. Here is where Lee is surreptitiously seeking recognition from Grey. For what is Grey's response to Lee's typos and other mistakes? He abhors her dress, her sniffling, the way she plays with her hair, her foot tapping, and what she does with her tongue when typing. He hates these attributes but he fully recognizes them; Lee realizes that he observes—and possibly finds himself obsessed—with every move she makes that, in his eyes, trespasses on his "stencil" of complete self-mastery.

Lee makes the same point by cutting out the fabric. The cutting out, itself a form of "cutting," is like a typing error that leaves a conspicuous gap. Lee wants Grey to know that the missing piece of fabric is *she*. And what's more she wants to sacrifice herself—to throw herself away—to render herself abject—for Grey. That is she wants him to know that she was *disposable*, expendable. Certainly, the entire practice of typing aims toward self-effacement. This dark motive could, at this point, evolve in three possible directions: a truly suicidal impulse; dedication to a revered "Other"; or the eroticization of submission, a change that might temporarily dispel inertia.

Grey's proposal of an exchange of symptoms

The idea of a proposal germinates in Grey's mind when he happens to see Lee bending over to replace a mousetrap on the floor of his office. His eyes drawn to her backside, he notices to one side a series of five small band-aids on the back of her right knee, stacked in a vertical line. Lee meets his eye, and in that look, Grey knows that she cuts herself and that Lee knows that he knows. And in the same instant, Lee realizes that the sight of her buttocks arouses Grey and that he knows that she knows. Hence when Grey—shortly thereafter—catches her in the act of laying out her cutting paraphernalia, the implications are clear. In her embarrassment, Lee tries to deflect attention by busying herself with pencils and papers, semi-acknowledging both her cutting and its autoerotic significance.

Once having established his credibility in Lee's eyes, Grey issues the following command: "You will never, ever cut yourself again." "It's in the past," he adds. Lee accepts the command without protest. Grey certifies her consent by taking a Polaroid snapshot of her. He then couples this prohibition with the permission to walk home from work by herself instead of being chauffeured (chaperoned?) by her mother. Lee enjoys the walk. She explains that: "Because he insisted on it, I felt held by him" (Winnicott, 1960b). Thus in her mind, there is a connection between Grey's "insistence" and being "held." And she makes the further connection that such support facilitates her freedom to act on her own.

For the first time, we discern that Grey's proposal sets a firm boundary, in keeping with his policy of a "pre-scribed" relationship. This boundary sits at the crossroads of at least four currents. First, it acts to separate Lee's own desires from those of her mother's. Up till now, Lee had acted as the vehicle of her mother's expectations—that she submit to normalization—that she remain passive. Only her cutting countermanded her basic passivity. And yet by "cutting too deep" she may have awakened her mother's desire that she *live*, or at least, gotten her to acknowledge that she wanted her daughter to live. Second, the boundary delineates Lee's private interior world from her public interactions with others. Her deep wish to protect and safeguard—if not bury—her secret "box" implies a fear that even something this "deep" is not really hers to keep. And third, the boundary acts as a buttress or stand-in for the incest taboo. Thus, we could view the proposal as another version of the one made to the oedipal child: give up the satisfaction of possessing or being possessed by the parent, and you will be allowed a future life of your own.

And finally, fourth, the boundary has a purely somatic reference. It suggests that as a child Lee was unsure which body parts—organs—were her own and which were her mother's (or her father's). In particular, there may have been ambiguity over her genitals: Had an organ been taken away from her that was originally hers, or alternatively, was there an organ of her mother's (the breast) that is now claimed by Lee? And in the incestuous fantasy with the father, does the idea of him sticking his penis "too deep" risk the sacrifice of this organ to the mother? And for this was she willing to "sacrifice" a little piece of herself to her father as now she is willing to do for Grey? Indeed, if we were to link the last two examples, perhaps Lee needs to stage a mini-castration in her own flesh in order to force acknowledgment of the sacrifice necessary on the part of her parents and herself to seal the oedipal bargain.

The first erotic encounter

At this point the groundwork has been laid for the movie's first erotic encounter. But the director's "painstaking" build-up to this point should caution us not to view the S and M scene as a cliché. For, as played by James Spader, E. Edward Grey is anything but glib or "slick" as he leans against a wall and clenches his fist (in anguish?) before making the first move. He then orders Lee to enter the office with the letter occasioning the multiple typos and corrections. Thus he makes an immediate connection between the letter with its slips of the pen (keys) and the anticipated erotic encounter. He demands that Lee bend over the desk with her eyes on the letter. She places both her hands palms down on the desk. Since she was not required to do this, we must assume that in placing her hands so, she is taking up a position (confirmation of which will come later). When Grey delivers the first blow, it is like an awakening jolt, for up until this instant Lee did not quite know what was about to happen. For just a moment she seems to waver, but then she grasps Grey's intent. The encounter—a patent transgression—is "framed" as a sort of contract (or compact)—and therefore as the imposition of some kind of law—by the requirement that Lee read the letter's analysis of a client's "rights" (animal rights?). Moreover, it is clear that part of the contract entails the exchange of one method of inflicting pain for another.

As the blows continue, Grey seems more and more caught up in the process, hitting with the open hand and on the backswing, and accelerating until he reaches the number twenty-one. Towards the end, Grey places his two hands, palms down, next to Lee's. She puts her little finger over one of Grey's fingers in a tiny moment of tenderness that contrasts with the violence of the blows. They both appear to reach a near-simultaneous orgasm. In the post-coital moment, Grey tells her to return to her desk and retype the letter. Thus the letter frames the beginning, middle, and end of the encounter. Back in the work area, Lee pulls down her clothes to reveal a large red bruise on her buttocks. She needs to witness this visible sign or stigmata. Her relief at the sight of this mark is as palpable as her orgasmic release. Clearly, the vivid bruise takes the place of the former lacerations. Later, having already brought him the corrected letter, Grey compliments her work. She is pleased and that pleasure cannot be readily distinguished from pain. Thus for both parties, and probably for different reasons, the erotic encounter conveys a subtext of enforcing "discipline," establishing a written compact, reinforcing a boundary, and paradoxically, pre-scribing a remedy for pain.

Yet as noted, the scenario stages an encounter that breaches or goes beyond the boundaries it is attempting to set. Both parties enter into the act with trepidation as if aware of the obvious transgression it represents. Both parties—and especially Grey—seem slightly overwhelmed by the power of the experience. Moreover, the violence of the blows seems more than either partner expected. Surely, the goal of leaving a mark would have necessitated fewer blows. Interestingly, the beating is never administered again—exactly as if Grey applied the prohibition against cutting to his own infliction of bodily harm. And just as the typos indicated a part of Lee's mind that resists definition, so the element of the encounter that went "too far" suggests a portion of their relationship not containable or classifiable within the strict confines of S and M practice.

In one sense the erotic encounter serves as a sort of consummation of Grey's proposal regarding Lee's self-cutting. In its aftermath, she feels free to indulge in erotic fantasies about Grey. In the same vein, she tells her mother that she no longer has to keep the knives under lock and key. Joan responds by embracing Lee from behind. Lee hugs her back because her temporary liberation from the burden of her mother's scrutiny frees her to re-experience affection for her. As a final step, she throws her sewing kit into the nearby river.

Grey retreats and Lee takes the lead

But in the immediate aftermath of the erotic encounter, three brief scenes effect a radical change in the film's tone. These scenes depict fanciful versions of the dominance/submission scenario (but not the spanking). In the first, Lee is depicted wearing an outlandish yoke tied to her neck and wrists, forcing her to go through contortions in order to perform simple tasks. The second has her crawling on the floor with the corrected letter in her mouth. And the third poses her on all fours while Grey places a saddle (that he just happens to have handy) on her back and cinches it tightly. Incredibly she is kneeling on a bed of straw. Whether we view these scenes as unmarked fantasy, magic realism, or comic relief, their effect on viewers is that of parody. Hence their inclusion at this point in the film suggests a "distancing effect."

The imaginary scenes introduce a phase of retreat and withdrawal on Grey's part. Lee sees evidence of the change the very next day when she marches into her employer's office, letter in hand, with a confident almost triumphant look. Yet Grey pointedly ignores her, rudely handing back the letter and announcing: "I have to work." Deflated, Lee tells him she is leaving for the day, giving her boss the option of calling her back if he "needs more typing done." This is code for "let me know when you're ready to resume our arrangement." In thanking her, Grey reverts to the formal address of Ms. Holloway. He cringes, perhaps at his own abruptness, then doubles down with: "That'll be all."

Later that same day, Lee learns that her father has been hospitalized. In obvious distress she takes the bold step of visiting Grey at his home. She knocks on the door and Grey—on his treadmill—almost falls over in surprise. He treats her with reserve but addresses her as Lee. Both his fall and "slip"—his "slip and fall," as it were—reveal his imbalance and discomfiture. Flustered as well, Lee goes completely off-script, muttering broken sentences: "I needed you ... I wanted you ...," half-acknowledging her need and desire for Grey himself. And despite being affected by her emotional appeal, Grey chooses to hear her words purely in a task-oriented sense. Lee picks up Grey's cue immediately, and "dials back" her original message, reminding him of a work-related matter. In parting, Lee feels demoted—like Cinderella after the ball—to being just an "ordinary secretary."

But she is far from giving up. At first she tries complimenting her boss on his tie adorned with incongruous little golfers. Then she brings him flowers and a framed photo of herself in alluring attire. These ploys fall flat, however. Then an idea occurs to her on the way to work. She sees a purplish worm on the ground and picks it up. At her desk, she carefully lays out the worm on a blank sheet of paper, folds the paper and inserts it in an envelope. She addresses the envelope to Grey. Grey's curiosity is already aroused when he sees her licking the flap from the doorway. At some point, Grey opens the letter, sees its contents and is moved by it. He starts to do pull-ups in his office—either as distraction or to work-off his accumulating libido.

Then he gingerly carries the worm to his desk and places it on a sheet of his personal stationery, and with one of his markers, draws an oval around it. Then he draws a series of loops, transforming the oval into an agitated vortex. What are we to make of this strange rite? In his first loop, Grey seems intent on "circumscribing" the worm and establishing a perimeter around it. Then his increasingly agitated repetitions suggest a need to wall it off completely. Yet the completed drawing implies a torrent of emotions that are about to overwhelm him (he had already admitted that "the office is overwhelmed"). Perhaps the worm represents Lee "worming" her way into his affections and burrowing into his defenses? Yet the vehicle for the worm—the letter in an envelope—suggests its function as a "joist" supporting the weight and pressure of the vortex and preventing internal collapse. And finally, Grey's action brings together symbolically the two organs—penis and vagina—whose contact has, by unspoken agreement between the pair, been proscribed, prohibited, and ruled out in advance.

The second erotic encounter

When Grey next orders Lee into his office, she senses a breakthrough. She tests his resolve by informing him that Mr. Marvel—a client—is sitting in the waiting room. Grey repeats his demand and Lee responds with an enthusiastic: "Yes, sir!" She dutifully bends over the desk and places her two palms face down on the top just as in the first encounter. Then Lee's friend,

Peter, rings himself into the waiting room, bringing Grey's only potential rival for Lee's attention to the fore. Grey directs Lee to ignore the interloper. Grey will not be distracted—and in this moment that is what Peter literally is: a distraction from the main action. Thus Grey's rapt focus on Lee contrasts with his earlier withdrawal and his attempts *to distract himself.*

Let us first consider Grey's side of the encounter. He asks Lee to pull up her skirt, and to her question: "Why," he responds with: "You're not worried I'm going to fxxx you, are you?" He then reassures her he has no such intention. That is to say, he will not have intercourse with her and neither will he do her harm. Perhaps the episode with the worm tempted Grey to have rough intercourse with Lee and, given her position over the desk, might have prompted a fantasy of either *coitus a tergo* (vaginal intercourse from behind) or anal penetration. Indeed, his reassurance may reflect revulsion at such an act. And his recoil may have led him to pause at the instant Lee— and the audience—expects him to start whaling on her buttocks, perhaps with even greater force than before. Instead, he unzips himself and masturbates. The scene reaches its climax in a monumental ejaculation that stains his pants and overflows on to Lee's blouse. The experience leaves him feeling drained and stuporous. Afterward, he tries to remove the residue from his clothes. We cannot escape the image of a man overwhelmed by a physical and emotional deluge.

But if Grey gives the impression of a man in the grip of a compulsion, Lee approaches it with the wide-eyed awareness of having made a choice (despite her submissive stance). But when the powerful slaps fail to occur she is taken aback. While certainly titillated, she misses the expected orgasm. She masturbates alone in the bathroom. When so occupied, she vocalizes the phrase, "cock in mouth," hinting at another meaning of the worm-in-the-oval: fellatio. In this context, perhaps Lee has become a phallic woman in Grey's eyes, making him the one harboring the fellatio fantasy. But even in the face of her mild sexual dissatisfaction, the second encounter demonstrates the degree to which she has drawn him to her and gotten under his skin.

Nevertheless, for both partners the second encounter fails to defuse the underlying instability plaguing their relationship. For Grey, the encounter proved an even greater threat to his self-autonomy than the first encounter. It re-ignited his primal fear of being "flooded" and "wetted." One could speculate that he feared wetting the bed as a child, and that this specific worry extended to a fear of emotional incontinence of any kind, as if his feelings comprised a witches brew of gall, bile, and blood. The fear of wetting would also apply to wetting a woman during intercourse, along with the messy results of insemination and impregnation.

For Lee, by contrast, the encounter didn't go far enough. It amounted to parallel masturbation rather than a true transaction or engagement. She has yet to secure any lasting commitment from Grey. But she has established the importance of the partnership as a portal to a richer and more intense existence. For the sake of their joint psychic survival, therefore, the pair must find a way to surmount Grey's obsession with mastery and free Lee from her suffocating familial entanglements.

Lee and Peter: an alternative history

Lee has had a pre-existing relationship with Peter since her sister's wedding day, and that relationship continues until just before the movie's finale. In many ways, the story of Lee and Peter parallels the one with Grey and addresses many of the same sexual conundrums. It provides a kind of alternative version of Lee's love life, with its own pleasures, impasses, and potential solutions. Yet almost from the start, Lee uses Peter as a "foil" for Grey, like Laertes to Grey's Hamlet. Making Peter the foil involves setting him up as a rival who differs from Grey in almost every respect. By convincing Grey that Peter is a legitimate rival, she defines Grey's choice of rejecting her (against his own powerful inclinations) as a failure or forfeiture. Then she dangles Peter like a puppet in front of Grey at every turn. The threat posed by Peter forces Grey towards a commitment that otherwise he might have postponed indefinitely.

In stage one, Lee and Peter meet as fellow oddballs at her sister's wedding. Both have been recently discharged from a psychiatric hospital. Peter thinks he understands Lee and the two develop a rapport. Peter is warm and empathetic, perhaps a little clingingly so. A few days later, they meet at a cafe and Peter confides to Lee that he would like to get married and have children. Lee almost chokes on her wine when she hears this. For Peter the chief goal of a relationship is "compatibility"—being at one with each other. Yet there is an unforced emotional spontaneity between them. At a laundromat, Lee makes gentle fun of Peter's desire for children, joking that his briefs will constrict the flow of sperm. This "joke"—which includes stretching the briefs in order to make room—expresses Lee's wish for a barrier against impregnation, of which the briefs are but one inadequate example. Peter—in a flourish—throws the briefs into the trash. They kiss, and in so doing take the relationship to the next level.

At this stage, their rapport is at the level of siblings. Peter's first appearance at Lee's sister's wedding suggests he is a "friend of the family." Peter is in some ways the sibling that Lee never had. Her relationship with her actual sister—now living in the family's backyard—is almost non-existent (the two never actually hold a conversation). The rapport between siblings is often based upon their common experience living with the same parents. This connection is implied by the fact that Peter's parents and Lee's parents are acquainted. Moreover, both Lee and Peter are struggling with their respective parents' expectations of them, one of which may be that they become friends. In another scene, for example, Peter's mother speaks for him, telling Lee—quite prematurely—that in her, Peter has found his "soulmate." But Lee's closeness to Peter must remind her of the inadequacy of boundaries within her family (or within the "blended" families of Peter and Lee). In resisting Peter's wishes to have children, Lee seeks to re-establish a barrier against brother–sister incest. The kiss with its promise of greater intimacy serves as a warning.

In stage two, Lee and Peter, "making out" on a bed, are on the verge of having sex. But as they approach the act, an almost comical misunderstanding ensues. Lee keeps guiding Peter's hands toward her buttocks in hopes that he will get the hint and spank her. Doesn't she see that such an activity is antithetical to Peter's character? Peter thinks she is merely signaling a desire for sex. He shows her a prophylactic, but she says: "That's not what I meant." Peter concludes she is simply not ready, and he throws the rubber on the floor, just as he previously threw his briefs into the trash. But Lee is moved by Peter's sincerity and obvious affection for her. She agrees to have sexual intercourse on two conditions: she wants to keep her clothes on and the lights out. When Peter enters her, she utters a word that could be either "oh" or "ow". The "oh" is spoken with a slight indication of surprise or perhaps disappointment. It is clear, however, that Lee is emotionally disengaged during the act while Peter is "all in" so to speak. Thus we suspect that their superficial rapport is complicated by their desires being at cross purposes.

Lee's reaction begs the question of her virginity. There is no other evidence that this is Lee's first time. Yet the film leaves the possibility open. The "oh" could signify: so this is how it is. The "ow" could signal slight pain. In a bit of irony, Peter asks her: "I didn't hurt you did I?" to which she answers: "No." The "no" expresses mild disappointment and boredom.

Yet, Lee's show of modesty concerning her clothes and the lights suggest sexual inexperience, while her obvious desire to be spanked suggests greater sophistication. Nevertheless, we must keep in mind that this sophistication originated with her erotic encounters with Grey. Thus in Lee's mind, her true loss of virginity may have occurred in Grey's office. Yet Lee's pose of being demure and innocent continues as a feature of her erotic encounters with Grey, suggesting that she is re-enacting her loss of her innocence, whether literal or figurative. Indeed the film symbolizes that innocence in the images of flowers and butterflies on Lee's "box" and the orchids in Grey's office. With both men, therefore, Lee may be reliving a fantasy in which her innocence is cherished by an idealized father figure as a magical and beautiful part of her whose boundary is respected and which is allowed to remain *virgo intacta*.

Be that as it may, Lee's affair with Peter shows the importance of barriers to direct sexual contact. She might have wanted Peter to spank her in order to evade sexual intercourse. The spanking would also add an edge to her feeling of being "blanketed" by Peter. Her desire to keep her clothes on ensures a barrier against full skin-to-skin contact, just as darkness avoids visual contact. The probable use of a condom adds another barrier; as does the hymen, although the latter remains moot (or muted). Certainly, the tenderness of Peter's penetration lessens the possibility of his going "too deep" and drawing blood.

Lee and Peter's growing involvement can lead in only one direction: engagement and marriage. And this possibility is staged in the movie even though its fulfillment is thwarted in the end. In marrying, Lee and Peter would satisfy their parent's expectations, including the prospect of grandchildren. And by marrying Peter, Lee would share in the nurturing relationship he enjoys with his parents. She would henceforth be included in a familial embrace, albeit one that is saccharine, cloying, and clinging. Indeed, she would be welcomed as a kind of "step-sibling." The director expertly captures this moment in the scene where Lee is trying on the wedding dress originally worn by Peter's mother. The latter notes that she was "a little lighter than you when I wore it." Her efforts to fit the dress show her subtle contempt for Lee as a lesser version of herself, as well as the lack of separation between herself and Lee, and the ill fit between Lee and the "slot" she is about to fill. That discordance is played back to her in the image reflected in the mirror.

The use of Peter as a foil emerges in the moments when the two alternative histories intersect. Grey early on witnesses Lee and Peter kissing and is
distressed by it. Here the desire to arouse Grey's jealousy is patent. Grey's
tirade over the typos stems in part from anger at Lee's "infidelity." His insistent question: "Are you pregnant?" only makes sense in regard to Peter. Later
Grey teases her over her "date" with Peter and the probability they had sex.
Lee is delighted with the question: it proves Grey's interest in her. In a show
of modesty and demureness, Lee gives their exchange a flirtatious gloss.
When Lee calls Grey a voyeur, it means, in part, that she is using Peter to put
on a little show for him. In yet another intersection, Peter rings himself into
the waiting room right before Grey and Lee's second erotic encounter. Now
he occupies the role of impotent witness to the act. At Grey's insistence,
Lee dismisses Peter. Thus Grey chooses Lee and Lee endorses his choice.
Toward the end of the film, it is Lee who finally rejects Peter while sitting at
Grey's desk, *ex cathedra*, so to speak.

Existential impasse and corrective (erotic?) third encounter

The second erotic encounter leads to an immediate existential impasse
for both partners. Grey attempts to disown Lee, to undo his ties to her, to
expunge her from the record, and to reset his personal history back to square
one, as if his liaison with her had never occurred. Accordingly, he smashes
Lee's framed letter and/or photo. He burns the snapshots of Lee, as he had
done with the snapshot of his ex-wife. He uses the shredder on other letters.
The floor is now littered with the detritus of their relationship. Then he calls
Lee into his office for a formal "undoing" or "divorce" ceremony. Ignoring
Lee's confusion over what has just happened, he asks Lee once again if she
is pregnant or if she plans on getting pregnant. Setting aside other factors,
Grey is attempting to reset their shared history by restarting his initial interview with her. As a test, he asks her if she really wants to be his secretary
and the kicker: This really isn't just about pencils and typing, is it? It's as if
he wants her to formally confirm that their relationship goes beyond the
professional and to use this fact to justify firing her. Of course Lee answers
in the affirmative. Grey then says: "I like you Lee, but I don't think I'm going
to offer you the job ... You can collect your things." And here note the dis-
missive "I like you but," Grey wants not only to dismiss her from the job but
also from his heart and mind.

But against the idea that Grey is merely being heartless and devoid of feeling for Lee, there is the evidence of his barely contained emotion. No sooner had Lee exited his office after their last erotic encounter than Grey sits down heavily as if stunned and overcome by the encounter. He types a letter to Lee saying: "This is disgusting," and admitting: "I don't know why I'm like this." This turn of events represents an about-face for Grey. He types the letter on his personal stationery and he expresses his feelings more openly than before. He puts his head down on the typewriter in shame. Disgust and shame are primal reactions to sexual excess, and moreover feelings Lee shares. He may, therefore, think that he is protecting both of them from the full impact of their sexual drives.

Lee, for her part, realizes that nullification of her secretarial position would rob her of her newfound identity and thus re-consign her to the limbo where she is neither dead nor alive. This dread combined with Grey's ambivalence leads to an irruptive and brilliant exchange—what I call a corrective third encounter. When Grey dismisses her, Lee cries out: "Time out!" She is for the first time interrupting the "game"—the highly scripted interaction between them. "Time out" constitutes her first "meta-communication" as it were. She is not only refusing to "play along" this time, she is making an appeal to his emotions—an *argumentum ad passiones*. All her emotions are right on the surface. He responds: "You're fired," and she throws his words back in his face: "You're fired." By giving tit for tat, she declares her refusal to submit. And when he tells her to get out, she slaps him hard across the face. This slap brings about an emotional climax that represents the high watermark of the movie. It echoes the erotic charge of the slaps to her buttocks but with a difference. In this instance, the slap takes place within an authentic emotional context and establishes Lee as an equal party in the encounter.

The slap also works as a wake-up call—a breaking of the spell that compelled the couple to lose themselves in the enactment of a shared fantasy or waking dream. Indeed it seems to dislodge some cog in Grey's mind. He reveals that Lee's every small action unsettles him: the way her feet smell, her sniffling, the little shavings produced when she uses an eraser, the Walkman that distracts her from answering the phone, her spilling glue on documents. In his hyperaesthetic sensitivity to her every move, he reveals his obsession with her. Yet he also divulges his deep aversion to the little quirks that comprise her "what-ness" (latin, *quidditas* per James Joyce) (theliterarylink.com). And two of these traits—sniffling and spilling glue—reaffirm his dismay at any sort of emotional and bodily incontinence. And let us keep in mind that all these quirks are associated with her typos. Additionally, the slap allows Grey to step back from his usual *modus operandi*, and admit: "You have to go or it won't stop, I cannot do this anymore." In other words, he feels so "possessed" by Lee—so tied to her body and soul—that his identity as a self-autonomous being is jeopardized. Thus the slap in the face helps to disabuse him of the fiction that has guided his life to date.

In a manner analogous to the first erotic encounter's sexual discharge, the slap triggers the release of previously blocked emotion. Grey is moved to tenderness as he moves his face closer to Lee, as if considering whether to kiss her. Yet at the last second, he moves away. He sits down heavily as if emotionally drained. Lee tells him she wants to know him better and she runs her fingers through his hair. Grey closes his eyes as if overtaken by rapture. However, the interrupted kiss demonstrates the couple's basic conundrum: the extreme proximity to full intimacy once again trips that switch in Grey that catapults him backwards. He hands Lee an envelope containing her severance pay and tells her in no uncertain terms to get out. This time Lee accepts defeat. She packs up her things and leaves the office.

The apparent failure, however, differs from earlier deadlocks. This time Lee has established a place for herself in Grey's mind analogous to her place inside his inner sanctum of an office. Grey can certainly try to expel her from this "place" but he cannot erase her from the map. In a short while Lee will experience an epiphany that prompts her to invade Grey's office unannounced and to forcefully "occupy" her place there.

Lee's last stand: the fourth encounter

For a short interval, Lee vacillates between self-effacement and a dramatic act of self-definition. The first "path"—"limbo"—takes her toward a place where she is just one in a long line of generic secretaries rather than "Secretary" with a capital S as the movie's title implies. This track entails drifting along in a watery medium—such as her swimming pool—like a piece of flotsam and jetsam, and in general following the path of least resistance. Thus she reverts to her previous role as dutiful daughter, helping her father maintain his sobriety for example. And when Peter proposes marriage she accepts. And before she knows it she is standing in her future mother-in-law's dress as if she were fitting a slot labeled "Peter's wife and soulmate."

But from early on Lee has been searching for ways to shore up her position and enhance her self-definition. While reading dating advice in *Cosmopolitan* magazine, for example, Lee imagines herself as a "Cosmo girl"—an urban sophisticate in matters of love and sexuality. The scene presages her entrance into the public sphere as a platform for "self-promotion." In a related scene, Lee listens to a tape about how to "come out" as a proponent of S and M, embracing the full range of one's sexuality. "Coming out" implies fitting into a pre-existing "slot" or at least one in the process of formation. Later she puts an ad in the paper seeking like-minded S and M types who together might comprise a community. However, this last effort fails.

And soon the two parallel paths meet in the moments preceding Lee's marriage to Peter. In publicly identifying herself with the S and M bond that ties her to Grey, she has already distanced herself from her future life with Peter. Then, while her future mother-in-law attempts to stuff her into her old wedding gown, she has an epiphany that the person she sees in the mirror is no longer herself. In that instant, she throws aside her vacillation and hesitation. Pulling off her veil and dropping her garter, she dashes downstairs, passing Peter and his dumbfounded parents, and leaving the ring on a side table.

She sprints to Grey's office and barges in. Without pause she says: "I love you!" In a flash she discards her carefully rehearsed and pre-scripted persona and shows Grey her unalloyed metal. In so doing, she puts herself (and possibly her life) on the line. Perhaps more than others who have uttered these three words, Lee is willing to let them fully define her. For her, the words declare: This is *everything* I am and this is *all* I am. And part of Lee's gamble lies in the performative effects of her utterance: in pronouncing the words she in effect creates a bond with Grey—a bond that she stakes her life on—and which constitutes a form of "bondage." This "bond/bondage" builds upon the sexual bond but goes beyond it; for whatever the outcome of this exchange, Lee will always be known and recognized for having taken a stand.

Grey of course responds with his usual indecision and irresolution. At first he appears crushed and at a loss for words. But then he tries to deny Lee's feelings, while she remains adamant. He claims that the severance check effectively dissolved their relationship. Lee must repeat, "I love you" several times before the words sink in. Grey soon drops his pretense of a nice clean separation between them. He opines that: "We can't do this twenty-four hours a day, seven days a week." That is, we can't sustain this level of erotic and emotional intensity all the time, nor can I handle the weight of a full-time commitment. Lee challenges him with: "Why not?" In combatting Grey's increasingly anemic objections, she finally feels secure in her "place" and she will not budge from it.

Lee and Grey then move towards a new rapprochement built on their previous erotic encounters. In a dramatic departure with the past, Lee now sits in Grey's chair. She fixes Grey with a devastating stare that he cannot escape. He suggests their standard opening move: Lee placing her hands palms down on the desk. She complies but adds: "I want to make love to you." Again, she lays her cards on the table and resets the stakes of the game. Grey tells her to "keep your feet on the floor until I return." While still vacillating, Grey no longer dismisses her. Indeed, he seems to acknowledge her steadfastness. While "keeping one's feet on the ground" denotes calm practicality, it *connotes* an unwavering sense of all one's parts hanging together. Lee holds that position at the desk with grim determination.

Grey sets the next phase in motion by calling Peter and informing him that his "fiancée" is sitting in the office. He seems to be inviting him to retrieve her. Meanwhile, he situates himself as witness to whatever is about to transpire. Addressing Peter as "fiancé" suggests Grey wants Peter and Lee to either claim what is rightfully theirs or to renounce it. Significantly, he leaves the choice to them. And Peter does indeed assert his right as "fiancé." But Lee denies the legitimacy of that right. She counterclaims that Peter is trespassing upon her domain. That is, he is encroaching on the space and position she has just established for herself. Peter tries to dislodge Lee from her position and space, by literally trying to carry her out of the office. They struggle. At one point Peter is lying on top of her, a pose that shows him "blanketing" her and crushing her personal space.

It is for this reason, I would argue, that Lee must be so merciless in her denunciation of Peter. As viewers we may be shocked by what appears as gratuitous cruelty. In fact, for someone supposedly into S and M, this act represents her only such act. But Lee knows that in order to maintain her identity, she must be decisive: the boundary must be clear for all to see. And that boundary she now defines as a "cut"—perhaps "the unkindest cut of all"—but nevertheless a severing—like Grey's severance check to her—that creates separation. When Lee kicks Peter in the balls, she is echoing one particular result of the castration complex: a "cut" of incestuous ties to the mother and of a complete overlapping ("blanketing") of their own desires.

Lee goes public

In the midst of what was at base a private transaction between Lee and Grey, the space now transforms into a public forum. This change gives Lee the opportunity to refine her position with respect to others. For the first time we see her holding court as if from a regal throne, as a succession of persons seek an "audience" with her. The first to visit is her mother, bearing "peas" (a "peace" offering) for her increasingly frugal meals, and establishing her as the one who can give or withhold nourishment. Next in line is a therapist, counseling her that "there are more conventional ways of expressing your feelings." Another visitor, a scholar, notes the longstanding use of whips and chains in the history of Catholicism. Other visitors raise similar questions about whether Lee's stance is "feminist" and whether love can be expressed in suffering. What stands out in these brief exchanges is the recognition that Lee occupies a particular, definable, and legitimate position, one that can be approved or opposed.

From her position *ex cathedra* Lee is able to reach an accommodation with her father. As if reading from a biblical text, her father states that: "Your soul and your body are yours to do with as you will." In effect he endorses her status and recognizes her right to live her own life. And he specifically mentions her body as an area over which she holds exclusive rights. In articulating these words, the father enacts a new compact with his daughter that obviates her need for further "cutting" behavior. We could say that Lee's "chair" props up the father's faltering official function. Lee thanks him for his words and her face reflects the requisite mixture of joy and sorrow.

By now her family is camped out outside the office and a crowd has gathered. Lee's cause has struck a chord with the public at large. She stops eating (or restricts her intake to three peas a day), and the media interpret her stance as a "hunger strike." In one sense, she has exchanged "cutting" for starvation—a transient eating disorder. Within the tableau she creates for the cameras, her fast represents the "cutting edge" between life and death. Its beauty consists in the simultaneous joining of tenacious resolution— she will not be moved from her spot—with extreme self-abnegation. Thus she announces to the world that "this is not about me"—"this is much bigger than me" as if the bond between Grey and herself originates in a vast collective Otherness.

The attachment transformed

Grey re-enters his office and sees Lee asleep at the desk. Amazingly, he holds her chin and feeds her coffee like a mother suckling her infant. His lips brush her cheek in a show of tenderness and a preface to their first kiss. Then he carries her out and deposits her on a bed. Incongruously she is still in her wedding dress. Grey draws a bath and unhooks her dress. Lee is still half-asleep. Cut to Lee sitting passively in the bath while Grey washes her hair with meticulous care. For the first time in the movie, her breast is exposed, a cue to maternal nurturing. Lee can now acknowledge her attachment to the earth—the earth mother, that is. And after a while, the first question she asks Grey is: "What was your mother like?"

Then we see Lee standing up in the nude, without fear or shyness. She exposes herself fully to Grey and he is no longer tempted to flee. Lee's nudity flows from her stance of putting all her cards on the table. It is a way of announcing: this is me in the "all together." For the first time she appears to fully inhabit her body. Hence she is finally able to grant her lover access to it in a way that was previously impossible. As he explores her body, he re-discovers and locates each of her scars—the traces of all the cuts and burns. Now, however, the traces undergo a change of function: they are no longer simply the jagged edge of a boundary; they are mementos and reminders of past events.

Interestingly, this line of thought prompts Lee to question Grey about his own past history. Her interest in getting to know him attempts to rebalance the scales, for, while we know quite a bit about Lee's past history, we know almost nothing about Grey's. Indeed, his history has been a closed book—a file cabinet where every snapshot and relevant document has been "filed away." We do not learn the answers to her questions save one: to Lee's query, "Where were you born?" He replies: "Des Moines, Iowa." And here the film discloses its sly comic tone, for Grey answers the one question that reveals the least about him. Even in the act of self-revelation he withholds. We get the impression he will remain somewhat of a mystery.

Conclusion: the S and M cure?

The abrupt and almost miraculous marriage of its two protagonists makes for a baffling ending to *Secretary*. Jarringly, but perhaps not illogically, the movie jump cuts from our two protagonists "making love" to their life as a married couple. We see them making up their bed on a typical workday morning, with Grey the more fastidious of the two. The voiceover narration tells us that they had a June wedding followed by a honeymoon in the mountains. There is a brief clip of them making vigorous love with Lee's hands tied behind a tree. Then back at the house, Grey is leaving for work, while Lee lounges on the front porch. What could be more stereotypical? In contrast to earlier bold color choices, the hues look faded here. The element of fantasy is muted, if not missing entirely. And in concert with these changes, the camera focuses on Lee looking outward with a bland, neutral expression. Her eyes slowly pivot until she is looking directly at the viewer with a quizzical air.

The handling of this scene contradicts the tone of its "happy ending." Here everything has returned to blandness, not unlike Lee's previous limbo while floating in the pool. Yes there is still a remnant of the couple's former S and M practice in Lee's being tied to a tree, but this bondage seems merely to add spice to their conjugal relations. In the final scene, moreover, the honeymoon is clearly over in every sense, so that even this remaining prop may have fallen by the wayside. And with Lee languishing on her front porch, can mutual boredom be far behind? Who is Lee, now that she has traded her role of secretary for that of dutiful wife? And, by the same token, who is Grey? Are these roles sufficient to sustain their newfound identity?

A single discrepancy in their seemingly idyllic marriage offers a hint to Lee's disaffection. Looking at the perfectly made bed, she casually drops a cockroach on it, as if commenting in a sly manner on her husband's compulsive neatness. The message could be: things are not as neatly resolved between us as you—the audience—may want to think. Indeed, the cockroach recalls the purple worm that penetrated Grey's impervious façade, implying that perhaps the whole bourgeois marriage is mainly a "façade" hiding the true psychic reality just beneath the surface. Therefore, by casually inserting a "bug" in the system, Lee may be offering up a harbinger of things to come.

Certainly her act is meant to raise questions in our minds. The important question, it seems to me, is whether an S and M sexual practice can produce a "cure" for the protagonists' suffering. In other words, is the film's happy ending justified? It would seem at this stage of the argument that the question is left open. While retaining a skeptical eye toward the happy ending, the filmmakers do not discount the possibility of a cure. In juxtaposing both sides of the question they amplify the film's ambiguity and emotive power.

The potential pathways to cure have been implicit in the couple's progress toward rapprochement. And although the "cure" can be viewed as a simple transference cure—or the "cure by love" recognized by Freud as an alternative to the therapeutic or psychoanalytic cure (Freud, 1914), I would suggest that it more closely corresponds to Lacan's notion of the *sinthome* (Evans, 2006, pp. 188–189). According to Lacan's usage, this term differs from the more common use of the word "symptom." In psychoanalysis, a symptom represents a point of access for verbal exploration and interpretation. In the best of cases—such as that of a transient phobia—thorough analysis of the symptom results in its dissolution. That is, the symptom will have been replaced by the patient's words—words addressed to the analyst. The *sinthome* by contrast resists all such efforts. Instead, the *sinthome* functions as a "kernel of enjoyment" that provides a "unique organization of jouissance" (Evans, 2006). Most important, it offers the patient a way to keep on living, a mechanism for psychic (and possibly literal) survival. In other words, the *sinthome* acts as a kind of buttress holding body, mind, and spirit together.

The *sinthome* helps to organize the various strategies employed by our protagonists. In its role as an "organization" the couple's S and M practice is conducted with a material restraint embodied in the yoke Lee bears while performing secretarial tasks. The filmmakers depict the yoke as a rigid material object that is also comical in its impossibility. But its reality consists in the bearer—Lee—accepting it as an absolute constant that she must work around, by picking up objects with her mouth, for example. Moreover, Lee does not view the yoke as a burden but rather as a path to happiness and liberation (women's liberation?).

And within the framework of S and M practice, the *sinthome* promotes the transformation of symptoms but never their elimination. Thus the crucial transformation of "cutting" to S and M practice places the symptom within inter-subjective space and furnishes the partners greater erotic freedom while minimizing the possibilities of self-harm. Indeed for both parties, the S and M practice and its variant in domination/submission opens a space for playfulness, emotional expression, and spontaneity heretofore missing in their lives. And finally it presents a locus for identification that stabilizes each of their shaky identities. Thus Lee allows her S and M practice and later her hunger strike to represent her, while the bond with Lee offers Grey a "container" for his overflowing emotions and libidinous yearnings. Indeed their partnership begins to function as the couple's unique means to love—a strange courtship if you will—a love that defines and sustains them—and which permits them to see each other as characters in a love story.

But like the proverbial image that oscillates back and forth between two gestalts, we must end our discussion on the skeptical note already implied in the final scene. It is not only that the film's ending is too neat. It is that the viewer seems the victim of a sleight of hand whereby the S and M practice is replaced with conventional love and marriage. The edginess has been replaced with schmaltz. Their *sinthome* might have been more convincing if they had returned to the hard-edged "love" of their unadulterated S and M practice. As it is, however, Lee and Grey's marriage could fall prey to the same fuzzy complacency that brought them to this pass in the first place—a limbo that lacks the knife-edge of being bounded, bonded, and banded.

In one scene in particular, Lee is warned against expecting too much of her arrangement with Grey. The rather somber paralegal issues a warning: "There are no statutes capable of controlling relations between men and women." Regarding sexuality, therefore, laws and norms go only part way in curbing the unruly nature of sexual drives. In the long run, no amount of restraint can fully rein them in. Moreover, the constraints of civilization such as the institution of marriage leave a residue of malaise that cannot be eliminated.

This warning implies that the organization or set of restraints established by Lee and Grey is incapable of fully containing and regulating the couple's "psychosexual disorder." The movie depicts this impossibility as the ongoing struggle over the typos. It seems that no matter how many times Lee corrects her typos, they keep cropping up. The typos represent that residue of the real that resists being scripted. Thus in yet another sense, the typo is the true *sinthome*—the symptom that resists correction or reduction to "sense." For this reason, Lee's scars should not be regarded as mementos of her past but as points where memory has failed to integrate events within a scripted narrative.

Hence, I propose Lee's dropping the cockroach as a fitting and ironic coda to the more conventional Hollywood style kiss that seems to bring both the movie and the protagonists' love to consummation.

CHAPTER SEVEN

Sexual Undertow in *Little Children*

In the opening scenes of *Little Children* (2006), a placid American bedroom community is driven to the edge of panic by the discovery that a convicted sex offender is living among them. His offence is "exposing himself to a minor." That is, the man in question exposed his penis in front of a child and masturbated. The filmmakers, I would argue, were deliberate in the way they present the offender's actions. They could have characterized the crime as murder, rape, or physical assault, as other movies involving pedophiles have done (as does the book of the same name on which the movie is based) (Perrotta, 2004). And they make sure that never during the film will Ronnie—for that is his name—actually menace or endanger a child. So we have to at least consider that the local media, in raising the alarm about him, might be exaggerating the threat he poses to others.

I begin here because it is important for the filmmakers that Ronnie not be entirely unsympathetic, that the threat he poses remains non-specific, and that the universality of his plight be highlighted. In one of the early scenes, for example, Sarah—the lead character—chides three mothers she meets in the playground for their draconian suggestion that Ronnie be castrated for his crimes. Then—perhaps feeling chastened—one of them confides that her brother used to expose himself to her in the same manner, implying that such occurrences do occur in the course of family life.

Indeed, we know from observation that small children display their genitals to others gleefully and without shame.

Accordingly, in this chapter, I posit that sexuality itself constitutes the real threat. And by "sexuality" I do not mean the watered down, domesticated version to which most people are accustomed. I mean sexuality as a shocking intrusion of the "perverse" and the "infantile" that threatens to dethrone the subject's mastery of her own narrative and destabilize relationships between marital partners, family members, and neighbors. In other words, it is not just Ronnie who is suffering from, in his own words, "a psychosexual disorder." Ronnie is merely the focal point of a roiling state of "psychosexual disorder" threatening to engulf the entire community.

In the following discussion, I will try to show how the filmmakers break down the barriers separating Ronnie's pathological condition and the unresolved sexual dilemmas facing its main characters. The film constructs multiple lines of association between Ronnie's "perversity" and perverse elements permeating the sex lives of the others. The criss-crossing of these lines reveals the influence of such sexual factors in love, in work, and in play. At first Ronnie inspires universal repugnance for embodying those sexual attributes that are problematic for most people: perversity, infantilism, and excess.

And in repudiating Ronnie, the citizenry reject him as a person and sever all their ties to him. Thus while he lives among them, he dwells in a kind of internal exile. Ronnie himself promotes his own exile by discounting the possibility of any adult relationship. Indeed, the film shows how the irruption of sexuality in its raw form, far from encouraging human ties, actually weakens them. In order to re-establish such relationships, each of the main characters must make a personal renunciation of the satisfaction afforded them by their sexual adventures. In so doing, the four reach a kind of rapprochement at the movie's end, with their own thwarted desires and with Ronnie, who now elicits their compassion.

The kiss

The first sexual irruption occurs with a playfully innocent kiss at the children's playground. On a bench sit a trio of obsessive mothers—Cheryl, Mary Ann, and Theresa. These mothers have sacrificed their desires on the altar of motherhood. Feeling thwarted in their other desires, they cope with their frustration through fantasy. Cheryl entertains them with a story about "eight couples at a spa in Mexico" that offers escape from their quotidian lives. But their most active fantasy involves a man they call "the prom king." On this particular day they see him enter the playground, his son on his shoulders, the boy wearing a jester's hat. The three women smile as the sight of him triggers the fantasy, and the effect is amplified by the man's recent absence from the park leaving a "gaping hole in the emotional lives" of the trio. It is assumed that in the fantasy, each woman is the "prom queen" to Brad's "king." Each in their own way is reliving the appreciation of their femininity in a way that contrasts with the unglamorous reality of caring for toddlers. And in order to safeguard the purity of the fantasy, the women have exchanged nary a word with Brad and actually know nothing about him. On some level they realize that such knowledge—such contact with reality—would only deflate the reverie.

Off to the side sits Sarah Pierce, mother to Lucy, who sets herself apart from these obsessive mothers as the rebel in the group: the one who refuses to merely comply with what is expected of her. She sets herself up as the sexual "liberal" of the group in order to show that she is not like them. Feeling challenged, one of the women dares Sarah to get Brad's phone number and offers her five dollars if she can bring it off. Sarah accepts. She engages Brad in conversation and she and Brad find an immediate rapport. Brad notes that, in all his visits to the playground, Sarah is the first person to actually talk to him.

Just as Brad is about to leave, Sarah draws him toward her by speaking in a whisper. She tells him about the "prom king" and the five-dollar bet and solicits his help in "freaking out" the women. Brad is intrigued. They hug. Sarah ups the ante with: "You know what would really freak them out, if you were to kiss me." They kiss tentatively and then they kiss for real. All the while, Cheryl, Mary Ann, and Theresa are watching intently from their perch.

The kiss starts out as an act of defiance against the trio's self-righteous moralism. Sarah is also, no doubt, defying the web of expectations in which she herself feels trapped. And we cannot discount the delight she must feel at "dethroning" her rivals for the prom king's affections. And for both Sarah and Brad, the kiss provides the pleasure of "getting a rise" out of their audience. Indeed, the shock it induces in the adult women and in their eyes, the danger to children, echoes the general horror and panic over Ronnie's crime.

But the little scene's most significant effect is transformation of sexual fantasy into action. It is a piece of "acting-out" such as might ensue during psychoanalytic therapy. What is not known is: Whom is the message meant for? In Brad's case it will become plausible that the message is addressed to his wife, but for Sarah we can only speculate that her absentee husband is the addressee, or possibly her MIA mother, as hinted in her subsequent encounter with Ronnie. However, it is only retroactively, when the four major characters confront the real losses they have suffered, that their actions appear staged for the benefit of a person missing in their lives.

From another angle, the enactment of the fantasy raises the level of satisfaction by an order of magnitude. The sexual fantasy entertained by the three women was mildly satisfying in and of itself. But that satisfaction depends on the non-realization of the fantasy, for only the knowledge that the longed-for tryst will never happen allows the daydreamer to imagine the fantasy in all its vivid detail. The structure of the fantasy helps to "contain" the various desires within defined limits. With the breaching of those limits, we are dealing with the *realization* of the fantasy. The realization of the fantasy pushes satisfaction to the limit and pushes the limit of satisfaction. The resulting erotic charge crosses the oral boundaries of the two soon-to-be lovers. That energy swells to near orgiastic proportions when the kiss expands into the full expression of sexuality.

Sarah and Brad's thwarted desire

The kiss and its aftermath raises the question: What primes the pump? What factors in the pair potentiate the kiss and light the fuse of their sexual yearnings? The answer is surprisingly clear in the movie's exposition. Both Sarah and Brad are thwarted in their innermost desires to the point where they are not getting what they want out of life.

Let us review the state of their desires starting with Sarah. In the area of work, Sarah had many intellectual interests while she attended college. As an undergraduate she shared an intense interest in feminism with a like-minded group of women. But having lost touch with her old friends, her interests have shrunk down to a tiny study furnished with a small library. This study is a narrow space within a cavernous house owned by her husband, Richard. Other than her study, there is nothing in this vast space she can call her own.

There are two small events within the house that highlight the sad state of her desire. While trying to steal a few minutes in her study, Lucy raps on the door. Rather than opening the door immediately, Sarah asks her child for "a minute." In that moment we see that Sarah views Lucy primarily as an impediment to her own desire. Indeed, if it were not for Lucy, she would have all the time in the world for her intellectual pursuits. Moreover, in all the early scenes between the two, Lucy fails to elicit excitement, enthusiasm, or joy from Sarah, although she does evoke an almost slavish compliance with her demands—demands that include not sitting in either the stroller or the car seat. Thus, Sarah does not reject Lucy; she deals with her paucity of desire by dutifully fulfilling her maternal duties. And interestingly, she is not at all devoid of maternal feeling or of the capacity to love.

Within roughly the same time frame, Sarah raps on the door of her husband's study, where he is often holed up. When she finally opens his door, she finds him masturbating while sniffing a pair of underpants he got from a woman named Slutty Kay. We will have more to say about the fetish theme but for now, let us simply note how the tables have turned. In a flash she realizes that she is not the object of Richard's desire, and probably never was. She is no more than an impediment to his self-absorbed quest and a footnote in his life. And unlike the case with Lucy, Sarah realizes that Richard is incapable of love for anybody but himself. Her marriage is therefore unsalvageable.

Sarah's attitude toward the other mothers at the playground reveals her protest against this state of affairs. She makes that protest explicit at a book club meeting attended by Mary Ann, her arch-rival at the playground. In many ways she identifies with Emma Bovary, the subject of the discussion, in her refusal "to accept a lifetime of misery." Like Emma, she wants to "reclaim her sexuality" in order to validate her desirability. And in pursuance of this aim, she is captivated by the idea of challenging sexual boundaries and norms as a means of breaking free of societal expectations.

Turning now to the state of Brad's desire, we find the same thwarted desires in the areas of love and work. Just as Sarah does not desire her "job" as mother, Brad—a law school graduate—has no desire to be a lawyer. He has failed the Bar exam twice and he regularly "plays hooky" during the afternoons he is supposed to be studying for his third attempt. It is Kathy, his wife, who wants him to be a lawyer, in part so he can support her career as a documentary filmmaker, an endeavor she pursues with passion. What does excite Brad is the fluid grace of a group of teenage skateboarders or his soon-to-be-discussed participation in a men's touch football game. We are led to infer that Brad would much rather work at something involving physical skill such as sports, police work, or firefighting. However, to pursue or even acknowledge these wishes, Brad would have to negotiate a rather thorough-going realignment of his marriage. Up to now it just seemed easier to comply—superficially at least—with Kathy's demands.

Brad perceives that he is not the main object of Kathy's desire. Her primary object of desire is Aaron, their three-year-old son. Kathy is besotted with her son and sees him as perfect. One night when Brad sees a rare opportunity to make love to his wife, he asks her if they can move their sleeping son to his own bed. But Kathy demurs. Thus Aaron becomes a literal barrier between the two spouses. But more than this, Brad senses that Aaron—at least at this time—completely fulfills Kathy's desire and there is little if any left over for him.

Let us note that for both Sarah and Brad desire means to a large extent *being desired*. The kiss brings together their mutual yearning to be desired by the other. And a strong component of "being desired" is being desired as a man and as a woman. Interestingly, one of the first things Brad shares with Sarah is that he "doesn't wear the pants in the family." Sarah, however, is not at all put off; she rather likes the fact that Brad is not the usual macho guy, despite his enviable physique. And for her part, Sarah is flattered that Brad chooses her over Kathy, whom Brad describes as a "knockout."

Indeed, Sarah's slightly disheveled and unglamorous appearance is supposed to suggest a "manly" aspect that attracts Brad. And for Sarah's part, the fact that Brad "does not wear the pants in the family" may be precisely the thing that attracts her. Thus the subtext of their desire may involve a reversal in which Sarah is desired as a man and Brad as a woman. Or just to complicate matters, each may desire a different version of the phallic woman: Brad the woman with a phallus; Sarah, the feminized male with a phallic member.

Brad and Larry

The affair between Sarah and Brad intersects with two other relationships that share the same tension between desire and orgiastic release. The first of these begins when Larry, a police officer on medical leave, pulls up in his car and jovially calls Brad a "pervert" just as the latter is thinking about his kiss with Sarah. Brad bristles at this accusation and the added remark that maybe "he likes little boys." Larry had seen Brad staring intently at the young skateboarders.

Nevertheless, the two men who had up until this moment been distant acquaintances develop an unlikely (and at first grudging on Brad's part) rapport. In Larry, Brad discovers a kindred spirit whose desires are also thwarted at work and in his marriage. Larry immediately recruits Brad as a partner in his crusade to protect the community from Ronnie's "perverted" predations. At the same time, and almost as an afterthought, he invites Brad to play quarterback in a night-time hard contact touch football league. Brad had played quarterback for his team in college.

Thus the men bond over actions that will elevate their deflated sense of masculinity. Brad is skeptical about the mission to "save" the community from Ronnie, but he appreciates Larry's need to protect families. And perhaps the focus on Ronnie's perversity deflects attention from the muted homoeroticism between the two, hinted by Larry's jokey accusation that Brad "likes little boys."

The football league on the other hand affords socially acceptable "hard contact" with men alongside the pleasures of physical skill and movement. And for Brad, the chance to regain some of his status as a star quarterback offers a powerful boost to his sagging male ego. On the field, under the bright lights, Brad feels "the same excitement as when he kissed Sarah. It was as if his world had cracked open revealing a previously undisclosed possibility." Hence the "bromance" between Brad and Larry emerges as a male version of Sarah and Brad's affair. There is the same instant rapport, the same thwarted desires, the same erotic charge—this time displaced onto the playing field—and the same powerful release. The director emphasizes the intense physicality through shots of men hitting and being hit, all the while emitting grunts, groans, and roars.

These trends reach their apotheosis late in the movie during the team's final game. In the interim they had played a game, which they lost, although Brad acquitted himself well. In that game, Brad passes a test of male tenacity and is fully accepted by his teammates, who are all cops. The final game, however, is a veritable orgy of male physicality and aggression. We hear primal yells. And then Brad has his moment of triumph, throwing a pass for a last-minute touchdown that wins the game.

Unexpectedly, the scene shifts to Sarah in the stands whooping and cheering, and wild with joy. For Brad, this is like the icing on the cake. He basks in Sarah's adulation. He admits that he wants to stay in this moment forever, as it represents "infinite possibility"—and we may add: the infinite *fulfillment* of those possibilities, in a word, perfection. Brad and Sarah then kiss on the field, in effect consummating this merger of male triumph on the field with sexual fruition.

Ronnie enters the pool

Earlier, when Brad and Sarah were on track to reaching the climax promised by their first kiss, Ronnie intersects their storyline with a public spectacle of his own. Having no life of his own and feeling like a virtual prisoner in his mother's house, Ronnie decides to take a swim in the town pool. In the summer heat, everyone—including Ronnie—wants to "cool off." But his perfectly understandable desire to exercise the same freedom as his neighbors becomes freighted with sexual significance in the set piece that follows.

Ronnie enters the pool area with snorkel gear. He puts on the mask and flippers and then jumps into the pool. It is not at all clear why the gear is necessary. Maybe it just makes it easier for him to swim underwater. The mask permits him to see bodies—including those of children—close up. And it momentarily disguises his identity like any mask would. The gear itself poignantly alludes to adventures exploring coral reefs that Ronnie will never have. And where Ronnie is concerned, the flippers suggest a rubber fetish or alternatively a condom. In a strange way the equipment insulates Ronnie from others and they from him, which is just the way he wants it. And decked out in his gear Ronnie resembles an "alien"—a creature from the black lagoon, for example.

When Ronnie takes off his mask, the first person to recognize him is Sarah, sitting on the grass with Brad, Lucy, and Aaron. "Its him," she says with a tone of contempt. Now consider that her indignant response is similar to that of Mary Ann and her cohorts after witnessing the kiss at the playground. The analogy is supported by the parents' mad dash to remove their children from the pool. Then we see them arrayed around the pool's edge, staring at him like a monster in their midst. Ronnie swims a few desultory laps but he probably realizes that the show is over. Two cops are called in to politely escort him away from the area. Ronnie raises his arms shouting: "I was only trying to cool off!" Was he being disingenuous?

Swiftly, the film cuts to a gathering thunderstorm prompting the lifeguards to evacuate the pool in the interest of safety. The lightning storm has the same disturbing effect on the swimmers as Ronnie's presence a few moments before. The sudden downpour leads Brad and Sarah to run with their children to Sarah's house. The exhausted Lucy and Aaron are put down for a nap. All these changes serve as prelude to Brad and Sarah consummating their affair. Wandering in the house, Brad comes across a book of poems with the line "love is like a fever." When their two wet bodies finally come together, the clothes dryer in the laundry room buffets loudly back and forth. When its buzzer goes off, Sarah and Brad reach orgasm.

Thus the sexual imagery suggests that Ronnie—despite his declaration of innocence—entered the pool with a burning need for sexual release. He must have known on some level that his visit to the pool would trigger panic, so we can postulate that he did it in part to cause a stir. And that momentary "tempest"—perhaps equivalent to his masturbatory excitement—represents one of his few remaining pleasures.

Ronnie and May

The pool escapade illustrates a basic fact about Ronnie's life: he has given up the possibility of pursuing his own desires as opposed to his immediate gratifications. His plight is partly due to the external restrictions imposed upon him: his registration as a sex offender, the requirement that he live with his mother in his mother's house in a state of virtual house arrest, and the obvious impediments to his obtaining a job or making friends. Thus we could view Ronnie's visit to the pool as a desperate attempt to break out of the prison of constraints and negative expectations under which he lives. Most of the time, however, Ronnie simply succumbs to his terrible lot in life.

But for the main cause of his inertia we need look no further than the *arrest* of Ronnie's relationship to his mother in early childhood. This arrest is indicated by the décor of May's house, with its antique clocks, and her collection of figurines depicting "little children." May herself looks "arrested" at the age of forty (although she appears closer to eighty) with her long grey hair falling about her shoulders. And Ronnie reveals his true age when he calls her "mommy." When May declares him to be a "miracle"—a view at odds with current reality—she could easily be talking about her feelings for him at the moment of his birth.

We can describe the cloying intimacy between May and Ronnie as the mutual saturation of desire. That is, Ronnie represents for May the absolute fulfillment of her desire—in Bruce Fink's words—the "be-all and end-all" of her life (Fink, 1999), despite his all too obvious imperfections. And Ronnie identifies completely with May's static image of him. He is totally dedicated to satisfying May's every wish. His mind is like a "supersaturated solution" of his mother's desires that crowds out any wishes of his own. Like an impish genie, his motto is: "Your wish is my command."

However, the simultaneous awareness of the reality of their lives together adds poignancy to their bond. May knows full well what Ronnie is up against and she worries how he will fare after her death. And Ronnie, as we have noted, has a brutally realistic appraisal of his lot in life. In an attempt to allay her concerns about Ronnie's future May suggests that Ronnie place an ad in the personal column of the local newspaper with the aim of meeting a woman his own age. The viewer must judge how serious are the pair in actually taking a step toward separation.

Ronnie agrees to May's proposal but will only promise to go on one date. May helps Ronnie craft a positive description of himself, and when a suitable woman responds to the ad, she advises Ronnie about what to wear. May acts as if Ronnie is taking a date to his high-school prom. The viewer may well ask: is he a fractured version of the "prom king" or just a laughable "court jester" à la Aaron with his jester's hat?

The scene then shifts to Ronnie dining at a restaurant with his date, Sheila, nicely played by Jane Adams. At the table, Ronnie queries Sheila about her past life and does not shirk from asking about her mental breakdowns, starting when she was in college. Sheila also admits she hasn't had a serious boyfriend in six years. At this stage it appears as if Ronnie is making a genuine effort to communicate with Sheila. He expresses solidarity with her dysfunction and social rejection. When Sheila disparages her potential as a mother, Ronnie replies: "You're not so bad."

What seems strange, however, is Ronnie's almost preternaturally self-assured demeanor. He appears utterly devoid of anxiety, an odd reaction in someone who probably never had a girlfriend. It is possible that his calm derives from the mental distance he takes from the encounter: perhaps he never had any intention of seeing Sheila again, after his promise to his mother of "just one date" was fulfilled.

And this possibility is confirmed the moment Sheila says to Ronnie: "You seem like a nice person." She implies that perhaps—just perhaps—he will be different from the many men who have treated her badly and abandoned her. Ronnie "answers" her not in words but by masturbating in front of her. Sheila is hurt but not overly surprised. This would have been enough to signal that whatever she thought they had is over. However, Ronnie gives the knife an extra twist by threatening to "getcha" if she ever tells on him.

Ronnie's sudden reversion to type calls for comment. First, there is the possibility that—whatever his intention—Ronnie did feel a moment of connection with Sheila. We could then posit that Ronnie sabotaged the relationship out of fear of it becoming real, or just from the sadistic delight in deflating Sheila's hopes. Perhaps both causes were in play. Yet he might also have staged the encounter entirely for May's benefit as if she were looking on from above (as she does in the frame when Ronnie re-enters her home). He might have thought that sabotaging the relationship was exactly what May desired in her heart of hearts. At the same time he could ridicule her pretense of wanting Ronnie to succeed with another woman. In this respect, his masturbation is also for his mother's benefit, as proof of his infantile bond with her, as provocation to her façade of moral rectitude, and as the culmination of his physical perfection in her eyes.

In this light, it must be understood that Ronnie's dark warning to Sheila is also strictly for his mother's benefit. For May is the only law that Ronnie recognizes. Her desire has the force of law for him. In Ronnie's mind nothing must mar or deface his mother's little icon. This logic, namely that one may murder someone in order to prevent them from "tattling" to other "little children," suggests an underlying vein of psychosis.

Larry goes on a rampage

In the latter third of the film, the director stages a third set piece on the order of "the kiss" and Ronnie's swim in the town pool. However, this scene adds two crucial elements: the turning point in the movie's plot, and the introduction of the element of loss. In addition to the perverse, infantile, and irruptive aspects of psychosexuality, there is also its propulsive aim to recreate the lost object in all its plenitude and therefore to disavow the possibility of loss.

In the preamble to Larry's rampage, little cracks in the surface begin to emerge. They all arise out of Larry's ongoing crusade to harass Ronnie and to trumpet his perversity to the world. In his campaign, Brad plays the role of confidant and male ally. However, after the first football game with Brad as quarterback, Larry makes a surprising confession: he felt "slow and fat" on the field and therefore inadequate as a man. Then he reveals that his wife, Joanie, left him and took their two kids to her mother. This happened after he called her a "slut" in front of the kids. This episode in itself crosses the line into "indecent exposure." Larry has no ready explanation for his behavior.

But the only explanation that makes sense is that he wrongly suspected his wife of sleeping with another man—another man better equipped than he.

Brad, feeling uncertain over how to respond to Larry's disclosure, shifts the conversation to Ronnie's swim. But apparently Larry knew nothing about this and the fact that it occurred behind his back, so to speak, adds fuel to his growing frustration. Larry enters a state of frenzy, yelling at Brad and driving the car with reckless disregard for safety. All along he has harbored a "hard on" for Ronnie, and now he can hold back no longer. He stops by May's house and bangs on her door, demanding to see Ronnie and issuing vague threats.

May, however, refuses to be intimidated and suddenly turns into Ronnie's protector and avenging angel. She accuses Larry of being a bully and immediately the impact of her word is apparent. Larry appears chastened. Then May reminds Larry that he shot an unarmed black teenager at the local mall—a fact that was unknown till now. As the *coup de grâce*, May declares: "My Ronnie would never do that." Thus even though it is doubtful whether May has taken the moral high ground (it is not out of the question that Ronnie is incapable of murder), she at least exposes the murderous rage behind Larry's crusade.

Once again, Larry tells Brad the backstory. He calls the boy he shot by his name, Antoine Harris. Afterwards, Larry was diagnosed with PTSD and, because of his dysfunction, had to resign from the police. This admission, compared with his earlier claim to be on "medical leave," testifies to the significance of his loss: giving up the only job he ever wanted and the one pursuit that gave him true satisfaction. But the enormity of what Antoine's parents must be going through is still too much for him to take in. Yet he has at least registered the loss of his wife, his kids, the boy he killed, and his beloved job. In formally recognizing the dead boy as Antoine Harris he makes a first tentative step toward reconciliation.

But it is insufficient to quell the climactic rampage, triggered by a further rejection of Larry's manhood. After the final game, scene of Brad's triumph, Larry interrupts Brad and Sarah's blissful reunion with the expectation that Brad join him at the local bar to celebrate. Brad, however, rebuffs him, promising vaguely to meet him there later. Brad's tone is unduly harsh, and it causes Larry to question whether Brad is a true friend. Larry waits for him at the bar until the bartender literally throws him out. Thus the final prop supporting Larry's manhood gives way.

At this point Larry goes on his final rampage. He once again drives to May's house. On this occasion, he wields a bullhorn, and his warning that "there is a pervert in our midst," reverberates throughout the block. May comes out shouting and the pair fight over possession of the bullhorn. Neighbors, including children, are witness to the fracas. Everybody senses that Larry has gone too far. In contrast to Ronnie's relatively impassive reaction, Larry's disturbing outburst seems more alarming than Ronnie's presence in the neighborhood. Then May falls to the ground from a heart attack or stroke—an intimation of her death. The neighbors rush to her aid and call an ambulance.

What stands out in this final confrontation is Larry's utter lack of restraint and his need to stage a spectacle in front of the children, echoing the earlier incident with his wife. The sight of him and May wrestling over the loudhailer is like a darkly comic primal scene in which the man and the woman appear to be struggling for possession of the one phallus. When Larry wins this battle with overwhelming force, his adversary/lover falls dead. And with this denouement, his "fever" breaks and he is left to contemplate his impotence in the wake of yet another loss.

Brad and Sarah go their separate ways

Potential fissures in Brad and Sarah's sexual liaison arise almost from the start, for they approach their first tryst with some trepidation. Even as they embrace, Brad breaks the mood slightly, admitting he feels bad about what they are doing. In a later scene with the couple lying naked, Brad hesitates before "doing it again." He shares with Sarah his worries about that night's football game. Thus on some level—and in addition to his anxiety about sexual performance—Brad may wonder if their tryst alone can restore the physical exultation he enjoyed when playing college football or recover the lost sense of "infinite possibility" he felt as a child.

Later, while wandering through Sarah's house, he discovers a cheesecake snapshot of himself taken near the pool with his shirt off. He pauses over this photo. We sense that pause reflects the gap he feels between this image and his more realistic self-appraisal. It might also lead him to wonder who is the object of Sarah's infatuation: Him or his sexualized double? The pause meshes with his qualms and hesitations.

However, it is not long before Sarah introduces qualms of her own. In one of their lovemaking sessions, Sarah asks Brad—seemingly out of the blue—if Kathy (Brad's wife) is pretty. Thus she immediately inserts another party—her chief rival—between herself and Brad, and in so doing dampens their mutual self-abandonment. Brad reports that Kathy is a "knockout" but that—in his mind—"beauty is overrated." Now it is not just Kathy's looks but Brad's attitude that acts as a wedge issue between them. From Brad's point of view, he is being honest because, as we have noted, the relative attractiveness of the two women is not the primary factor at play. However, for Sarah, his attitude reflects complacency born of his own beauty. For Sarah, Brad's infatuation with her represents recognition of *her* beauty as if in a magic mirror, and a belated victory over the "prom queens" from her high school days.

The wedge widens when Sarah sees Kathy for the first time, dropping Brad off at his house before the weekend. This weekend is one of several intervals when she feels the pain of being apart from Brad. And that distress—and now an element of grief—is compounded by her dawning awareness of Kathy as an interested party in their affair. Her fantasy that she and Brad can love each other freely with "nobody to answer to but themselves" is wearing thin.

And indeed, Kathy is already suspicious. After Brad and Sarah make the reckless decision to go away for the weekend when Brad is supposed to be taking his Bar exam, Kathy asks Brad why he didn't call in the night before. She no longer takes his "absences" for granted. At home, Aaron has been telling Kathy about his friend, "Lucy," yet Brad says he doesn't even know Sarah's name, a claim Kathy finds doubtful. She proposes they invite Sarah and Lucy over for dinner to see what falls out. Brad reluctantly agrees.

The dinner conversation that follows stages the developing wedge issues in stunning fashion. The presence of Richard, Sarah's husband, at the table is already jarring because he has been absent from the movie since Sarah's discovery of his fetish. He describes his work as a kind of packaging or "branding" that—like his fetish—deceives the buyer about what's inside. And his deceptive pitch intersects Brad and Sarah's efforts to deceive Kathy.

But then there is one beautiful moment when the façade dissolves. Somehow the conversation had turned—as it always does—to talk of the predator/pervert. Sarah offers her opinion that people are overreacting to him, lighting fires on his porch, for example. Kathy, seeking to bring Brad into the mix, contends that her husband is biased because of his friendship with Larry, the very person responsible for "overreacting" (as well as being

Brad's teammate on the football squad). Without thinking, Sarah says to Brad: "I didn't know you knew that guy".

In that moment, Sarah unconsciously reveals that she knows Brad. But she is so shocked by his lack of transparency she still doesn't get it. She blurts out: "He was on your team, you never told me that!" From this point on, we know that Kathy knows. The dinner conversation will galvanize her to take a more active role toward Brad, who at this juncture still holds on to the illusion of Kathy's ignorance (or perhaps, in his mind, her indifference).

Despite these chinks in the wall of their solidarity, Brad and Sarah make one more desperate and ultimately futile attempt to rekindle their fantasy of running away. They conspire to meet at the park from whence they will flee the scene with their children. But this meeting never takes place. Brad becomes diverted and Sarah waits in vain. And that dis-synchrony between their two time lines, that expectation that is never fulfilled, that plenitude that is never attained, breaks the erotic circuit. It means the two are not, and never really have been, "on the same path." In accepting this reality now, they choose to go their separate ways, acknowledging Sarah's warning that what they had is "wrong and its not real."

Ronnie commits an unthinkable act

At the hospital, Ronnie is informed of his mother's death. At first he is at a complete loss. At home he goes through May's belongings and among them finds a letter addressed to him. Before reading it, he washes and neatly stacks the dishes, almost as if he were putting his affairs in order. The letter consists of just one line: "Please be a good boy." The apparent impossibility of complying with this last request sends him into a frenzy of grief, fury, and despair. He gives out an agonized howl. Then as if cued by the chiming of one of the clocks, he begins smashing his mother's figurines of "little children" in a frenzy of iconoclasm.

To understand this act, we must return to the opening sequence of the movie when these figurines are shown in close-up. On first glance these doll-like figures appear "cutesy," sentimental, and innocent. But Todd Field has shot them in such a way that their hidden concupiscence stands out. Some are arranged in boy and girl pairs. Their lips are painted bright red. Their gazes all point askance, never toward the viewer. Their eyelashes are impossibly long. In several, the mouth is half-open in a pout. In one case, the child's buttocks are exposed. In another, the little girl is vainly trying to prevent her skirt from riding up over her thigh.

Seen in this light, we can think of the figurines as both miniature sex-dolls and kitschy religious icons. Consciously, May wants Ronnie to "be a good boy." Unconsciously, she wants him to expose himself to her and to the world. Ronnie feels torn apart by his inability to reconcile these two demands. And with his last desperate act he vainly attempts to break free from his position as object of May's religiosity and sexual ardor.

And in his grief, frustration, and despair, Ronnie sees only one path forward. In his mind, the logic of the situation requires—indeed demands—that he undertake the one single action that guarantees he will be a "good boy." We see him picking up a kitchen knife and know that he is about to castrate himself. In this moment, we recall various characters such as Mary Ann and Larry recommending castration as the ultimate solution to Ronnie's perversity. And now he in effect enacts what they want—and what in his heart of hearts he thinks everybody wants. His act thus takes on the significance of a collective rite—an act of bodily sacrifice for the good of the community.

From another angle, however, Ronnie, with one stroke of the knife, renders himself capable of entertaining a desire; while simultaneously nullifying his ability of satisfy it. In this regard, let us note that self-castration only eliminates sexual satisfaction for *him*. As we have just noted, his act may satisfy the desire of the *Other*. Moreover, the dimension of desire still lives on as "impossible desires." As we saw in the case of the trio of mothers, knowing that a desire is impossible to fulfill is not a deterrent to fantasy, indeed quite the opposite: Ronnie's capacity for fantasy could actually be enhanced. Self-castration is not unknown among psychotic individuals (as are other forms of self-mutilation, such as putting out one's eye), a fact that suggests Ronnie lacks the mental resources to make an act of separation on the symbolic plane. However, his action—at least within the film's domain—opens the possibility of recognizing a lack within himself and of reaching out to others to fill it.

The foursome of Brad, Sarah, Ronnie, and Larry re-establish ties

It is revealed almost in passing about halfway through the film that Brad lost his mother when he was a teenager. In retrospect, we can view his affair with

Sarah as an attempt to master this loss by re-establishing that state of "infinite possibility" that, in his mind, held sway in the frozen moments before
she died. He therefore reacted to his wife's besotted attachment to their son,
Aaron, as a repetition of the original loss and his "acting out" sent a message
to her that he felt taken for granted. Indeed the real possibility she could
lose Brad rekindled her desire for him—a desire that had been displaced by
her "love affair" with her son, but never extinguished.

However Brad needs a near fatal mishap with a skateboard to fully realize the reality of loss. The loss of consciousness is at once a final moment of
supreme bliss, a wake-up call, and a second chance. That is, it replaces the
repletion of "infinite possibilities" with "lack" and the promise of rekindled
desire. Hence upon awakening, Brad asks the EMTs to discard his farewell
letter to Kathy and "call my wife." And with these words, he re-commits
himself to his wife.

The deaths of Brad and Ronnie's mothers, Larry's separation from his
wife, and the absence of parental involvement in Sarah's life introduce the
dimension of loss and specifically the role of the lost object in the psychic
life of all four. In Sarah's case, for example, her friendship with Jean, an
older neighbor, recapitulates in reverse her feeling of never having been
the object of her mother's exclusive attention. As a babysitter, Jean is the
good mother to Lucy that Sarah is not. She is excited at the mere sight
of Lucy, for example, and unlike Sarah, engages her in stories, play, and
art projects. Toward the end when Sarah lies to Jean about her tryst with
Brad, Jean signals disappointment that Lucy is not receiving the mothering
she deserves.

If we reverse the situation, we can guess that Sarah is playing out the
role of Lucy, the unwanted child deprived of her mother's attention. And
like Brad, she seeks to recover the caring mother she believes she never had.
Mostly she tries to bring her to life in the affair with Brad. One might think
that in Brad she was looking for a father figure, and this could be true on
some level. But the movie emphasizes mothers by calling the women at the
playground and those at the community pool, "mothers." We had noted that
Sarah's attraction to Brad was partly based on his maternal aspect—the fact
that he is a good and competent mother to Aaron, for example, and initially
supports and assists Sarah in caring for Lucy.

Now cut to the final scenes when Sarah is pushing Lucy on the swing,
waiting for Brad's return. But while praying for Brad to reappear, she is interrupted by Ronnie moaning in pain. Ronnie has come to the playground

right after castrating himself. Sarah asks him if he needs help. He nods. Then the following interchange takes place (Field & Perrotta, 2006):

Ronnie: "She's gone."
Sarah: "Who's gone?"
Ronnie: "Mommy—Mommy's gone."
Sarah: "I'm sorry."
Ronnie: "She loved *me*. She was the only one."

In this moment Ronnie engages all of Sarah's empathy. The words "mommy's gone" strike a deep chord in her. We are justified in thinking that she is reliving the loss of her own mommy. When she apologizes, she is approaching her own sense of remorse at neglecting Lucy. Ronnie's last words are devastating. When he lays stress on the word "me" he refers to his mother's absolute devotion and preoccupation with her child, a hoped for and expected emotional state for new mothers (Winnicott, 1958). And his last words suggest, not only that she was the only one to love him; but that he was the object of her *exclusive* love and desire. This idealized and now unrecoverable lost object is exactly what Sarah had been praying for a moment ago.

And then in a great cut, we see that Lucy is missing from the swing. Sarah frantically calls her name. Her raw and powerful calls to Lucy echo Ronnie's recent *cri de cœur*. When she finds Lucy a moment later, the weight of her potential loss falls on her with a thud. She begins to see that only by devoting herself to Lucy can she hope to ameliorate the losses she has suffered. And the immanence of loss has shown her the depths of her previously suppressed love. In her profound apology to Lucy, she reveals an immediate connection to what Ronnie had stirred in her moments before. She recommits herself to Lucy as Brad had recommitted to Aaron and Kathy. And in so doing, she relinquishes the futile search for the lost object and accepts the sacrifice of some of her own satisfactions that parenthood requires. In asking Lucy if "she would like to go home" she intimates that Lucy's mother has returned and that *she* can return to the place at which her mother abandoned her.

In a similar storyline, Larry reaches out to Ronnie. He also encounters him at the playground—one of three crossroads in the community where people meet and mingle. He offers a sincere apology for harassing Ronnie and for whatever role he may have played in May's death. Shortly, he will take Ronnie to the hospital in an effort to compensate for the boy's life he took at the mall.

Receptive to Sarah and Larry's overtures, Ronnie drops the blanket covering him. In a shocking instant, he "exposes himself." We see bloodstains on the back of his briefs. Larry cries: "Oh no." The actual sight is left to the viewer's imagination and evokes a combination of revulsion and compassion. Yet in a way this poignant scene makes for a suitable coda to the other set pieces where a sexually charged spectacle is staged. This is its other side: the reality of loss—of the lost organ, the lost satisfaction, and the lost object.

Indeed, the film's conclusion offers a cautionary tale on the dire consequences of sexual undertow. Each of the four lead characters come close to being carried away by it. Only a last minute reassessment—a stepping back from the brink—saves them. In that act of separation, sacrifice, or retrenchment (in Ronnie's case, literally a pound of flesh), the protagonists realize—that is, actualize—the impossibility of neatly integrating sexuality into their lives. Late in his life, Freud (1940a [1938]) noted that full satisfaction of the sexual drives is impossible because such satisfaction depends upon the full recovery of the lost object. In keeping with this idea, the film's final image of a dark and deserted "playground"—a playground without children—conveys better than words the somber and elegiac mood conducive to an acceptance of loss.

CHAPTER EIGHT

The Camera as Psychotic Object in *Peeping Tom*

Long after its clash with British censorship and its drubbing by critics, *Peeping Tom* (1960) continues to exert a deeply disturbing effect on us today, despite our belated recognition of its artistic merit. The film makes us feel that angst—indeed makes us participate in it—by transporting us down the rabbit hole of psychosis, until we—like its victims—feel the "walls closing in." Indeed, right from the beginning we are catapulted into one of the most chilling and disorienting segments in all of mainstream cinema. The first two screen images are especially ominous: a target with six arrows in the inner ring and one at dead center, and an eye in close-up, its lid twitching, its pupil adjusting. The eye is unsettling because we do not know where its gaze is coming from. Does it reflect our eye—as if we are looking in a mirror—or rather an all-seeing eye watching us?

Then cut to a deserted street in a sleazy neighborhood. It is night-time. A woman in a fur stole—likely a prostitute—is looking at items in a store window. The window display is scattered with broken manikins: female legs, torsos, arms, and breasts. Are we to infer that the woman has been reduced to a jumble of fetish objects? All at once she senses somebody watching her. A man—apparently a passerby—enters the frame. But as soon as we see his triple lens 16 millimeter camera "peeping" out from his logan coat we know he is the observer. The woman acknowledges him and offers her price: "Two quid."

We quickly infer that the man is filming her when the movie shifts to his point of view behind the camera. The lens zooms in and depicts her at the "cross hairs"—the two intersecting lines traversing the frame. The man holds her there as she enters a building and climbs the stairs. This crossing of lines will become a recurrent motif in the movie, and already offers us a hint to the observer's mindset. The compulsive need to precisely locate his subject suggests a need to pinpoint something elusive, to draw a sharp line of demarcation in a "fuzzy area." Perhaps the grid lines divide up the woman's body like the broken parts of the manikin.

With the camera focused on the woman's ankles, the man sees another woman coming down the stairs. The two women exchange complicit looks. These women crossing paths—like the crossing of lines—will assume importance later as a second recurrent motif. It opposes a young woman marked for murder by the "taint" of her sexuality and an older maternal figure who is spared this fate.

But we—and by we I mean male viewers—are too focused on the prostitute to notice her neighbor. The woman—Dora—enters her bedroom and as she turns up the electric heater, the erotic charge heats up. She throws her fur on a chair to reveal a blue top and an eyecatching red skirt. She removes her anklet—another seductive prop—and places it on the mantel. Then, just as we see her reach behind to lower her zipper, the camera abruptly pivots left and we hear a noise. This interruption alters the mood. The woman senses something amiss. The man swerves back into the frame with a long pointed spike emerging from one of his camera pods. We remain unaware that he has also affixed a circular mirror to the camera lens. A look of horror appears on Dora's face as she leans away from the point. Then we hear a scream. For reasons both practical and thematic the sight of the spike plunging into her body is not shown.

The emergence of the spike—a feature missing from the shooting script—signals a sudden intrusion into the frame and a kind of penetration of the imaginary "screen" that protects us viewers from the "reality" being projected upon it. The spike is impressively long and thin like an arrow. Is it meant to suggest the arrow hitting the bullseye in the first image? The spike is certainly phallic but does it qualify as a "phallic symbol"? Yes, it suggests the state of male erection but the immediate question is: Does it carry sexual significance for Mark Lewis, the wielder of the spike? We shall suggest that—if we see it as an erection at all—it is one split off from the mind of a man for whom sexual thoughts are unthinkable. Thus it could function as a kind of "prosthesis"—or "extra limb"—for this man whose self-image does not include a phallic member. And in the context of the camera lens, we might think of the spike as a "ray" (as in "ray of light") or laser beam that gives material form to a fatal gaze.

The appearance of the spike also springs a trap for the male gaze. The promise of illicit sex—even if this promise is purely voyeuristic—and the woman in a state of undress—lure the viewer's gaze toward the "mark," the woman in the cross hairs, the one who will become Mark Lewis' first victim. Inexorably he is seduced into sharing the camera's point of view. Then, before he can extricate himself from this position, the spike flashes before his eyes and the scream reverberates in his ears. For many, this intrusion will trigger an involuntary erotic thrill before moral scruples can be mobilized. The result is horror—not just for the victim—but also from our complicity with the impulse, if not the crime itself. In either case, the viewer feels like an accomplice.

The effect invites comparison to being forced to watch a snuff film. A snuff film refers to the filming of a murder, usually of a woman. What shocks us about such films is the inability to distinguish the filming of a simulated murder—especially with today's technology—from an actual one. Late in *Peeping Tom*, Helen Stephens—the second lead character—pleads with Mark: "Tell me this is only a film!" Thus we have to allow for a scintilla of doubt over whether the murders in *Peeping Tom* are real or imagined. And can we conceive a better prognostic for psychosis than the inability to distinguish impulse from action, thought from deed, or simulation from "reality"?

Even the first sequence, therefore, raises the question of seeing and being seen, of lines intersecting, bodies fragmenting, women crossing paths, spikes elongating, and viewers colluding. In this chapter, we will address these questions and others such as: What precipitates the psychotic state and propels Mark Lewis—the protagonist—to murder young women? What features identify his behavior as psychotic? How can psychosis coexist with a non-psychotic part of his personality capable of human relatedness? And given such relatedness, is he treatable? And, finally, just who is the "Peeping Tom" of the movie's title?

Mark Lewis versus the typical male voyeur

The following day, Mark Lewis resumes his part-time job as a pin-up photographer. His boss runs a newsagent shop that serves as a front for girly photos sold under the counter. While Mark peruses newspaper photos of his victim in the *Daily Mirror*, an older man approaches the owner and expresses interest in what he calls "views"—a euphemism for girly photos. The owner shows the man samples and we watch his face go through contortions of delight. The anonymous man's comic state of arousal contrasts with Mark's detached bemusement, as does the man's shame when, just at that moment, a fresh-faced schoolgirl enters the shop to buy candy. We sense his relief when the owner wraps the photos in a plain brown envelope labeled "educational books." In his haste, the man forgets his newspapers until the owner reminds him, and we chuckle at the depth of his sexual preoccupation. Thus the anonymous man displays all the features of a typical voyeur, and we might add, of a typical man of his time and place. Indeed, his visit to the newsagent is not unlike the moviegoer's experience watching *Peeping Tom* from his private enclave in a darkened theatre, where he can vicariously enjoy titillating images without fear of exposure.

But I would posit that the director—Michael Powell—had a more radical purpose in mind in juxtaposing Mark Lewis and the anonymous man in this scene, namely, that the vignette is there to showcase the man's sexuality, especially his attraction to its more prurient aspects. He functions, therefore, as a stark contrast to Mark's apparent lack of erotic interest. Not only is Mark not a typical voyeur, but his desires and aims in stalking and killing his victims point in another direction.

Note, for example, that while proximate to the man in the scene, there is no connection or relationship between Mark and the anonymous man. Mark repudiates such a connection. For him all other men are anonymous because they are motivated by the prospect of sex with a woman. (Interestingly, the possibility of sex with a man never comes up, but even so, it is not so much the object but the sexual aim that Mark finds repugnant.) To him, men are more or less clones (or drones) of each other. If we enumerate the other men in the movie—the man at the newsagent, the man on the movie set who asks an extra for a date, the man who lives in Mark's building, and the co-worker who questions Mark on the set—we find not the slightest suggestion of an ongoing relationship with Mark. Indeed he seems incapable of fraternal bonds.

Moreover, we must not forget that Mark helps to produce the pin-up photos. He will soon enter the back room of the newsagent in order to photograph Milly, a model who will later become his third victim. Hence the anonymous man may have in his recent possession an erotic photo of Milly that implies a distant sexual hook-up. In Mark's mind, there is a presumed link between his victims, all of whom he assumes to be sexually available, and the male drones drawn to them as bees to honey. Thus while he dismisses his male counterparts as easy "marks," he abhors the women who, in his mind, are "tainted" with sexual desire. And on a fundamental level—as we shall try to show—he repudiates the idea of the sexual couple and even of coitus itself—the literal act of coupling.

Milly and Lorraine

In a makeshift studio, Mark sets about photographing Milly in various erotic poses and states of undress. In the background stands Lorraine, an aspiring model standing with her back to the camera, her apparent nudity draped only with a shawl. The two women are immediately set apart from each other despite their obvious similarities of class and modest aspirations to "fame." Their positioning in the scene offers clues to Mark's point of view behind the camera. Milly's gaze, for example, is direct and challenging; Lorraine's, modest and demure. Indeed, from the moment of his entry, Milly assumes a taunting, teasing attitude toward Mark, comparing him to the famous fashion photographer Cecil Beaton, asking him if he has a girlfriend, and concluding that he is: "A puzzle and a half." Thus Mark may interpret Milly's boldness as an attempt to provoke sexual thoughts or to literally force such thoughts into his mind.

Then it is Lorraine's turn to be photographed. When called, she stiffens. Milly notes that this session is "her first time." She is obviously shy in contrast with her co-worker. She is further set apart by the classical beauty of her profile compared with Milly's earthier charms. Yet the impression is marred by what the script calls a "harelip" that "twists and distorts" the right side of her face. But the malformation on her upper lip is not so well defined in the movie. It could be a scar, a mole, or a birthmark (of which a harelip would certainly count as an extreme example). The director opted to leave its exact nature unexplained so that what stands out is its "thingness." Lorraine's expression is one of defiance—but not one of sexual provocation. She defies us to see her "thing"—the thing that may suggest the vulva (as if it were a genital wart)—but whose brute reality inhibits any aura of eroticism.

The most telling difference between the two women lies in Mark's ardent response to Lorraine's "look." Seized with admiration for her, he immediately wants to photograph her, that is, capture her look in a photograph.

Clearly the nevus on Lorraine's lip attracts Mark in a way that Milly's state of déshabille does not. For him, it evokes wonder and near-adoration. He points his 16mm camera at her, exclaiming: "It's my first time too." While the context of photography is obvious, Mark treats the encounter with Lorraine as a courtship dance between two innocents. He moves the camera toward her until the lens is almost touching her face. He swoons on the edge of ecstasy. The exchange amounts to a kind of lovemaking without physical intimacy. In that respect, the little pantomime is like a consummation of first love in which no virginal blood is shed, and thus the benevolent counterpart to the unseen pooling of blood around the murder victims.

Perhaps it is not too far afield to view Lorraine's nevus as a "mark" in which Mark sees himself, his birthmark, so to speak. Mark responds positively, in part because his image in the mirror of Lorraine's face pleases him and because it commemorates his existence. On the other hand, the malformation might represent him as an amorphous stillborn child—the child he wishes had never been born.

In any case it is clear that Mark grants Lorraine exalted and protected status in his eyes. He will murder Milly but spare Lorraine. And although Lorraine disappears from the movie at this juncture, she serves as a prototype for Mark's more developed relationship with Helen Stephens. So it is to that relationship that we now turn.

Mark and Helen

Helen Stephens, Mark's downstairs neighbor, accosts him on the stairs of their building. In a forthright manner, she extends her hand in greeting and introduces herself. He accepts it. She invites him to her birthday party. He demurs but wishes her a happy birthday. He is not just being polite—although he possesses fine manners—for his words express genuine feeling. He wants her to be happy that it is her birthday and he wants to share in that happiness. And in a more literal sense, Mark expresses joy that Helen was born—for that is after all what a birthday celebrates—that she is *here* talking with him. And his joy might also imply its mirror reflection: that he feels glad that he was born, that he too exists. When he utters the word "Mark" seemingly out of nowhere—*ex nihilo*, as it were—and then clarifies with: "I am Mark," he may be naming his own coming into being in the presence of Helen.

A bit later in the evening, Helen knocks on Mark's door. She brings him a large slice of her birthday cake with a candle in it. Mark responds by offering Helen water, then milk. This exchange, already foreshadowed in their initial exchange of offer and acceptance, initiates what will become a custom of gift giving. Once having learned of Mark's moviemaking, Helen pleads with him to show her his work, framing her request as: "It would be a birthday present from you to me." He could thus give the gift of his work in exchange for the cake. After screening one of his home movies, he remarks: "This is the first 21st birthday present I've ever given," to which Helen responds: "And it's the first 21st birthday present I've ever asked for." Note here the similarity with his comment to Lorraine: "This is my first time too," and the association of "first" with "birth" and new beginnings.

At this point we may ask what functions do these exchanges serve in the nascent relationship between Helen and Mark. Taken together they establish a clearly defined arrangement—a kind of formal scaffolding as it were—that holds together (and apart) the emotive aspects of their growing intimacy. And this at times ritual scaffolding is entirely *symbolic* in nature. Like traditions of gift giving in diverse cultures, the objects exchanged have no monetary or use value, or their use values are immaterial to the practice (Lévi-Strauss, 1963). Thus objects of trivial value, like a slice of cake, serve the purpose and often the "object" consists only of words, the classic example being the phrase "thank you," universally regarded as "the giving of thanks." Note also that in the practice of giving, the act of receiving, when formally acknowledged, counts as a gift. Thus "thank you" is a formal acknowledgment of a gift and a gift in itself.

Moreover, the symbolic nature of gift giving helps to prevent exploitation from playing a part in the relationship. It does so in part by emphasizing *being* over *having*. Having is the opposite of giving, since the former's only aim is acquisition. Also the exchange of non-use objects renders the two subjects of the exchange "non users," thus reducing the possibility of them using each other (the very definition of exploitation). Hence Helen makes no obligatory demands on Mark, sexual or otherwise. Their pact is based solely upon what each is willing to give.

The symbolic apparatus emphasizes the significance of seemingly minor actions and small gestures. Even the simple action of crossing a threshold takes on importance. Recall that Helen first accosts Mark on the stairs, in the public space of their building. In public space, it is far easier for Mark to follow the rules of social decorum and to relate to Helen in a warm but formal manner. But crossing the boundary into private space calls for a different approach. The slice of cake, for example, that Helen presents Mark with at the door to his apartment prompts Mark to invite Helen into his "darkroom"—his *sanctum sanctorum*. In the language of cinema the "darkroom" is the area of psychosis and Helen's proximity to this space puts her at great risk. In this space the slightest wrong move could "switch" Mark into frank psychosis. When Mark is deciding which movie to show Helen, he shines a light on her and the discordant music swells. We sense he is struggling with the urge to show her his footage of the murder, to film her reaction, and perhaps kill her as well. Luckily for Helen, he steps back from the brink.

For this reason, however, Helen must be vigilant in her awareness and enforcement of boundaries. In the midst of showing her home movies, for example, Mark suddenly shines a spotlight on her and starts filming her reactions (just as he was tempted to do when she first entered the room). Helen immediately puts her hand in front of the camera, creating a makeshift barrier. We can say that her gesture carries weight and that it helps Mark to re-establish the boundaries between him and Helen as well as the boundary between the psychotic and non-psychotic parts of his personality. Mark appreciates Helen's efforts, for at one point—near another breaking point—he advises Helen to leave the room. Helen's decision to stay is risky but ultimately convinces Mark of her position as a bulwark against his chaotic emotions. When Helen senses that Mark's emotions have reached "critical mass" she demands that he "switch it off." She means: "switch off" the projector but also, "snap out of this trance-like mental state" and switch back to non-psychotic Mark. Once again her words carry weight they would not otherwise possess. In the pause opened by her demand, Helen and Mark flee the "darkroom" together.

As their relationship deepens, Helen continues to support proper boundaries and in so doing, to demand adherence to certain basic prohibitions. The most stringent and most wide ranging is the prohibition against sexuality in all its explicit forms. This especially applies to any sexual consummation of Helen and Mark's relationship. Therefore it must also apply to any act that raises the possibility or "promise" of such a relationship, such as kissing. And it applies just as resolutely to flirting or indeed any trace of the prurient or the illicit in their growing intimacy.

The other restriction applies to Mark's camera. Helen has already blocked the lens with her hand, and in all subsequent interactions with Mark she discourages filming. Before leaving on their date, for example, Helen asks Mark to leave his camera at home. She had noticed that Mark treats it like an "extra limb" and perhaps she feels that its presence would inhibit Mark from placing full faith and trust in her. Thus her request takes the form of another exchange: leaving the object (his surrogate) in a safe and secure place in exchange for herself as an equally secure object of trust. Later she tests Mark's resolution by allowing him to bring the camera, but he trusts her enough to decline. Later, returning from their date, Helen playfully points the camera on herself. Mark recoils and pushes the lens aside, admonishing her to never point the camera at herself. Then Helen extends the rule to include looking at footage after their "date."

In planning their first and only "date," Helen seeks a pretext that fulfills all these requirements and also appeals to Mark's sensibilities. She finds it in the idea of collaborating on her project of writing and illustrating a children's book. Mark accepts with alacrity the task of taking the photos for the book. In the context of their gift giving, he agrees to do the work for nothing, as if it were a sacred duty. Thus the pretext gives the meeting a legitimate basis and Mark's response elevates it to a special—albeit platonic—place in his mind.

Yet the prohibition against sex must be continually reasserted as their rapport deepens. The urgency escalates the moment Helen sets foot inside her bedroom. As she locks and stows the camera, Mark hesitates on the threshold of her room. He tells Helen that this was his mother's room. Thus he hesitates to enter the bedroom in part because it implies the possibility—even if distant—of sleeping with Helen and because it veers too close to the thought of incest with his mother. On her way out of the room, Mark blocks Helen's passage with his arm. He seems on the verge of kissing her but holds back, drawing near the threshold of physical intimacy without breaching it. Thus the blocked kiss expresses Mark's tender feelings within a narrow zone of safety.

These emotional currents reach a crescendo at the threshold of Helen's apartment and the moment of parting. This time Helen moves to kiss Mark and her lips barely touch him. Is this not the perfect "threshold" gesture? Neither an "air kiss" nor a smooch, it lingers on the edge of both. Mark's eyes close in a kind of romantic swoon, as if the two had just made love.

In a symbolic sense, they have. And as confirmation, Mark brings the camera lens to his mouth and face, caressing it and miming the kiss that didn't quite happen. In caressing the camera lens, does Mark cross over into what I would call masturbation at one remove? Certainly the camera, in addition to its other meanings, seems to embody his split off sexuality in a detached member, prohibited on pain of death from touching any woman.

Mark's mangled history

In the context of his therapeutic give and take with Helen, Mark shows her some of his home movies. These clips offer a glimpse into Mark's disturbing history. He presents the clips in four batches. Let us review the first group with minimal commentary. In it, we see Mark in bed asleep, a light—as if from a flashlight—playing over his face. Then cut to a shot of him crying (but not wailing). We naturally assume a connection between the two shots, inferring that Mark is crying directly after and *because of* the light. In the shooting script, however, the light is pointed directly in Mark's eyes and when he awakens, he sees something that arouses terror and he screams. Both these elements are deleted from the film. Mark's crying indicates distress but not necessarily terror.

The second subgroup seems completely unrelated to the first. It shows young Mark atop a high wall looking down on a couple lying on the ground kissing. Mark is smiling. This clip is so obviously out of order (an order that could have been verified since all the clips are dated) that it casts doubt on the connection to its antecedent. Moreover, since all of the clips are supposed to show the effects of fear on the boy, according to adult Mark, this shot appears thematically irrelevant.

The third batch seems—and I stress "seems"—to show continuity with the first. Mark is once again in bed and the light shines on his face. Then a small lizard drops onto the bed. After a pause it starts moving toward Mark's outstretched hand. But just when we expect to see Mark's reaction, a floodlight blots out the scene. We see Mark starting to cry. The script, however, describes this shot as Mark screaming in terror *with no sign of the lizard.* Again the discrepancy casts doubt on whether Mark's distress is caused by the lizard directly. The viewer will note that the lizard doesn't appear particularly frightening, a fact that makes it all the more plausible that Mark could be reacting to some other factor or factors.

Then without supplying much in the way of explanation, Mark shows a fourth batch of clips with more explicit historical referents. Now we see a somewhat older Mark dressed in a coat and tie slowly approaching screen left. Then cut to a corpse laid out—it is his mother. He touches her arm and says the word "mother" followed by a rushed view of the funeral and burial. Thus, unlike the previous batches, we have a verifiable, dated event and, moreover, we do not doubt the continuity of the sequential cuts. And the same applies to the following shot showing a much younger woman whom Mark calls his mother's "successor." In the next shot we see the same woman holding Mark's hand while he looks down. Mark clarifies that his father married his second wife six weeks after his mother's funeral. The final shot occurs when the couple returns from their honeymoon. We see Mark's father give him his first camera and his son's happy expression. The script (but not the film) describes Mark "watching himself being born."

At this point, we can draw one broad inference from the clips: we cannot assume we understand them, or as Helen puts it: "I like to understand what I'm shown." Nor can we assume a connection—chronological or otherwise— between any two shots. And we cannot assume that a given shot is simply a "record" of what the camera sees. There are simply too many questions left unanswered, such as: Why is young Mark crying? If it is from fear, then what is the source of the fear? The lizard that Helen thinks of as a "pet" seems an insufficient explanation. Not only does Mark not supply answers to most of these questions but we cannot always rely on the explanations he does provide.

Consider that these clips provide the primary source of Mark's memories. It is therefore just a short step to thinking of them as "screen memories"— since they are literally screen memories—memories projected on a screen. Such a hypothesis would explain their being out of order and deprived of context. The scene of Mark witnessing the couple making love, for example, is split off from all Mark's other memories and from his conscious self-image. And the content of the shots further support the condensation of multiple events and layered meanings. The function of screen memories (Freud, 1899a) would also account for their obvious fantasy content. The lizard, for example, could be blown up to gargantuan proportions in a child's dinosaur fantasies. The movie *Godzilla* (1954) would have been familiar to the filmmakers.

The clips as a whole also remind us how little we really know of Mark's past. The portrait of Mark's father that emerges is so persecutory that we wonder why Mark harbors no feelings of (conscious) hatred toward him. Nor do we know how he viewed his mother while she was alive. He says nothing about her role or attitude toward what the father was doing to Mark. Again we can surmise that he had feelings about his father's second wife, but significantly she drops out of the narrative after the two "snapshots" of her, never to be heard from again. We shall gain some hints into these omissions through Mark's interactions with Helen and with her mother, as well as the "acting out" of the murders. But the biggest omission in Mark's history is his own role in it, for it largely records *what happened to him* rather than depicting him as an agent in his own right.

Peeping Tom goes mainstream

A subplot features a mainstream movie being shot on a soundstage. With a leading lady whom everybody on set treats as a prima donna, a director at his wits end over her gaffes, and an attractive stand-in for the lady during her frequent absences, the segment brings needed comic relief to *Peeping Tom*. Yet this "film within the film" also works as an alternate version of motifs just highlighted in Mark's history. Moreover, plot and subplot are intertwined. Each requires multiple "takes" in order to satisfy the director/serial killer. Mark, for example, can be seen going about his work as a cameraman on the "mainstream" set and later directing his "home movie" with his 16mm device. Both movies are filmed in the same studio. Vivian—Mark's next murder victim—plays a "stand-in" on the professional set and a star of Mark's "independent film." Mark kills Vivian there and her corpse turns up later in a steamer trunk on the set where she played the stand-in.

The subplot revolves around a leading lady whose flubs drive the director to distraction. When the scene opens, he has been trying to get her to "faint" in a credible manner. He tells her to forget to look stunning and to try to look "stunned." He seems to be saying that she should worry less about her effect on others and more about the effect of whatever she has seen on *her* (we do not know the stimulus for her fainting). After several more takes, she grouses that: "If I have to do this once more, I *will* faint." In her joking way, she refers to something real—an actual faint—intruding into the make-believe. And consider that if she were to drop dead—surely the most definitive intrusion of the Real—everyone on the set would just think she was doing a better job of fainting. In the aforementioned retake after the murder, the lady looks inside the trunk, screams, and then faints dead away, this time for real. Thus the fainting represents death as "absence" while the actual dead body "stuns" the leading lady and causes her to fade from the scene.

During an earlier hiatus, Mark chooses his next victim when he sees Vivian flirting with a co-worker on the set. And here is where the structural similarities of this scenario and Mark's "home movies" begin to emerge. The "leading lady" enacts the role of Mark's dead mother—the "leading lady" in his life for sure. She is "stunning" to Mark because of her beauty and the beatific aura surrounding her. And we can surmise that Mark was "stunned" to see her in death and that, in a certain sense, he has remained "stunned" and fixated on this picture. Vivian—the youthful and beautiful extra—stands-in for the leading lady, his mother. She represents the young woman Mark calls the "successor"—his father's second wife and his putative stepmother. Hence Mark's choice of Vivian as his second victim arises, not on account of who she is, but because of her structural position as sexual usurper of the maternal role.

Finally, there is the matter of the retakes whose swelling number adds to the subplot's comedy. It invites reflection on the murders that, while few in number (three), were in principle unlimited until Helen's intervention and the efforts of the police to bring them to a halt. The meaning of the "retakes"—besides indicating the compulsion to repeat—can best be expressed in the form of questions. Does each murder leave a residue in Mark's mind that can only be resolved with the next (n +1) murder? Does Mark need to seek new victims because the act fails to obliterate the memory of his dead mother, fails to dissipate her haunting presence, and utterly fails to lay her "corpse" to rest? And, at the most extreme, does each murder fail to annihilate the sexually obscene act that produced Mark in the first place?

Vivian's final performance

With Vivian's entrance onto Stage E for her upcoming role in Mark's film, we sense a looming contest of wills between the two figures, representing radically different modes of being. Their clash begins when a spotlight flashes in Vivian's face followed by a discordant clang. Then a second, third, and fourth light and sound appear. These intense lights momentarily "stun" Vivian. In each instance she calls out Mark's name. And with each exclamation she seems to stop in her tracks. In so doing she "marks" those moments of stoppage when her sensory awareness blanks out. And she in effect "names" that blockage: "Mark." Later the same word will name the "X" on the floor where she is to stand. Of course, we cannot omit the obvious: that she wants to know where Mark is and why he is doing this to her.

Mark finally announces his presence from above, atop a moveable scaffold that now begins to descend. It is as if he is alighting from on high and returning to the human realm. Yet his original elevated position will define all his interactions with Vivian. His lordly position, for example, helps to explain his mildly condescending attitude toward Vivian, whose concerns seem trivial to a man who by his own admission has nothing to lose. And from his ceiling perch, she cannot see him and only hears him as a disembodied voice. She looks all around trying to find him but she doesn't think to look up. The ceiling is also the ideal place to see everything—the big picture—from a commanding position. Moreover it holds that perspective from a single point—the point where all lines of sight converge. That point is defined as Mark's place behind his 16mm camera. And given his camera's easy portability, that place and that "point" are located wherever he happens to be.

The aptly named Vivian (meaning life) presents a contrasting modus vivendi exemplified in her dance routine. The original British audience would have recognized the actor playing Vivian as the great dancer Moira Shearer and would have understood the allusion to Michael Powell's great film *The Red Shoes* (1948). Their eyes would have been riveted on her free-form movement and its implied message of freedom from constraints. In contrast to Mark's fixed position, Vivian reveals herself through movement. She will not stay put. She postpones standing on her "mark," refusing to be pinned down to any one place, or for that matter, any one role. If she finds herself in one spot, she steps aside. While dancing to the jazz beat of her portable tape player, she makes it hard for Mark to keep her in the cross hairs of his camera lens. And she continues to defy his tightly planned agenda when she playfully jumps inside the steamer trunk at the wrong time (it is set up to catch her body after the murder).

Yet when Vivian lies inside the trunk, the camera shows Mark looming over her and looking down at her. Her dance routine over, she finds herself once again at the cross hairs of Mark's camera. And while she ponders her next move, Mark invites her to stand behind the studio camera. In so doing he aims to stabilize her location and limit her movements that up till now have zigzagged over the entire set. But once behind the big lens Vivian exclaims: "I can see you Mark, perfectly." That is, she can see Mark from the same elevated vantage point that Mark claims for himself. Then, in a direct countermeasure, Mark moves toward her with his camera, "photographing you, photographing me." Thus he attempts to regain mastery by incorporating Vivian's viewpoint within his more comprehensive overview. But from the point of view of Mark's camera, her face is blocked by the big camera's viewfinder and pushed off-center from his smaller camera's cross hairs. He responds by pivoting screen right so he can film her in profile, prompting her to concede: "I've lost you." Now she finds herself back in the cross hairs because Mark has moved into her blind spot. But suddenly she shifts away from behind the camera and gazes at him straight on.

At this point, Vivian's impish playfulness seems to run out of steam and—after a few more attempts to "step aside"—she succumbs to Mark's request that she stand on her "mark." In asking for his help in setting the mood, she yields to his authority. She and Mark are both standing yet he seems to loom over her as he gains the upper hand. He asks her to imagine "someone coming toward you" and his tone of voice turns icy. He walks slowly toward her, the camera invading her personal space. We see her feet rising as she leans backward over the open trunk. When she asks: "A madman?" he replies: "Yes, but he knows it and you don't."

In these words, Mark articulates his superior position towards Vivian. What does he know? He knows that the madman knows he is mad, and that *he is the madman*. Ergo he knows that he is mad. And his embrace of his own madness makes him all the more menacing, for if he were unaware of his psychosis, we might see it as a kind of irresistible impulse over which he has no control. But in double-downing on his awareness he in effect identifies his "I" with the "it" of psychosis, lending him a "laser-like" focus and shattering any illusion that he doesn't recognize the consequences of his actions. Referring to himself in the third person also puts him in the position of a god who knows exactly what he is doing and possesses absolute freedom to make it happen. Moreover, the use of "he" allows Vivian to cling to the *idée reçue* that Mark is only speaking hypothetically. Thus he sees without being seen; because Vivian remains captive to the "film" scenario.

And once Mark has Vivian in the "cross hairs" both literally (in his camera) and figuratively, he decides the time for talking is over. He grabs his intended victim by the throat, holding her at arms length (the right focal length?) and squelching her last question. The sudden and almost simultaneous unsheathing of the spike, and the unseen affixing of the mirror to the lens act in concert to stun Vivian and render her immobile. We can view this effect as primal and instinctual like a deer caught in the headlights. Or we can conceive her reaction as the primal response to trauma: a cessation of all thought and action while in the grip of an altered state of consciousness. And her response amplifies the chilling effect of Mark's murderous action by nullifying Vivian's subjective freedom even before she has literally faded from the scene. *And rendering Vivian immobile is especially significant because she expresses who and what she is through movement.*

But Mark's ability to cast a spell on his victim doesn't fully explain Vivian's victimhood. Consider that she has already proved herself lithe, flexible, and capable of dramatic leaps. We know she can jump and pivot on a dime. So we have to ask why the camera only shows her toes upraised as if her body was stiffly leaning backwards over the open trunk. Yet with her skill set she could have leaped backwards over the trunk, twisted to the side, or dropped to the ground and rolled. In fact, almost any movement on her part might have deflected the spike from its path. And even if escape proved impossible she could have shoved her two hands upwards under the pointed blade.

So perhaps the bigger question is why Vivian appears to surrender to her fate at the last possible moment? An answer suggests itself if we consider that perhaps she was a little bit in love with Mark, or at least infatuated with him. After all he was her director and she drew inspiration from filling what she took to be a "lack" (or desire) in Mark, namely, a woman to star in his film. She maintained this connection and the associated "positive transference" right up until the end. Indeed the last word she utters is "Mark!" vocalized in a plaintive, longing tone. In that moment, she realizes that she has fallen to nothing in his eyes and it is as if the very basis of her being had been pulled out from under her. Hence in a moment of extreme deflation of the Eros invested in her name, Vivian, she dies.

The police investigation

The discovery of Vivian's body inside the blue trunk launches a police investigation and opens the possibility that the two murders are connected. In the back seat of a police cruiser en route to the film studio, two inspectors are discussing the murder of the prostitute. One confesses that he has never seen such fear on anybody's face. The other responds: "Surely it can be explained by someone coming at her with a sharp weapon." The chief replies: "I'm familiar with that kind of terror but this is something new to me." In his statement he refers to the "face" of terror—its "emoticon" if you will.

Apparently this victim's face points to something else—something "other"—that resists capture in word or image. When the two open the blue trunk, they note that the late Vivian's face is "exactly the same," by which they mean that it exhibits the same unfathomable look.

In a later scene they are viewing the body in the trunk with the medical examiner. He confirms their hunch that the women were killed with the same instrument. However, he says nothing about the nature of the wounds or the weapon's point of entry. His omitted description corresponds to the elided shot of the death blow. The ME further notes that both women were "subject to the most violent shock." And in stressing this effect, he seems to imply they died from the sight of something incalculably horrific rather than the death blow itself. Perhaps they were already dead when the blow fell. Although all evidence points to their being stabbed in the throat, the ME's lack of confirmation doesn't rule out the eye or eyes as point of entry. The police urge him to specify the nature of the shock, but he says: "That's for you to find out." However, instead of pursuing this line of thought, the police treat it as a dead end. It is as if, faced with the "unthinkable," they look elsewhere.

Meanwhile, Mark has already inserted himself into the police investigation and made little effort to hide the fact. Indeed his entire strategy with regard to the police is to hide in plain sight by appearing in contexts that will not arouse suspicion or undue scrutiny. In this respect, the police tolerate his filming because there is nothing strictly illegal about it and after a while they simply take his presence for granted. He reveals to a co-worker on the movie set, for example, that he is filming the investigation in order to create a complete documentary and that he doesn't care about the risks. His nonchalance prompts his acquaintance to remark: "Are you crazy?" to which he nods, saying: "Think they'll notice?" He even films the two officers interviewing him. In a clever ploy, he hands over his camera to them and offers to give them the film. Disarmed by his candor and apparent lack of guile, they hand it back, tacitly condoning his project.

Asked whether he knew Vivian, he replies "mainly by sight," and in this cryptic response provides the police with the key to his strategy and thus the solution to the crime. The word "sight" hints that he is hiding in plain sight at the moment he pronounces those words. That is, he is literally telling the truth—he certainly did know Vivian by sight—in order to hide his role in the crime. And what does it mean to know somebody "by sight"? It implies that one has seen that person before and recognizes their face.

But it also implies that you can take that "face" for granted in all future encounters. This is what we mean by accepting something or someone at "face value." But when that assumption becomes axiomatic, it cannot be challenged. Indeed this error is exactly what the chief and the ME had warned against when viewing the "face" of the victims: that "face" did *not* fit the familiar picture of someone in the grip of fear. That "sight" was unrecognizable. Thus the word "sight" offered the police—if they had been able to question what appeared to them self-evident—the connection between seeing/filming and the shock of the unfamiliar. Hence in the words "mainly by sight," Mark replicates the truth of his words in the act of pronouncing them: the police know him "mainly by sight" since he has been filming them all along and they therefore accept the assumption that he is exactly what he appears to be.

The power of this illusion is made manifest when Mark is filming the police on Stage E from above. In the rigging just under the ceiling he has found the ideal hiding place, for as we saw in Vivian's case, he can only be seen if someone looks straight up. Yet he almost betrays his presence when, leaning too far out from his crow's-nest—several small items fall to the floor in full view of the police. And for an instant they look up, but to them the idea of somebody being ensconced up there seems so unlikely and so antithetical to common sense, they turn back to their examination ignoring what they have seen and failing to consider the logical possibility that somebody could be up there.

Indeed it is only out of the need for thoroughness and abundance of caution that they finally put a tail on Mark. And as we suspect, he leads them right down the garden path. The plainclothes cop (a visual pun on hiding in plain sight) sees Mark enter the newsagent where he will assault his final victim. Now we already know that this shop is a "front" or façade for the taking of "indecent" photos. Thus when the cop sees Mark filming the front of the building covered with nudie photos of women, he pegs Mark as a typical voyeur planning either to buy photos or take some of his own. In this respect, Mark's actions are familiar and recognizable because the cop harbors the same desires. And because he cannot see inside the building (Mark has lowered the shades upstairs) the officer sees nothing amiss when Mark exits the store. Ergo he has become so caught up in his imaginary scenario, he makes the fatal error of not looking inside the building. On the basis of his false conclusion, the police call off the surveillance as unproductive.

Mark meets his match in Mrs. Stephens

Our first acquaintance with Mrs. Stephens reveals her capacities as a clairvoyant, despite her obvious blindness. She and her daughter Helen live in the same building as Mark, and his name has just come up in conversation. Mrs. Stephens immediately intuits that Helen likes Mark, while noticing a "stealthy" quality to his quiet footsteps. She senses something fishy about the possibility that he knew Vivian. Thus she identifies the precise spot where the police are "blind." To Helen's amazement, she discerns Mark at the window in the act of surreptitiously peering in through the mullion crossbeams. And with this epiphany, she captures Mark's customary position behind the camera and its link to Vivian's demise. Helen asks how she knew. She replies: "The back of my neck told me," which is tantamount to claiming: "I just knew."

Later Helen introduces her to Mark, and when he extends his hand in greeting, she grabs it with both hands. She holds it for a long beat and Mark doesn't pull away. And just from his touch, she infers that Mark has been running. The clasping of hands affects Mark. To him it is not just a gesture of greeting but a genuine "joining of hands" and an "attachment" as real as an extra limb. The intimacy forged by the hands will become a channel of communication. Mark doesn't deny that he has been running—perhaps from the scene of the crime? And on the basis of their tentative connection, she asks the key question: Did he know Vivian? His denial carries little conviction. It confirms what she already suspects: that he knew Vivian and therefore he could have killed her and the thought prompts her to remark: "Pity, I prefer first-hand information." The reference to "hand" hints that the more reliable information came via the hand-to-hand connection. In fact she is already so attuned to Mark that when he pops his head back inside the room after departing, she turns toward him as if she had eyes in the back of her head. In parting she prophesizes: "I expect we shall meet again."

That meeting does indeed take place later that evening in Mark's darkroom where he is poised to screen the footage of Vivian's murder. After discovering Mrs. Stephens seated in the corner of the room, he tries to fend her off with a spotlight. She is not put off, however, and boldly approaches him with her cane extended until the end touches him. When he thrusts himself forward, he finds his path blocked by the now visible sharpened point of the cane. For once it seems that Mark has met his match—that he has encountered his mirror image and formidable female counterpart. The significance of the confrontation lies in his finding "his path blocked"—perhaps for the first time in the film. On the offensive now, Mrs. Stephens informs Mark that she can hear his movements from her room underneath his when he is loading the projector. She demands to know what movies he sees there and specifically what movie sits in his projector as they speak.

Now he admits that there is "no point in lying to her" because she "would know at once." He is beginning to acknowledge her for the "Sybil" that she is. For the first time in his life he admits that his films fail to adequately capture some "essence" without which his entire enterprise must come to naught. "It's no use," he bemoans, "I was afraid it wouldn't be ..." Is he searching for the word "complete" or "perfect"? Apparently, "the lights fade too soon" before the thing he is looking for can be revealed. "Now I have to find another one," he says. Thus the prospect of yet another murder sounds like an admission of defeat.

But as Mark nears the point of acknowledging his fallibility, if not his culpability, he slides once again into psychosis. The shift to psychosis works like an "on/off" switch that renders Mark unreachable. It has apparently been triggered by his confession and the consequent need to complete the project his failure left unfinished. In the grip of his camera's compulsion—or so it seems in his dissociated state—he unsheathes the sharpened pod. But building on her previous efforts to block him, Mrs. Stephens commands him to put the camera aside. And those words cause the "switch" to flip back to sanity much like a hair trigger. He re-sheathes the spike, bends down (in a less imposing stance), and relinquishes the cane to her hands. In so doing, he formalizes his relationship with Mrs. Stephens as an act of "femme-age."

Mrs. Stephens solidifies—or perhaps a better word would be "solders"— her fragile affiliation with Mark by boldly taking his face in her hands and touching it all over. Her aim is clearly to cement the attachment initiated by the earlier hand grip. Mark reacts by closing his eyes and comparing her action to "taking my picture." In noting that nobody has taken the time (or interest) to do this in a long time he probably has in mind his mother, and the last time he held her lifeless arm in his hand. For her part, Mrs. Stephens views her action as one more way of gaining "first-hand" knowledge of Mark through emotional and sensory attunement. For Mrs. Stephens, therefore, the process of forging emotional connections, opening up channels of unconscious communication, and making inferences based on first-hand knowledge constitute different sides of the same object.

So, in holding Mark's face, Mrs. Stephens hopes to encourage *his* receptivity to mental events that, because they cannot be photographed, have never before been articulated in speech. In Mark's act of "femme-age" he accepts—at least for the moment—the "Other" that Mrs. Stephens embodies and thus gives a nod to the possibility of "otherness." It is from this standpoint, we would argue, that she exhorts him to seek out a therapeutic situation in which he can feel safe enough to say who and what he is. In discouraging Mark from filming and forbidding him to photograph Helen, she supports the non-psychotic part of Mark's personality from "flipping" into psychosis and creates a kind of "blindness" analogous to her own. That "blindness" would reduce his tendency to see the world as a comprehensive whole, "complete in every detail."

Thus, in her final communications to Mark, she outlines a path that could return him to sanity and restore his connection to others. It would then be up to others to decide whether he is a monster or simply a limit-case of what is humanly possible. And there would be at least one person in the world who cares whether he lives or dies. In this pyrrhic victory he would be granted the existential validation he never found in life.

Helen's blind quest for the truth

Mark finds the necessary conditions for truth telling in his ongoing relationship with Mrs. Stephens' daughter, Helen. The process begins when Helen enters Mark's darkroom—which we now know to be the cinematic equivalent of the psychotic core of his psyche. Helen sees the projector set up and her curiosity prods her to "switch it on." We also surmise that the "switch" objectifies the switch to psychosis signaled by the rising and insistent piano theme. Watching the unvarnished footage of the murder, Helen's face shifts from pleased anticipation to somber attention and then to abject horror, causing her to cry out. The script observes that: "She cannot stop watching." That is, she is both captivated and appalled by what she sees. When Mark touches her from behind, she screams.

Mark warns her not to let him see her frightened. He worries that her fear could trigger his automatic murderous rampage. On the psychic level, showing fear could indicate her incapacity to "contain" his chaotic mental state. The task of "containing" Mark's violence is synonymous with accepting the painful truth about who he is. Helen senses his desire to protect her from that truth but she refuses to leave until she "knows." Although she cannot hide the fact that she is frightened, she surmounts this drawback with her steadfast refusal to abandon her post as Mark's "firewall" against a gathering storm. And it is within this emotionally fraught context that Mark finally confesses that: "I killed them."

After a sketchy account of Mark's history of abuse at the hands of his father, Helen reframes her desire to know in a way she hopes that Mark will understand. She now explains it—not as a drive—but as a means to "not being tortured for the rest of my life" by what she imagines he did. "But what if you're frightened," Mark opines. "Show me," she says, "or I'll remain frightened for the rest of my life." Thus Helen appeals to Mark's solicitude toward her. But in quite another sense, she is following up on the idea of a limit—a limit to the unfettered proliferation of her own terrible imaginings—her most violent unconscious fantasies. In Mark's case, such a limit would "contain" the psychosis that has already engulfed his life and those around him. That is, it would prevent it from escalating further and would confine it to the therapeutic space of the darkroom. We can add that, for Helen, telling the truth translates the real into a shape and form that can be mentally processed.

Helen's imperative, "show me!" propels Mark to act out the murders and their accompanying madness. But the enactment differs from the actual murders in so far as it is staged for Helen's benefit, with the hope that she can make sense of it. And this time we are privy to a feature of the murders that previously went unseen: the affixing of the circular mirror. We see a distorted image of Helen's face reflected in the mirror, but that reflection is not an exact replica of her face because there is a small round blot near her cheek reminiscent of Lorraine's nevus that must be the aperture of the camera lens. The blot can be read as a sign of incompleteness, since the gap opened up by the aperture would seem to indicate that a piece of the face is missing.

The spike having been once again unsheathed, Mark touches the tip against Helen's throat, causing her to lean backwards just as in the previous murders. However, in this case we see that Helen's eyes are closed, and in fact have been closed from the moment Mark affixed the mirror. It is as if Mark doesn't realize—and has never realized—that Helen's closed eyes constitute a rejection of the entire basis of his quest. For in the moment of closing her eyes—the one remaining means of exercising her subjectivity—she refutes his argument that "the most frightening thing in the world is fear"—or we might say, the "face" of fear. In that instant, she refuses to see what Mark wants her to see, refuses any longer to be deluded by the projected image of herself. Instead she—and by extension, her fellow victims—*see nothing at all*.

And with the outcome resting on a knife-edge, the stage is set for the denouement of Mark's suicide. For at the moment we expect the spike to plunge forward, he draws back and averts his camera away from Helen. We have to assume that at the last possible instant he remembers the prohibition transmitted to him via Mrs. Stephens against filming Helen. She gasps out the words "frightened *for* you" and in these words places her anxiety inside the crucible of their emotional attachment. Yet in a cruel irony, that life-affirming note hastens and solidifies Mark's intention to kill himself. For despite having envisioned this act well in advance, it is Mark's love and concern for Helen that *precipitates* the act. Knowing that his mental state sits on a hair trigger between homicide and suicide, he rushes to perform it before he can succumb to another fit of homicidal rage.

Nevertheless, Mark also wants to show Helen the truth in its stark reality and thus bring his and her ordeal to an end. Thus he reveals the nature of his suicide as a pure act of self-annihilation—analogous to the so-called ouroboros—a snake eating its own tail. Such an act breaks all ties with others and all meaningful associations. It is therefore pointless to ascribe a motive to the act such as, for example, gaining revenge against his sadistic father. Thus the act suggests not mere self-destruction but the condition of never having existed. The image of Helen's closed eyes at the critical juncture hints at the void lying just behind Mark's persona and behind the frightened faces of his victims.

These ideas are in keeping with Mark's strange and terrible ecstasy at the moment of death set against a fireworks-like display of timed light and sound—an explosion of non-being designed to obliterate all traces of him including the "mark" on the floor. In the final moments of *Peeping Tom* the film breaks. Then we see a pinkish red cloud filling the bottom of the screen reminiscent of a Mark Rothko painting. In its utter lack of boundaries and absence of linearity this final image contrasts with the film's opening image of an arrow hitting the bullseye. It implies that the movie's unknowns—the true import of the faces of the victims, the "X" that is Mark Lewis, and the "thing" that was the object of his terrible quest—must remain hidden from sight and inaccessible to formulation in word or image.

Conclusions: psychosis and sexuality

In this chapter I have argued that Mark Lewis' psychosis goes to the heart (if not the throat!) of this movie's disturbing effect on viewers. I would conclude that its shock effect ensues the moment the spike is unsheathed and *the psychosis is unveiled*. And this powerful effect, in turn, depends on the covert—shall we say "latent"—state of Mark's mind throughout much of the film. Mark himself contributes to the condition by deliberatively hiding his madness—at least up to the point where it usurps his personality. Indeed, its proximity to those of us who consider ourselves "normal" adds to the frisson when that line is crossed.

From the psychoanalytic standpoint, the questions posed by the film are: What structural elements permit us to characterize Mark as psychotic given the absence of florid symptoms such as delusions and hallucinations? What position does Mark occupy toward others and the world in general? And how does Mark "see" the world?

We can formulate tentative answers to these questions in a series of assertions, some stated by Mark himself:

1. I see from an elevated position above the human stage. No absolute distinction is made between elevation in height and an attitude of condescension toward fellow mortals.
2. I can see from all directions at once.
3. And given 2: I see from a single and unique point that only I can occupy.
4. The point defines a place from which I can see the world from every possible vantage point at one and the same time and place.
5. That unique "point" is located behind my camera at the intersection of its cross hairs.
6. This "point"—or point of view—is referred to as a "mark" and is called by my proper name: Mark.
7. I can see without being seen and therefore:
8. I can hide in plain sight.
9. Thus I see all: a panorama spreads out before me, complete in every detail no matter how small.

These assertions can be summed up in one phrase: I can do the impossible, for it is an article of faith for Mark that "nothing is impossible." We can, therefore, picture him as a kind of perverse Don Quixote tilting at windmills.

Like Quixote, he re-imagines harlots as noble ladies above reproach and perhaps dedicates his quest in their honor. When he finally encounters this figure in the person of Mrs. Stephens he abases himself before her and pledges himself to her—and by extension to her daughter Helen. Indeed, we can conceive his quest as ridding the world of fallen women whose very existence threatens to taint the image of sacred womanhood.

Yet the attentive viewer can discern two major fallacies in his quest that go beyond the common sense objection that it is futile to attempt the impossible. The first involves Mark's view of mirroring, and analogous modalities such as "photographing you, photographing me." When he affixes the mirror to the camera he intends to force his victim to see her own expression of fear and horror at the moment of death. Mark would be able to see this mirror effect from a peephole in the mirror through which his camera lens protrudes. He thus preserves his position of seeing without being seen. But if we suppose that the victim's face acts as a mirror in its own right, then Mark is in effect watching a "hall-of-mirrors" (Wikipedia.org) effect as if his peephole operated as a one-way mirror. But as is well known, the reverberating light rays between the two mirrors produce a *mise en abyme*, an infinite regress that never reaches an endpoint or better yet, a throwing into the abyss. That is to say, the mirror fallacy also reveals the truth of Mark's quest: that behind the surface of his mind projected on a screen looms an abyss. Thus the truth of the mirror effect emerges in the void that appears when we see the first victim's open mouth expand to the edges of the screen, when we see Vivian's closed eyes, presumed to be looking in the mirror, and the fade out and pinkish cloud at film's end displacing any recognizable image.

But we see the best evidence of Mark's failed quest in his final exchanges with Helen. And it is not a coincidence that the two women in his life are the only ones who succeed in placing limits on his behavior. We recall that they both forbid him from photographing Helen. Before this moment, Mark cannot conceive of the possibility that he "lacks" anything. In his original quest, "doing the impossible" meant creating a complete and flawless picture of the world (and of himself). But once Helen sets some ground rules and imposes a prohibition, "seeking the impossible" is given a new meaning. In the light of restraints, it means *recognizing the lack*, which from his all-seeing position was impossible. And with Helen's guidance he proceeds to do just that: he opens up the dimension of loss (losing those I photograph), failure (I couldn't …) and the void at the center of his quest.

Nevertheless the shadow of Mark's impossible quest still hovers over his otherwise fruitful relationship with both women. Their living presence grants him a reprieve, but it also solidifies their connection to his dead mother; and facilitates the impossible goal of communing with her in death. Moreover he sees the opportunity of reversing the curse that has plagued his existence since childhood. In this scenario he allows his mother—in the guise of Helen Stephens—to live while he dies in her place. And in so doing he in effect returns to the era before his birth and uncouples his father and mother—repudiates the sexual act that produced him—and ensures his annihilation from the scene as if he never existed.

We are left at the end with a note of caution. Helen's quest for the truth of Mark's existence is psychoanalytic in spirit. Yet she is quite aware of its inherent dangers. For the most part, she succeeds in avoiding the triggers of Mark's psychosis. She and Mrs. Stephens have credibility either because they mirror Mark's all-seeing position or, in Helen's case, because her unshakable search for truth places Mark in the position of superior knowledge. Still, the risk of suicide is very real. The questions at the end are: Was Mark's suicide inevitable? Was it preventable? Or was it a paradoxical result of therapeutic success? Was his final act an exercise of free choice or simply the result of his repetitive psychotic enactment? In committing suicide, does he finally "do the impossible"—perform the act that gives him exactly what he wants and grants him perfect satisfaction? *Peeping Tom* offers no answers to these questions but they are bound to arise whenever therapists are engaged in treating psychotic individuals.

References

Akhtar, S. (2012). Normal and pathological generosity. *The Psychoanalytic Review,* *99*(5): 645–676.

Alien (1979). Directed by Ridley Scott. Twentieth Century Fox.

Alien 3 (1992). Directed by David Fincher. Twentieth Century Fox.

Alien Resurrection (1997). Directed by Jean-Pierre Jeunet. Twentieth Century Fox.

The Alien Saga (2002). TV documentary. Interview by Dan O'Bannon.

Aliens (1986). Directed by James Cameron. Twentieth Century Fox.

Anatomy of a Murder (1959). Directed by Otto Preminger. Columbia Pictures.

Bion, W. R. (1961). *Experiences in Groups and Other Papers.* London & New York: Tavistock Publications Limited.

Bion, W. R. (1962). *Learning from Experience.* London: Karnac, 1984.

Bion, W. R. (1978). Attention and interpretation. In: *Seven Servants: Four Works by Wilfred R. Bion.* New York: Jason Aronson.

The Blue Angel (1930). Directed by Josef von Sternberg. Paramount Pictures.

Boiler Room (2000). Directed by Ben Younger. New Line Cinema.

Boris, H. (1986). The "other" breast: greed, envy, spite and revenge. *Contemporary Psychoanalysis, 22*(1): 45–59.

Carnal Knowledge (1971). Directed by Mike Nichols. AVCO Embassy Pictures. dailyscript.com/scripts/alien_shooting.html

Days of Wine and Roses (1962). Directed by Blake Edwards. Warner Brothers.

"Days of Wine and Roses" (1963). Written by Henry Mancini, lyrics by Johnny Mercer.

Deep Throat (1972). Directed by Gerard Damiano. Bryanston Distributing Company.

Double Indemnity (1944). Directed by Billy Wilder. Paramount Pictures.

Ebert, R. (1994). Review at rogerebert.com

Evans, D. (2006). *An Introductory Dictionary of Lacanian Psychoanalysis*. New York: Routledge.

Field, T., & Perrotta, T. (2006). *Little Children*, dailyscript.com/scripts/Little_Children-script.pdf, p. 107.

Fink, B. (1999). *A Clinical Introduction to Lacanian Psychoanalysis: Theory and Technique*. Boston, MA: Harvard University Press.

Freud, S. (1899a). Screen memories. *S.E., 3*: 299–232. London: Hogarth.

Freud, S. (1900a). *The Interpretation of Dreams. S.E., 4*: ix–627. London: Hogarth.

Freud, S. (1905d). *Three Essays on the Theory of Sexuality. S.E., 7*: 123–246. London: Hogarth.

Freud, S. (1909b). *Analysis of a Phobia in a Five-Year-Old Boy. S.E., 10*: 1–150. London: Hogarth.

Freud, S. (1910h). A special type of choice of object made by men. *S.E., 11*: 163–176. London: Hogarth.

Freud, S. (1913f). The theme of the three caskets. *S.E., 12*: 289–302. London: Hogarth.

Freud, S. (1915a). Observations on transference-love. *S.E., 12*: 157–171. London: Hogarth.

Freud, S. (1916–1917). Introductory lectures on psycho-analysis (Parts I and II). *S.E., 15*: 1–240. London: Hogarth.

Freud, S. (1920g). *Beyond The Pleasure Principle. S.E., 18*: 1–64. London: Hogarth.

Freud, S. (1940a [1938]). An outline of psycho-analysis. *S.E., 23*: 139–208. London: Hogarth.

Godzilla (1954). Directed by Ishirō Honda. Toho Studios.

Greed (1924). Directed by Erich Von Stroheim. Metro-Goldwyn-Mayer.

Invasion of the Body Snatchers (1956). Directed by Don Siegel. Allied Artists Pictures.

It Happened One Night (1934). Directed by Frank Capra. Columbia Pictures.

The Kiss (1896). Directed by William Heise. Thomas A. Edison Inc.

Lacan, J. (1953). The function and field of speech and language in psychoanalysis. In: *Écrits: A Selection*. New York: W. W. Norton, 1977.

Last Tango in Paris (1972). Directed by Bernardo Bertolucci. United Artists.

Laura (1944). Directed by Otto Preminger. Twentieth Century Fox.

Leaving Las Vegas (1995). Directed by Mike Figgis. United Artists.

Lévi-Strauss, C. (1963). *Structural Anthropology*. New York: Basic Books.

Lewin, B. D. (1946). Sleep, the mouth, and the dream screen. *The Psychoanalytic Quarterly, 15*(4): 419–434.

Little Children (2006). Directed by Todd Field. New Line Cinema. theliterarylink.com/joyce.html

"Lonely Teardrops" (1958). Written by Berry Gordy, Gwendolyn Gordy, and Roquel Davis.

The Lost Weekend (1945). Directed by Billy Wilder. Paramount Pictures.

M (1931). Directed by Fritz Lang. Nero-Film A.G.

The Maltese Falcon (1941). Directed by John Huston. Warner Brothers.

McLuhan, M. (1964). *Understanding Media: The Extensions of Man*. New York: The New American Library.

The Moon Is Blue (1953). Directed by Otto Preminger. United Artists.

Naremore, J. (2019). *Film Noir: A Very Short Introduction*. New York: Oxford University Press.

Nosferatu (1922). Directed by F. W. Murnau. Prana Film.

On the Waterfront (1954). Directed be Elia Kazan. Columbia Pictures.

Pandora's Box (1929). Directed by Georg Wilhelm Pabst. Süd-Film.

Peeping Tom (1960). Directed by Michael Powell. Astor Pictures.

Perrotta, T. (2004). *Little Children: A Novel*. New York: St. Martin's Press.

Rear Window (1954). Directed by Alfred Hitchcock. Paramount Pictures.

The Red Shoes (1948). Directed by Michael Powell. J. Arthur Rank Film Distributors. Rogerebert.com/reviews/secretary-2002

Scarface (1932). Directed by Howard Hawks. United Artists. scifi.stackexchange.com/questions/127767/in-the-movie-alien-why-did-ash-use-a-magazine-to-try-to-kill-ripley

Scott, A. O. (2014). A brief history of kissing in movies. *The New York Times Magazine*, 10 December 2014.

Secretary (2002). Directed by Steven Shainberg. Lions Gate Films.

Sun Tzu (2002). *The Art of War*. New York: Viking Press.

Sunrise (1927). Directed by F. W. Murnau. Fox Film Corporation.

The Thin Man (1934). Directed by W. S. Van Dyke. Metro-Goldwyn-Mayer.

The Thing from Another World (1951). Directed by Christian Nyby. RKO Radio Pictures.

The Treasure of the Sierra Madre (1948). Directed by John Huston. Warner Brothers.

Wall Street (1987). Directed by Oliver Stone. Twentieth Century Fox.

Wall Street: Money Never Sleeps (2010). Directed by Oliver Stone. Twentieth Century Fox.

Weir, D. (2018). *Decadence: A Very Short Introduction*. New York: Oxford University Press.

Winnicott, D. W. (1958). Primary maternal preoccupation. In: *Collected Papers: Through Paediactics to Psycho-analysis* (pp. 300–305). New York: Basic Books.

Winnicott, D. W. (1960a). Ego distortion in terms of true and false self. In: *Maturational Processes and the Facilitating Environment* (pp. 140–152). New York: International Universities Press, 1965.

Winnicott, D. W. (1960b). The theory of parent-infant relationship. In: *The Maturational Processes and the Facilitating Environment* (pp. 37–55). New York: International Universities Press, 1965.

The Wolf of Wall Street (2013). Directed by Martin Scorsese. Paramount Pictures.

Wolman, T. (2014). Primal greed, developmental greed, and terminal greed. In: S. Akhtar (Ed.), *Greed: Developmental, Cultural, and Clinical Realms* (pp. 43–67). London: Karnac.

Žižek, S. (1991). *Looking Awry: An Introduction to Jacques Lacan through Popular Culture*. Cambridge, MA: The MIT Press.

Index